Discover the
Northeastern Adirondacks

Four-Season Adventures from Lake Champlain
to the Rock-Crowned Eastern Slopes

Discover the Northeastern Adirondacks

Four-Season Adventures from Lake Champlain
to the Rock-Crowned Eastern Slopes

Dennis Conroy
James C. Dawson
Barbara McMartin

Backcountry Publications
Woodstock, Vermont

An Invitation to the Reader

Over time trails can be rerouted and signs and landmarks altered. If you find that changes have occurred on the routes described in this book, please let us know so that corrections may be made in future editions. The author and publisher also welcome other comments and suggestions. Address all correspondence to:

Editor
Discover the Adirondacks Series
Backcountry Publications
P.O. Box 175
Woodstock, VT 05091

Library of Congress Cataloging-in-Publication Data

Conroy, Dennis.
    Discover the northeastern Adirondacks.

    (Discover the Adirondacks series)
    Bibliography: p. 218
    Includes index.
    1. Outdoor recreation—New York (State)—Adirondack
Mountains—Guide-books. 2. Outdoor recreation—New York
(State)—Adirondack Park—Guide-books. 3. Adirondack
Mountains (N.Y.)—Description and travel—Guide-books.
4. Adirondack Park (N.Y.)—Guide-books. I. Dawson,
James C. II. McMartin, Barbara. III. Title. IV. Series.
GV191.42.N7C66   1987   917.47'53'0443   87-14458
ISBN 0-942440-37-4 (pbk.)

Published by Backcountry Publications,
Woodstock, Vermont 05091
Printed in the United States of America by McNaughton & Gunn
Typesetting by The Sant Bani Press

Series design by Leslie Fry
Layout by Barbara McMartin
Maps by Richard Widhu

Photograph credits
Dennis Conroy, pages 10, 24, 29, 37, 56, 61, 73, 79, 82, 92, 102, 130, 149, 150, 192, 202
James C. Dawson, 136, 169, 175, 186, 189, 196
Barbara McMartin, 6, 18, 42, 47, 49, 52, 115, 119, 140, 143, 157, 162
Patricia Collier, 2, 107

Photographs
Cover: *View from Nippletop toward Giant and Rocky Peak Ridge (Barbara McMartin)*
Page ii: *Waterfall East of the Dipper on Giant Mountain*
Page vi: *View from Baxter Mountain to the High Peaks*

Acknowledgments

The authors are indebted to a number of people who helped make this book possible. Barbara's husband, W. Alec Reid, assisted all three authors by expertly printing their photographs.

Randorf and Tim Barnett told us of a number of cross-country ski trips. Pat Flood of International Paper Company kept us informed on that company's Nichols Pond Tract. Jerold Pepper, librarian at the Adirondack Museum, and Francis B. Rosevear assisted with historical research. Paul Desjardins of Jay gave us permission to climb Saddleback from his land and to include that mountain's western route in the guide. DEC's Tony Tyrell briefed us on Valcour Island.

Jim Dawson received extensive assistance from a number of DEC personnel: Kenneth L. Kogut, Margaret L. Baldwin, John Maye, Richard Willauer, Sydney Maicus, and Terry Healey. Richard Ward and James G. Bailey shared information and historical notes. Morris F. Glenn, with whom Jim explored some of Essex County's iron mine area, gave him much valuable information.

Dennis Conroy is indebted to Don Greene who hiked a number of trails on Giant, Hurricane, Jay, and Pokamoonshine with him and shared his extensive knowledge of the area. Don also wrote the section on the slides of Giant. Evelyn Greene skied several trips and opened up the facinating world of mosses and lichens. Shirley Matzke shared discovery of the beauty of the Ausable River delta and other trips with Dennis and they skied much of the Nichols Pond area and checked mileages together. John Siau helped him understand the East Hill area and they climbed Clements together in the snow. DEC Forest Ranger Grant Thatcher was especially helpful in the large area around North Hudson and Paul Stapeley provided information on early settlers and old roads. Dennis was fortunate to have some time on Valcour Island with Wayne Byrne, past-President of the Adirondack Conservancy, who played a key role in acquiring land for public ownership and keeping the island undeveloped.

All three co-authors thank these individuals whose knowledge and varying perspectives add so much to the texture of this guide.

Contents

New Russia Area 75

Giant Mountain Wilderness Area 83

Keene Valley Hikes 111

Hurricane Mountain Primitive Area 121

Jay Mountain Wilderness Area 139

Introduction

THE NORTHEASTERN ADIRONDACKS is a realm of contrasts displaying the most spectacular scenery in the Park. You will find the disparity between kinds of outdoor activities within the region is as pronounced as the differences in scenery.

Level fields border Lake Champlain; small, mostly wooded hills range inland; and in the north some of the most rugged, rock-crowned mountains in the entire Park rise along the region's western border.

While there is very little public land close to Lake Champlain, there are a few lovely places to camp, canoe, or walk. The gentle, wooded hills were once peppered with iron mines and logging sites; today the roads that lead to them are wonderful routes for ski-touring. But the rock-crowned summits are the province of that most adventurous of hikers, the bushwhacker, and the reasons for this are many.

First, consider the nature of the mountains themselves. They are faced with sheer cliffs, having been given their present form by the glaciers. They were so steep and remote, most were not logged until the end of the nineteenth century or into the twentieth. Turn-of-century fires burned fiercely, taking away the thin mantle of duff that covered the even thinner layers of mineral soil—all that had been left when the glaciers scoured the peaks bare. Nature had to start again to cover these peaks from almost the same point it began ten thousand years ago when the glaciers retreated.

The Champlain Valley was settled early; pre-Revolutionary settlements grew to a row of charming villages that line the lake. Settlers were enticed inland to iron mines. Deep valleys close to the High Peaks attracted artists and adventurers. With the twentieth century advent of outdoors people who love to follow wooded trails to soaring summits, the High Peaks region developed a vast network of hiking trails. This is not the case with the northeastern slopes. It is almost as if they were bypassed, ignored, forgotten. That neglect has led to a dearth of trails. Half the mountains in this guide are trailless, reached only by bushwhacks; but the accompanying solitude is greater than you will find within much of the higher mountain region. A day trip will take you to almost any of these peaks, so you can wait for the very clearest weather to enjoy the panoramic views from the summits in the Jay, Hurricane, and North Hudson ranges.

This is the land of the middle mountains—summits from which to view vast distances down rolling hills to the long sweep of the Champlain basin

Conners Notch West of Hurricane Mountain

and east to the high mountains of Vermont while at the same time looking up to the Park's highest peaks. Looking at the High Peaks from these middle mountains is much more impressive than most vistas from their crowded interior. Many people agree that the most superb Adirondack views are those from the peripheral mountains, and certainly the best of the middle mountain views are encompassed by this guide.

This guide includes Giant, the Park's third tallest peak; and even though it has two popular approaches, many of the rest of the trails in the Giant Mountain Wilderness are rarely used. A few of the lowland places are very popular, but in general, there is much to be discovered. The opportunity for discovery is in sharp contrast with the accessibility of the region for it is bisected by the Adirondack Northway, I-87, and no corner is more than a few minutes from one of that route's many exits.

How to Use the "Discover" Guides

The regional guides in the *Discover the Adirondacks* series will tell you enough about each area so that you can enjoy it in many different ways at any time of year. Each guide will acquaint you with that region's access roads and trailheads, its trails and unmarked paths, some bushwhack routes and canoe trips, and its best picnic spots, campsites, and ski-touring routes. At the same time, the guides will introduce you to valleys, mountains, cliffs, scenic views, lakes, streams, and a myriad of other natural features.

Some of the destinations are within walking distance of the major highways that ring the areas, while others are miles deep into the wilderness. Each description will enable you to determine the best excursion for you and to enjoy the natural features you will pass, whether you are on a summer day hike or a winter ski-touring trek. The sections are grouped in chapters according to their access points. Each chapter contains a brief introduction to that area's history and the old settlements and industries that have all but disappeared into wilderness. Throughout the guides you will find accounts of the geological forces that shaped features of the land. Unusual wildflowers and forest stands also will be noted.

It is our hope that you will find this guide not only an invitation to know and enjoy the woods but a companion for all your adventures there.

MAPS AND NOMENCLATURE

The Adirondack Atlas, a map published by City Street Directory of Poughkeepsie, New York, is the best reference for town roads, and it has the added advantage of identifying state land. In spite of the fact that it has not been updated to show recent acquisitions, this is a valuable aid in the northeastern region where public and private lands are so intricately mixed.

This guide contains maps that show all the routes mentioned, but you may still want to carry the USGS topographic quadrangle sheets for the region, especially since most of the region is now covered by the new metric maps, printed in a 7.5 x 15 minute format. The larger scale (this guide reduces them by forty percent to give a standard 1 inch to 1 mile) is very easy to follow and many more features such as stream and old roadways now appear. However, the new contour interval, 10 meters, close to 33 feet, provides less precision than the 20-foot contours of the 15-minute series. There are times when these metric maps do not depict the lay of the land as well as the previous series and when greater detail would be helpful. In addition, many old roads are omitted from the new maps. Because this guide reduces the maps, if you are serious about hiking in this region, you may want to have one of the following: Witherbee, Elizabethtown, and Lewis. Small parts of Keene Valley, Mt Marcy, and Lake Placid are also used.

Most of the other maps used in this guide are not essential for safe hiking; the copies in the guide are adequate. The metric maps include Port Henry, Westport, Ausable Forks, and Willsboro Bay. Older 7.5-minute series maps are used for Peasleeville, Peru, Keeseville, Plattsburgh, West Chazy, Beekmantown, North Hero VT, Mooers, Champlain, and Rouses Point.

Maps are available locally at the Mountaineer in Keene Valley, at EMS in Lake Placid, and at Plaza Bookhouse, Plattsburgh Plaza, Plattsburgh. You can order maps from USGS Map Distribution Branch, Box 25286, Denver Federal Center, Denver, CO 80225. The new metric maps are currently priced at $3.60, though some discount rates can be found. Maps are currently more easily obtained from a private source, Timely Discount Maps. You can call them at 1-800-821-7609; with your credit card number they will ship maps within a week.

The guide uses the spelling given in the USGS but local variations are noted.

DISTANCE AND TIME

Distance along the routes is measured from the USGS survey maps and is accurate to within ten percent. Few hikers gauge distance accurately even on well-defined trails. Distance is a variable factor in comparing routes along trails, paths, or bushwhacks. Because the new maps are just as easily read in miles as meters, this guide continues to give distance in the more familiar miles. However, the metric maps give elevation in 10-meter contours, so elevation is given in both meters and feet.

Time is given as an additional gauge for the length of routes. This provides a better understanding of the difficulty of the terrain, the change of elevation, and the problems of finding a suitable course. Average time for walking trails is 2 miles an hour, 3 miles if the way is level and well defined; for paths, 1½ to 2 miles an hour; and for bushwhacks, 1 mile an hour.

Summaries for distance, time, and vertical rise are given with the title of each section describing a trail or path. These distances and times are for *one way only*, unless otherwise stated.

TYPES OF ROUTES

Each section of this guide generally describes a route or a place. Included in the descriptions are such basic information as the suitability for different levels of woods experience, walking (or skiing, paddling, and climbing) times, distances, directions to the access, and, of course, directions along the route itself. The following definitions clarify the terms used in this book.

A route is considered a *trail* if it is so designated by the New York State Department of Environmental Conservation (DEC). This means the trail is routinely cleared by DEC or volunteer groups and adequately marked with official DEC disks. *Blue disks* generally indicate major north-south routes, *red disks* indicate east-west routes, and *yellow disks* indicate side trails. This scheme is not, however, applied consistently throughout the Adirondacks.

Some trails have been marked for *cross-country skiing*, and new *pale yellow disks with a skier* are used. *Large orange disks* indicate *snowmobile trails*, which are limited to some portions of Wild Forest Areas. Snowmobiles are permitted on them in winter when there is sufficient snow cover. Many snowmobile trails on the interior are not heavily used and can be shared by those on cross-country skis as long as the skier is cautious. Hikers can enjoy both ski and snowmobile trails.

A *path* is an informal and unmarked route with a clearly defined foot tread. These traditional routes, worn by fishermen and hunters to favorite spots, are great for hiking. A path, however, is not necessarily kept open, and fallen trees and new growth sometimes obliterate its course. The paths that cross wet meadows or open fields often become concealed by lush growth. You should always carry a map and compass when you are following an unmarked path and you should keep track of your location.

There is a safe prescription for walking paths. In a group of three or more hikers, stringing out along a narrow path will permit the leader to scout until the path disappears, at which point at least one member of the party should still be standing on an obvious part of the path. If that hiker remains standing while those in front range out to find the path, the whole group can continue safely after a matter of moments.

Hikers in the north country often use the term *bushwhack* to describe an uncharted and unmarked trip. Sometimes bushwhacking means literally pushing brush aside, but it usually connotes a variety of cross-country walks.

Bushwhacks are an important part of this regional guide series because of the shortage of marked trails throughout much of the Adirondack Park and the abundance of little-known and highly desirable destinations for which no visible routes exist. While experienced bushwhackers could reach these destinations with not much more help than the knowledge of their location, I think most hikers will appreciate these simple descriptions that point out the easiest and most interesting routes and the possible pitfalls. In general, descriptions for bushwhacks are less detailed than those for paths or trails, for the guide assumes that those who bushwhack have a greater knowledge of the woods than those who walk marked routes.

Bushwhack is defined as any trip on which you make your way through the woods without a trail, path, or the visible foot tread of other hikers and without markings, signs, or blazes. It also means you will make your way by following a route chosen on a contour map, aided by a compass, using streambeds, valleys, abandoned roads, and obvious ridges as guides. Most bushwhacks require navigating by both contour map and compass, and an understanding of the terrain.

Bushwack distances are not given in precise tenths of a mile. They are estimates representing the shortest distance one could travel between points. This reinforces the fact that each hiker's cross-country route will be different, yielding different mileages.

A bushwhack is said to be *easy* if the route is along a stream, a lakeshore, a reasonably obvious abandoned roadway, or some similarly well-defined feature. A short route to the summit of a hill or a small mountain can often be easy. A bushwhack is termed *moderate* if a simple route can be defined on a contour map and followed with the aid of a compass. Previous experience is necessary. A bushwhack is rated *difficult* if it entails a complex route, necessitating advanced knowledge of navigation by compass and reading contour maps and land features.

Compass directions for bushwhacks are given in degrees from magnetic north, a phrase abbreviated here to *degrees magnetic*.

The guide occasionally refers to old *blazed* lines or trails. The word "blaze" comes from the French *blesser* and means to cut or wound. Early loggers and settlers made deep slashes in good-sized trees with an axe to mark property lines and trails. Later, hunters and fishermen often made slashes with knives and, though they are not as deep as axe cuts, they too can still be seen. Following an old blazed path for miles in dense woods is often a challenging but good way to reach a trailless destination. Remember, though, that it is now, and has been for many years, illegal to deface trees in the Forest Preserve in this manner.

You may see *yellow paint daubs on a line of trees*. These lines usually indicate the boundary between private and public lands. Individuals have also used different colors of paint to mark informal routes from time to time. Although it is not legal to mark trails on state land, this guide does refer to such informally marked paths.

All *vehicular traffic*, except snowmobiles on their designated trails, is *prohibited* in the Forest Preserve. There are some town roads or roads that lead to private inholdings on which vehicular use is permitted. These roads are described in the guides, and soon the DEC will start marking those old roads that are open to vehicles. Most old roads referred to in the guides are town or logging roads that were abandoned when the land around them became part of the Forest Preserve. Now they are routes for hikers, not for vehicles.

There has been an increase in the use of three- and four-wheeled off-road vehicles, even on trails where such use is not permitted. New laws will stop this in the Forest Preserve and make sure that some of the old roads remain attractive hiking routes.

Cables have been placed across many streams by hunters and other sportsmen to help them cross in high water. The legality of this practice has been challenged. Some may be quite safe to use, others are certainly questionable. Using them is not a recommended practice, so when this guide mentions crossing streams to reach some of the hikes, you are urged to do so only when a boat can be used or in low water when you can wade across.

The *beginning of each section describing a trail* gives a summary of the distance, time, and elevation change for the trail. For unmarked routes, such information is given only within the text of each section—partly to allow for the great variations in the way hikers approach an unmarked route, and partly to emphasize the difficulty of those routes.

Protecting the Land

Most of the land described in these guides is in the *Forest Preserve*, land set aside a century ago, where no trees may be cut. All of it is open to the public. The *Adirondack Park Agency* has responsibility for the Wilderness, Primitive, and Wild Forest guidelines that govern use of the Forest Preserve. Care and custody of these state lands is left to the Department of Environmental Conservation, which is in the process of producing Unit Management Plans for the roughly 130 separate Forest Preserve areas.

Camping is permitted throughout the public lands except at elevations above 4000 feet and within 150 feet of water or 100 feet of trails. In certain fragile areas, camping is restricted to specific locations, and the state is using a new No Camping disk to mark fragile spots. *Permits* for camping on state lands are needed only for stays that exceed three days or for groups of more than ten campers. Permits can be obtained from the local rangers, who are listed in the area phone books under NY DEC.

Only dead and downed wood can be used for *campfires*. Build fires only when absolutely necessary; carry a small stove for cooking. Build fires at designated fire rings or on rocks or gravelly soil. Fire is dangerous and can travel rapidly through the duff or organic soil, burning roots and spreading through the forest. Douse fires with water, and be sure they are completely out and cold before you leave.

Private lands are generally not open to the public, though some individuals have granted public access across their land to state land. It is always wise to ask before crossing private lands. Be very respectful of private landowners so that public access will continue to be granted. Never enter private lands that have been posted unless you have the owner's permission. Unless the text expressly identifies an area as state-owned Forest Preserve or private land whose owner permits unrestricted public passage, the inclusion of a walk description in this guide does not imply public right-of-way.

Burn combustible trash and carry out everything else.

Most *wildflowers and ferns* mentioned in the text are protected by law. Do not pick them or try to transplant them.

Safety in the Woods

It is best *not to walk alone*. Make sure someone knows where you are heading and when you are expected back.

Carry water or other liquids with you. Not only are the mountains dry, but the recent spread of *Giardia* makes many streams suspect. I have an aluminum fuel bottle especially for carrying water; it is virtually indestructible and has a deep screw that prevents leaking.

Carry a small *day pack* with insect repellent, flashlight, first aid kit, emergency food rations, waterproof matches, jackknife, whistle, rain gear, and a wool sweater, even for summer hiking. Wear layers of wool and waterproof clothing in winter and carry an extra sweater and socks. If you plan to camp, consult a good outfitter or a camping organization for the essentials. Better yet, make your first few trips with an experienced leader or with a group.

Jay Summits

Always carry a *map and compass*. You may also want to carry an altimeter to judge your progress on bushwhack climbs.

Wear *glasses* when bushwhacking. The risk to your eyes of a small protruding branch makes this a necessity.

Carry *binoculars* for birding as well as for viewing distant peaks.

Use great care near the *edges of cliffs* and when *crossing streams* by hopping rocks in the streambed. Never bushwhack unless you have gained a measure of woods experience. If you are a novice in the out-of-doors, join a hiking group or hire the services of one of the many outfitters in the north country. As you get to know the land, you can progress from the standard trails to the more difficult and more satisfyingly remote routes. Then you will really begin to discover the Adirondacks.

Sharp Bridge Area

THE SOUTHERNMOST SECTIONS of this guide fan out from the small valley through which meanders the upper reaches of the Schroon River. The valley is about a thousand feet in elevation; to the west, nearby peaks rise to three thousand feet, separated by several valleys whose clear brooks tumble eastward to swell the waters of the Schroon. These peaks and valleys are described in the chapter, "Under the Northway."

The eastern slopes are lower and contain numerous beautiful ponds that nestle among the hills an easy hike away from main roads. Some of these are described in "The Fishing Ponds" chapter.

NY 9, which runs from New York City to Rouses Point near the Canadian border, forms the transportation backbone for the trailheads in the Schroon Valley. The Northway is the quickest way to get to the general area, which lies between Exit 29 at North Hudson and Exit 30 ten miles to the north.

Deadwater Pond, the source of the Schroon River, was the site chosen by the first settlers in the area. Two brothers named Pond cleared land there sometime in the late 1700s. They came from Vermont by way of Fort Henry and Mineville, along Tracy Road, which is County Route NY 6 and sometimes designated Mineville Road, to the Old Tracy Place. The North Hudson Cemetery, beside Black Brook Road as you go east toward Port Henry, has Benjamin Pond's grave under tall white pines. He was born in 1768, fought with the Sixth Artillery New York Militia in the War of 1812, and died in 1814. There is a headstone for Benajah Pond, born in 1805, perhaps son of Benjamin. Other gravestones mark the resting places of MacIntyres, Chillis, Cumings—all of whom were early settlers in the valley. There is a "Challis Pond" not far away; and the names of other settlers survive in nearby mountains and ponds.

An exception to this mode of naming is Sharp Bridge, crossing the Schroon seven miles north from the intersection of Exit 29 and NY 9 in North Hudson. On the north side of the bridge is the entrance to the Sharp Bridge Campground. The old Sharp place was a backwoods farm northwest of the bridge on Gui Pond. It is difficult to find a trace of the buildings; but stone walls can be found among extensive pine groves, which must have been farm land a century ago. No working farms remain in this area now; income is derived from tourists who stay in the local motels and bed-and-breakfast inns. Summer visitors are wise to leave the Northway for NY 9 in order to discover this pleasant valley.

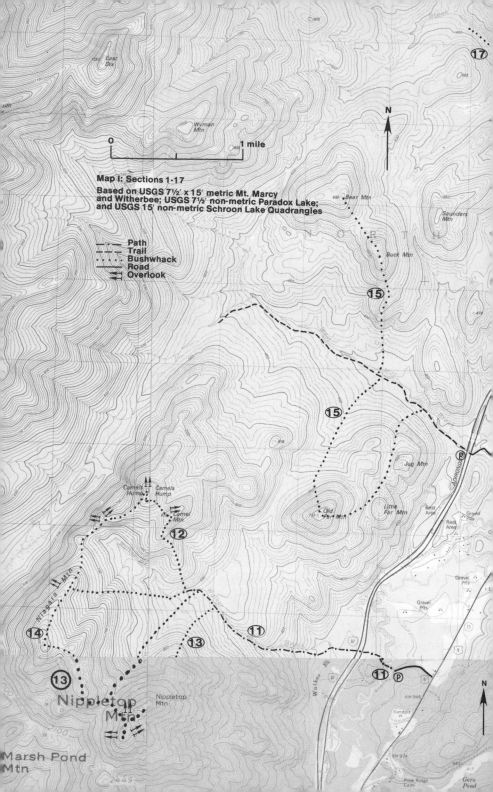

Map I: Sections 1-17

Based on USGS 7½' x 15' metric Mt. Marcy
and Witherbee; USGS 7½' non-metric Paradox Lake;
and USGS 15' non-metric Schroon Lake Quadrangles

Sharp Bridge Campground is the focus of several paths and trails. It is one of the first public campgrounds in the Adirondacks. (The other, also built in 1922, is on the Sacandaga River south of Wells). For years, this facility with its thirty-seven tent sites, widely scattered under tall white pines, was a favorite with hikers. Many campers returned each year to set up a base from which to hike in the area or climb in the Dix and Giant Ranges. There are fewer "regulars" now and it is used mostly for overnight stops, for a standard fee. The campground is open from Memorial Day to Labor Day, and you can usually find a vacancy and enjoy the sense of camaraderie which exists among those who frequent it. It is an enjoyable place to spend a week or so, and would make an excellent base for the southern portions of this guide.

A marked DEC trail starts at the campground and goes east to East Mill Flow, which becomes an important tributary of the Schroon River. Round, Moriah, and other ponds can be reached via this trail. Across NY 9, south of the bridge, another path leads under the Northway to Lindsay Brook Valley and Gui Pond (pronounced goo-eye). These are easy day hikes for fishing, swimming, or birding. The old tote roads are excellent for cross-country skiing and snowshoeing in winter.

There is a swimming hole in the Schroon River at Sharp Bridge Campground and fishing from the banks. In the spring, enough water flows under the bridge to float a canoe down the river, but unfortunately, there are so many trees across the river that a canoe trip is frustrating, and at times even dangerous. (Canoeists call such trees "strainers" because the water pressure forces a canoe or swimmer against the limbs and down under water, and rescue is very difficult.) The closest canoeing is further south, with the put-in at North Hudson Beach, about 6 miles south, and a take-out at NY 74.

1 Round Pond and Moriah Pond via East Mill Flow

Hiking, cross-country skiing, snowshoeing, fishing
5 miles, 2 hours, 420-foot vertical rise

A marked official trail begins at Sharp Bridge Campground on the Schroon River. More people use this route, summer and winter, than any other in the area. It is a wide, clear path that once was the old Moriah Road. It rises from 980 feet at the campsite to 1400 feet at Moriah Pond. At the beginning of the trip there is a steep section that requires intermediate proficiency on skis, but otherwise the slopes are gentle.

You reach Sharp Bridge Campground by going east toward North Hudson from Northway Interchange 29. In 0.2 mile, turn left onto NY 9 and go north for 7 miles. The marked entrance to the campground is just north of a bridge across the Schroon River. Alternatively, leave the Northway at Interchange 30 and go south on NY 9 for 2.6 miles. Park in an area on the left before entering the campground gate. Bear right, south, toward the river when you start and then walk east, parallel with the stream, to reach the trailhead. There is a DEC sign indicating (incorrectly) Round Pond 6 miles, Trout Pond 7 miles. The Sharp Bridge campsites are on the knoll to the left under tall, majestic white pines.

The trail goes east for several hundred yards between the stream and the knoll, crossing several small depressions on two logs that are sometimes difficult to negotiate on skis. After a twenty-five-minute walk, you are going up the steep section. Five minutes later, at 1.4 miles, the small, pretty stream on your left comes close to the old road you are following and you may note a small rock cairn on the left of the road. This marks one route to Clap Mountain to the north, section 2. The road gradually levels off and swings around to the northeast at about 1300 feet. There is a low rock ledge on the left and the evergreen polypody fern pokes through the snow on large rocks along the way.

Land to the right of the trail slopes down toward a wet area, which is in the East Mill Brook Valley. The way through the large hardwood forest is easy. In the springtime look for the dark, shiny leaves of trailing arbutus along either side of the trail. After a little more than an hour, at 2.6 miles, you reach East Mill Flow. It has been dammed by beavers, and in winter there may be an otter's opening near the dam and a hold under the roots of cedar trees on the shore. In spring, look for more trailing arbutus and other spring flowers along the bank to the left.

Cross-country skiers can traverse the ice to a path that goes northeast along the east side of the flow. Alternatively ski up the flow for perhaps 500 yards to the valley of a brook that flows in from the right. It is the outlet of Round Pond.

To reach the trail along the flow, hikers can usually cross the outlet of the flow on the beaver dam; if the water is high, cross about fifty yards downstream on a large tree trunk. Walk along the east side of the flow to Round Pond Brook at 3.4 miles. The trail to Round Pond from East Mill Flow follows up the north side of the brook. Three hundred yards from East Mill Flow, there are five red trail markers on trees indicating the beginning of the trail to Trout Pond, which goes off to the right. You

can ski or hike on this trail southeast to Trout Pond and out to the North Hudson–Moriah–Port Henry Road, section 10. Continue straight and you will be at Round Pond, at 3.7 miles, after a hike of two hours.

Round Pond is deep and clean, nestled among low hills. You can camp in a grassy area on this western shore, but the preferred campsite is on a rocky outcrop on the northeastern point.

The old road to Moriah Pond continues up a draw to the north of Round Pond. It crosses private land, and this is not marked as a DEC trail. Snowmobiles use this approach to Round Pond; the path is easily followed. Go north along the west side of the pond and up the draw, which has a small brook. You will see a cabin on the right as you climb. After climbing twenty minutes beyond Round Pond, the path levels off and there are signs of recent logging. A logging road goes off to the left, downhill, at about 4.3 miles. It can be followed in the winter to ski out to Crowfoot Brook. This is not an easy trip because the logging road ends short of the brook and you have to bushwhack the rest of the way by compass.

The path angles right, east, following the logging road toward the pond, which you reach at 5 miles after a forty-minute climb from Round Pond. Moriah Pond is a marshy body of water that can be reached by logging trucks and skidders from the east in winter. You can ski east around Broughton Ledge to Crowfoot Pond, but it is best to go with someone who knows the way. Alternatively, look north from Moriah Pond to a deep notch. A difficult but possible 200-foot climb, easier on snowshoes, up the notch will put you on a path to Crowfoot Brook and out to County Route 6, section 6.

It is, of course, not necessary to make a loop on skis. The trip back the way you came in—on skis or hiking—is enjoyable. It takes thirty minutes to ski back to Round Pond and an hour and a quarter to ski from Round Pond back to the campsite and your car. Hiking takes longer, as skiers can take advantage of several good downhill runs.

2 Clap Mountain and Triangle Pond
Trail and bushwhack, rock ledges, birding

The first Adirondack Mountain Club guidebook, published in 1934 and prepared by Orra Phelps, has a section on Clap Mountain, which lies just

Round Pond

east of Sharp Bridge and rises to 1700 feet. She mentioned it as having " . . . a beautiful outlook toward Dix, Macomb and the Great Range." The mountain is still there, but in fifty-two years forest regeneration has all but eliminated any views from the summit. The beginning of this trip is from Sharp Bridge Campground along the same marked trail that leads to Round Pond, section 1. Follow the trail for about an hour, approximately 2.2 miles; at this point it is at 1200 feet elevation and has a northeasterly and level course. There is a low valley on the left, northwest, and the trail goes between two large trees that partly constrict it. At this point, bushwhack northwest up the valley for fifteen minutes, 0.25 mile, to Triangle Pond. Its surface is small, with the shores ringed by small alders and other shrubs, but there are many birds to be seen and heard around the pond.

The steep ledges of Clap Mountain rise in the west just beyond the pond. Proceed southwest up a steep gully with the cliffs of the mountain on the right, then contour around the southern slope of the mountain to the west. You will cross several wet areas before reaching a rocky, pine-dotted slope. At this point, you climb in a generally northern direction and come to a rocky section that seems like a summit but is not. Continue north, dropping into a valley and then up to the highest point. You may see small, flat rocks that have been overturned—a sign of black bear searching for ants. In the winter and early spring there may be views to the north, but in summer there are none, nor is there a view of Triangle Pond to the east. Make your way back around the west side of the mountain, and there are fleeting views of distant peaks through the trees.

You start down from this western opening by contouring around to the south, and then making your way down over rocky ledges wherever you can. Keep going south and down; in forty minutes you reach a small brook. Follow it down to where you can continue south and you will reach the marked trail you came up on. Turn right, west, downhill and back to Sharp Bridge Campground.

Another way to the summit of Clap Mountain is directly up this south slope. It is a nice, open, rocky climb that is much easier than the previously described loop via Triangle Pond. The start of this bushwhack is up the trail, a thirty-minute, 1.4-mile walk from the campground where the brook comes close to the trail on the left. Look for a rock cairn on the left of the trail; there are old blazes on two yellow birches on the left, near the cairn. To the right there is a three-foot diameter rock and a hemlock tree with sapsucker holes. Go due north, left, here. At first there are old blazes on the trees, but these soon vanish. You make your way up the steep rocky section, bearing around to the west, left, near the top. It is a short climb of fifty minutes and not too difficult. You should have a compass, as it is easy to get turned around on top of the mountain. Reverse your direction to return as described above.

3 Courtney Pond
Canoeing, fishing

Drive south on NY 9 for 2.75 miles from Northway Interchange 30 or 6.45 miles north from the NY 9 intersection at Exit 29 and you will see a small pond on the west beside the road. There is a place to park under the trees and to sit beside the pond on the bank. If you want to get away from the road, walk down the path along the north side of the pond to some rock ledge outcroppings. You can picnic there and drop a fishing line in the water if you do not have a boat or canoe.

If you want to launch a rowboat, the easiest place is along the southern end of the pond. There are several obvious launch openings through the trees along the bank. The pond is stocked with trout each year by DEC. It is fished so extensively that there is no natural spawning, but it is a popular fishing place in the spring after it is stocked. Later on in the summer, it is a very accessible place to enjoy a quiet paddle in a canoe. Look for turtles sunning themselves on logs on the far shore.

4 Gui Pond
Bushwhack, birding

This pond appears quite large on older topographic maps. At one time, a backwoods farm, the Old Sharp Place, was located on it. In later years it had good fishing. Now the shallow bottom has begun to fill in and swamp bushes and water lilies are taking over. There are a profusion of redwing blackbirds and other water-loving species in this close, but isolated spot.

The beginning of the trip is along an old road with a DEC trail sign indicating Lindsay Brook Trail, 0.9 mile to Northway Underpass. It is immediately south of Sharp Bridge on NY 9, 2.5 miles south of Northway Exit 30, and 6.75 miles north of the NY 9 intersection at Exit 29. Park on the west side of the road and walk up the old road to the northwest with the river on your right. Within 100 yards, the road turns right across a wooden bridge. Beavers have dammed the flow under the bridge, flooding the road, so make your way along the high ground and bushes to the right of the road for the next fifty feet. After that the old road rises gradually through an attractive pine forest. Occasionally there are red DEC trail markers.

Within twenty minutes, 0.9 mile according to the DEC trail sign, you reach a Northway underpass. Do not go under, but look for a fisherman's path going north, parallel to the Northway. The area is fern-covered and damp. Within five minutes you reach Lindsay Brook where it flows from under the Northway. It is too deep to cross here, but follow it downstream about twenty yards and you will see a small stream coming in from the north. This is the tiny outlet of Gui Pond. Cross the brook on rocks at this juncture and go up the far bank to the northeast. From here continue northeast up a slight rise until you are into a white pine woods. Look for an old path through the woods, but if you cannot locate it, walk north-northeast, about 20° magnetic. You will see an old stone wall in the middle of the forest, testimony to the time that this land was cleared and farmed.

About forty-five minutes and 1.4 miles after leaving the car, you reach the pond. It is shallow, and in spring and summer the water is covered with white water lilies. Sheep laurel and other swamp bushes are beginning to fill in the center area. It is not a sphagnum bog, but it is too shallow for good fishing. The pond and the swampy area near the outlet to the west have numerous redwing blackbirds.

Retrace your steps through the pines, if you wish, or follow down the outlet brook to look for birds and wildlife. You can be back at your car in thirty-five minutes.

5 Deadwater and Joe Ponds
Old path, cross-country skiing, hunting

You can drive almost to the shore of Deadwater Pond, but there is little left of the large body of water shown on older topographic maps. This headwater of the Schroon River was dammed to provide the surge of water that floated logs downriver at the beginning of nineteenth-century log drives. Today only a little open water in a large marshy area remains.

Skiing from Sharp Bridge

A gravel road to the pond heads east 1.15 miles south of Northway Exit 30 on NY 9. After turning, you pass a house on the right and a garage on the left; the road continues into a field and curves around to the left, north. Park and walk east down the mowed path to the outlet of Deadwater Pond. You can see the remains of a dam and a bridge at the outlet, which gave access to the woods to the east in the old days. You can also walk along the high west bank of the pond, but there is no place to launch a canoe nowadays, since the shore is rimmed with brush.

Tiny Joe Pond is an easy hike of an hour and a quarter with an altitude gain of 450 feet. The faint path begins 130 yards south of the bridge over the Schroon on NY 9, which is 1.5 miles south of Exit 30. Park on the east side of the road near two large white pines. The path begins twelve yards south of the two pines; there is no marker and you will have to search for it. Walk east along the pine-needle-strewn path, which rises gently as it curves to a northeasterly, 40° magnetic direction. Walk or ski through an attractive thirty- to fifty-year-old white pine forest with low balsam undergrowth along the top of a hogback that parallels the river on your left. If you explore between the ridge and the river you will find a very old road and the abutments of a bridge that crossed the river 200 yards upstream of the present bridge. In less than twenty minutes of walking along the hogback, you go into a small gully. You can hear the gurgle of the outlet to Deadwater Pond on your left. Cross the gully and go up the other side toward 60° magnetic to the top of the next ridge, which runs northeast. Here very large pines are scattered among younger trees. Soon the path swings more easterly and passes an old fence nailed to large pines. Hardwoods begin here and the path is paved with leaves. On your right, spinulose woodfern grows profusely in a damp depression. Hunters have tied orange 'flags' along the trail in this area.

Thirty minutes after leaving your car, you will hear a brook ahead to the left. At this point, an old logging road goes uphill at 140° magnetic. Because there are several blowdowns across it, it is difficult to find. If you do not locate the road, go straight on to the brook, passing on your right a large rock capped with polypody ferns. When you reach the brook, follow it up going 160° magnetic, almost south. Within five minutes of hiking along this fairly large stream which flows around pretty moss-covered rocks, you will see a large rock outcrop to the left, east. This small cliff guards the bank of the stream, and in five more minutes forces you to cross the stream to the west bank. Continue west for fifty feet from the brook and you will pick up the old logging road, here heading 170° magnetic. The depression of the old road is quite visible as it heads uphill and crosses the brook twice.

A half hour after starting up the brook, you reach a fork. Go left to a large, fairly open, flat area. Straight ahead is a high ragged rock outcrop; on your immediate left is another smaller one—both are covered with a profusion of reindeer lichen. You climb up a well-defined draw running 60° magnetic, and in a few minutes you are at the beaver dam across the outlet of Joe Pond. At first it appears the pond is filled with shrubs, but if you walk around to the right you will see open water. Cedar and hemlock skeletons cast photogenic reflections on this clear, smooth surface. There are no open areas around the shore for lunch, so it is best to return to the clearing for a sunny log seat.

The path back to the car is easier to follow than the ascent. After leaving the clearing you cross the brook within five minutes and cross it again to the right a few minutes later, going due north. Cross again to the left at ten minutes, traveling on the old road with a bearing of 330° magnetic. After twenty minutes the old road will be blocked by blow-downs and the brook will be off on the right a ways. From here look for the path to the left along the ridge with Deadwater Pond down the hill to the right. You cross the gully and head up along the ridge picking up the path running 220° through the pines. It will take you out to the road and your car, forty-five minutes after leaving the clearing below the pond. The hike is about 1.5 miles one way. The path is gradual enough for cross-country skiing and snowshoeing, if you are willing to go around several blowdowns.

6 Crowfoot Brook to Crowfoot Pond
Hiking, cross-country skiing, birding, spring flowers
3 miles, 1 1/2 hours, 450-foot vertical rise

In winter this marked snowmobile trail has been so lightly used that it is an excellent low-intermediate cross-country ski trail. During other seasons the wide old road is a pleasant, easy walk.

The start of the trip is on County Road 6 that goes to Mineville and Port Henry from NY 9. Go east from Northway Exit 30 on NY 9 south; in one hundred yards turn left (north) on County Route 6 at a large sign that reads Mineville 9, Port Henry 12, Champlain Bridge 20. Drive 1.6 miles north on Route 6 to a place where the road winds left uphill. On the right (east) there is a metal signpost (no sign) and a dirt road; in summer you can drive 100 yards in and park.

The trail (marked for snowmobiles) begins on a new log and plank bridge across Crowfoot Brook that is easily seen from the parking area.

Across the brook, the path goes left to the southeast and rises gradually through dense hemlock. The old road, which once was a major wagon route going west from Moriah Center, is well graded with little signs of wash. As you walk up the first slope, there is a steep bank on the left with a pretty brook far down in the gully.

In ten minutes you move away from the brook. In spring red trillium, Solomon's seal, wood sorrel, and other blossoms push up through the leaves beside the road. After seventeen minutes you are back to the brook, crossing it on a bridge. In this area you may hear the melodious song of the winter wren.

After thirty minutes you cross a bridge over a tributary and then begin to climb more steeply. The main brook valley is to the right with the stream sheltered by interlocking branches of hemlock. Five minutes later, you cross the stream; it is especially attractive here where the brook falls over large rocks. The bridges on this stretch of road are well made, showing good stone work. After about forty minutes the trail levels off as it goes through a valley with low hills on either side. After fifty minutes you cross a small brook without a bridge. In just an hour, at 2.5 miles, an old trail goes right across the outlet of Crowfoot Pond but ends just beyond an old camp. You can see the pond ahead and are soon walking along the north side close to the water. At nearly 3 miles, about halfway up the long, narrow pond, state land ends. At the eastern end of the pond, which you reach in another quarter hour, there are a number of summer camps that are reached by road from Moriah Center.

Returning along the same route, the old road is clearly marked as a snowmobile trail. After walking downhill about 0.6 mile from the outlet, less than fifteen minutes, you will notice a cleared path going uphill to the southwest. It is unmarked and heads 220° magnetic, towards the notch between Moriah Pond Mountain and Broughton Ledge. The cleared trail stops before you get to the notch, but if you continue you can look down the slope and see Moriah Pond in the valley below. The ledge is steep, but in winter you could walk down it and ski out to the pond, making a loop down to Sharp Bridge Campground, section 1. This is an excellent, if somewhat strenuous, day trip, if you have a two-car shuttle.

Back on the Crowfoot Brook road, the return ski trip is easy. In spring, the same route offers yellow violets, wild oats, bluets, and fiddleheads. You can hear many warblers, and if the leaves are small enough, you may spot the black-throated green warbler. Walking this easy route in spring or early summer, you arrive back at your car relaxed and marveling at the beauty of nature.

The Fishing Ponds—North Hudson to Moriah Road

FIVE TINY PONDS are nestled in among the hills north of the Moriah Road. Driving along it, you will be totally unaware that there are paths to any of them, but fishermen know the way, and you can follow their routes.

The road is of relatively recent vintage. The original Cedar Point (Port Henry) Road apparently went west to Moriah Center and then continued past Moriah Pond, Round Pond, and down to the Schroon River, reaching the river at the north end of the straight stretch called McCauley Flats. From this point, well below Sharp Bridge Campground, the road turned south following the route of the present NY 9.

There is a very interesting boundary marker on the Moriah Road—an elaborately carved marble monument depicting a handshake. It is located just east of the parking place for Howard and Munson ponds. The marker divides the townships of Moriah and North Hudson, but for some reason it was erected 0.65 miles to the west of the boundary shown on the 1978 USGS map.

You reach the North Hudson-Moriah Road (also called the Ensign Pond Road) by going east from Northway Exit 29 for 0.35 mile, then north on NY 9. At 2.75 miles go right, east, on the road marked Port Henry, making a second right at 3.05 miles. You are now on the North Hudson-Moriah Road, which is County Route 4.

7 Twin Ponds
Bushwhack

There are two ways to reach the westernmost pond in this group. If you want a full day's hiking, combine this bushwhack with a trek to Howard and Brother ponds, section 8, and a 1.8-mile walk along the Moriah Road for a great loop. Take Northway Exit 29 to the Moriah Road, as described

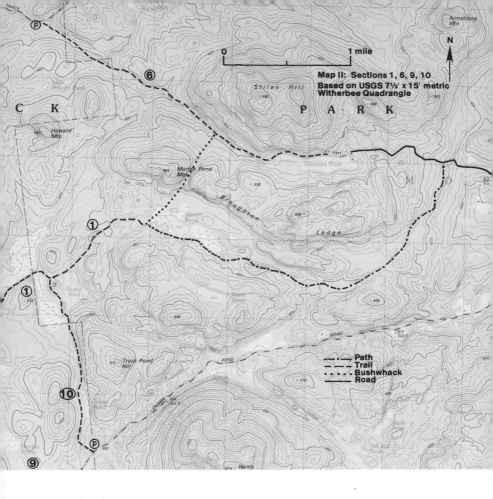

Map II: Sections 1, 6, 9, 10
Based on USGS 7½' x 15' metric
Witherbee Quadrangle

Path
Trail
Bushwhack
Road

in the introduction. You cross the second bridge over Black Brook 3.2 miles from NY 9. At 3.55 miles, after the road bends to the right, park heading uphill.

To begin the bushwhack to Twin Ponds, walk along the road for 100 yards, almost to the point it bends left. There is a large rock with a pine tree on the right. You head left, down across the tiny brook to start the bushwhack. Walk toward true north, 14° on your compass, along the slope of the hill down to a small brook filled with moss-covered rocks. Keep this course along the brook and in fifteen minutes you come through a very small notch into a flat area. The brook heads off to the northwest; you continue north.

A small stream drains the notch to the north, which lies between Claybed and Mile Square mountains. You will want to follow it. If you are hiking in midsummer, watch for rattlesnake orchids along the way. You cross two very small streams, then about a half hour into the bushwhack, 0.5 mile from the road, the steep slopes of Mile Square Mountain plunge down to the level of the stream. Crossing the stream, you will notice how much more open it is on the left.

Forty minutes into the walk, nearly 0.8 mile from the road, you might notice coral root orchids in profusion. (They like the wet meadow that lies in the draw.) The stream disappears as you reach the 384-meter (1260-foot) level. Notice that the hemlocks filling the deep valley give way to hardwoods in the draw. In fact, you will have to push through a beech thicket just before reaching level land at the top of the draw.

Continue north, reaching the end of the level after just an hour's walk. From here you can see both lobes of Twin Ponds, and draws lead left and right into each lobe. The western lobe at about 1.2 miles has a nice rock for picnicking; the view across the pond is of Nippletop Mountain, section 13. The Twin Ponds are filled with water lilies.

To make a loop you can continue bushwhacking around the eastern pond, close to the water. The shores are steep. Almost all the way around, beyond a ledge, at 1.45 miles, there is a draw filled with tumbled and broken boulders. Head up it, on a northeasterly course. There is a steep ledge to your right as you go through this clearly defined draw with large white birch and hemlock. The walking is open and easy. As you head down the northern side of the draw between the two unnamed knobs, keep to the flanks of the right knob in order to avoid a spruce and cedar swamp. Continue northeast to Munson Pond at 2.25 miles. The walk between the two ponds should take no more than fifty minutes. Head around to the south corner of Munson and return to the road, a mile northeast of your car, by the routes described in the next section.

8 Howard and Munson Ponds
Paths, hiking, camping, fishing

For such a well-used path, the beginning of this one is certainly well concealed. Park at the large turnout on the side of the North Hudson to Moriah Road, 5.45 miles east of the intersection with NY 9. This spot is just west of the town line monument. Walk back west 150 yards to a large pine tree on the north side of the road; further west the ground is very wet and boggy. Head into the woods and skirt the edge of the boggy area. Within fifty feet, there is a really good footpath heading southwest around a small hill. The path swings to northwest to contour around the hill then passes to the left of some steep rock ledges on the hill.

The path continues north-northwest along the outlet brook of Howard Pond and reaches a large cedar grove with hemlock at the foot of the pond in less than half a mile, a ten-minute walk. There are campsites to the right as you approach the pond and to the left near the outlet. Down the shore to the left there is a handsome rock slab site on the western shore. Up the eastern shore there is a lovely fishing spot near a campsite with fire ring. Paths lead along both shores to these camping spots.

The paths along both shores of this long narrow pond intersect at its northwestern end at the bottom of a steep draw that points to the northwest. Follow that draw for a ten-minute walk through fields of maidenhair mixed with the more common wood ferns. You reach and cross a height-of-land at 0.8 mile; the route is now well marked, albeit informally, with red disks. These direct you to a well-worn footpath and lead across a flat area, then down a steep slope to the southeast shore of Munson Pond at 1.1 miles.

From here, you can walk around the southern end of Munson Pond and then follow the bushwhack of section 7 in reverse or return to your car. If you start the full circuit by first going to Twin Ponds, you can find the red-marked path on the shore of Munson Pond by walking along its southeast shore to a small opening with a white birch felled by a beaver. Twenty feet inland, southeast of the clearing, you will see the first of the red blazes.

9 Brother Ponds
Path, nature walk

From the parking area on the North Hudson to Moriah Road, cross the road to the north side and walk a few feet east to a large white pine. If you enter the woods here, you will see a small brook on your right. Cross it, then head north along it through a lovely hemlock woods. Moss-covered ledges guard the west side of the brook. You can walk the 0.2 mile to the pond in five minutes.

The two ponds are true bogs stretching north for half a mile; no path leads along them. You have to push your way through leatherleaf and sheep laurel to reach the bog rosemary and rose pogonia orchid that grow on the sphagnum mats of the bog where a lonesome forest of stumps stands vigil.

Looking across Twin Pond to Nippletop

10 Trout Pond and Round Pond

Marked trail, hiking, fishing, camping, cross-country skiing

3 miles, round trip, relatively level

A good day's fishing and fun is in store for you on this outing, if you have a portable rubber raft or if you can carry a canoe for a quarter mile. In the winter, the clearly marked trail is an easy 3-mile round trip to Round Pond, or you can double that by going on to Moriah Pond, section 1. Better yet, if you want a downhill run, leave a car at Sharp Bridge Campground and you have a one-way 5.5-mile trip that drops 200 feet.

This trailhead has a new sign on a green, metal post that reads: Trout Pond 0.7 mile, Round Pond 1.3 mile, East Mill Flow 2.5 miles, and Sharp Bridge Campground 5.2 miles. The sign is on the north side of the North Hudson-Moriah Road 6.4 miles east of NY 9, or 1.7 miles east of the county line. You can drive a car in for a hundred yards or so on the narrow woods road. There are markers along the entire trail.

Walk northeast and in 200 yards you will cross a small brook, the outlet of Trout Pond. The path swings north and you will occasionally see red DEC trail marker disks. There are one or two recent blowdowns that must be negotiated, but generally the trail is wide and practically level. In 0.3 mile, less than fifteen minutes, you reach the southern outlet of Trout Pond. You can launch a canoe there but brush and logs make it awkward, so it is better to walk halfway along the pond and put in by some large pines. The pond is narrow but deep in spots, and you may catch trout or perch. It is a pleasant place for a picnic but the shoreline is mucky for swimming.

To continue on to Round Pond, 1.5 miles from the road, follow the trail along an almost level draw below Trout Pond Hill, which goes up steeply on the right, east. In forty-five minutes you see the large pond, and the trail goes northwesterly across its log-filled outlet. You follow the trail with Round Pond on your right, east, and in less than ten minutes at 1.8 miles join the trail that comes in from Sharp Bridge Campground to the west, left, section 1. The trail right, northeast, goes to Moriah Pond.

The best place to camp on Round Pond is on a rocky point on the east side. It is an easy bushwhack through relatively open woods around the east side of the pond as you approach it from the south.

Under the Northway

DRIVING NORTH ALONG the Northway between Exits 29 and 30, you are drawn to the visions of distant peaks and rocky crags, most seemingly cut off by the Northway itself. But wait. There are half a dozen underpasses accessible from NY 9, and each leads to a destination on the lower reaches of the High Peaks. The few real trails and old logging roads only extend into a small portion of the valleys and even these routes are seldom visited. The mountain tops are a bushwhacker's dream, and even the proximity of the Northway does not break the secluded spell cast by the remote wilderness on this unspoiled corner of the mountainous heart of the Adirondacks.

Many of the names found in this area can be seen on gravestones in the small Deyo Cemetery in North Hudson, opposite Pepper Hollow Road. Titus Walker, who died on March 5, 1842 at the age of 72, is buried there beside his wife, Hanna; it seems likely that Walker Brook was named for him. Also buried there is Steven Farr, who died at age 71 in 1820; George W. Farr and his two wives also lie there. The mountain today is called "Old Far" but the name is so unusual it must have come from the Farr family. Over by the bank of the stream is the grave of David, son of Daniel and Martha Lindsay, who died on March 30, 1825, when he was seven years old.

This beautiful hiking area was obviously settled in the late 1700s and early 1800s by sturdy stock who lived long lives in the valleys that bear their names.

Some of the routes to the underpasses traverse private land, so you must cross without leaving the roadways, whose beginnings are remarkably well concealed.

11 Walker Brook
Path, hiking, snowshoeing, camping

The path along Walker Brook, following an old tote road, leads you through one of the prettiest valleys bordering the High Peaks. From points high in the valley, you can easily bushwhack to three of the surrounding mountains, (described in sections 12 through 14).

To reach Walker Brook, drive north from the intersection where Northway Exit 29 joins NY 9 for 3.3 miles to a dirt road that heads west. From the north the road is 0.9 miles south of a bridge over the Schroon River. The road is marked by a metal post with three white signs hanging from it that read: JJC Ranck, SUERIG, Private Camps. Drive down the road for 0.3 mile to a fork with a large white sign indicating that the NY State right-of-way to the Northway underpass goes right. Go right for 100 feet more and bear right to the river. The bridge has washed out and was still out in early 1993, but it is scheduled to be replaced. The 20-foot wide stream is shallow in dry weather and can be waded at the ford.

Stop and set your altimeter, here at 900 feet elevation. The climb through the valley will take you up nearly one thousand feet in 2.3 miles. The tote road, which crossed at the ford immediately downstream of the bridge, angles uphill to the right then turns west. In 0.5 mile you turn right, within sight of the Northway underpass.

Once you are through the underpass, you are in the Wilderness Area. The tote road heads into a deep cedar and hemlock stand and immediately forks. The right fork disappears shortly; there are several places to camp along it, close to the brook but far enough (150 feet) away from it to be legal.

The left fork crosses Walker Brook. You hop across on the rocks and if the water is very high you will have to search a few yards upstream to find a dry crossing. The road heads away from the brook, then back toward it, as it begins the first of many zigzags up the steep slopes. At 1.2 miles, just over a thirty-minute walk, you will have climbed 500 feet to a small waterfall where the road and the brook almost touch. Opposite the waterfall on the south side of the trail there is a bank of rattlesnake fern.

At this point, the worst of the steep climb is over—the road and the valley now point to the northwest. You cross a tributary of Walker Brook about a quarter mile past the waterfall; in another quarter mile the road passes through a very wet area. The road is narrower and filled with witch hobble and maple starts. A fifteen-minute walk past the waterfall brings you to a wet, grassy area where the road seems to disappear. It does not; walk straight ahead to pick it up again. There are places in the next ten minutes of walking where the path seems to disappear in beech thickets.

You are at about 1700 feet and the valley appears much broader and more open. You leave the brook, to return to it and cross it at about 2.1 miles. However, the brook you cross is the tributary that comes from the saddle between Niagara and Nippletop mountains. Its confluence with Walker Brook is 200 yards downstream.

Follow the tote road west for another few minutes and watch carefully. Fifty yards from the crossing, there is a fork in the way marked by three blazed trees, a large yellow birch and two beech, one with a double blaze. The path left is the route to use for Nippletop Mountain. The way straight ahead leads into a high hemlock-and spruce-filled valley. The point 100 yards from the blazed intersection is the takeoff for the easiest climb up Camels Hump.

The tote road now continues west, crossing the real Walker Brook. It follows the brook past a good campsite into a cedar swamp where the brook turns sharply southwest into a steep gully.

If you are planning a weekend of climbing, you can set up camp high in this valley and have ready access to all three surrounding summits.

12 Camels Hump Mountain
Bushwhack

Hikers agree that the most spectacular views of the High Peaks are those from the lower, peripheral summits where vistas range from lake and river valleys, to the foothills, to the rugged panorama of the peaks themselves. This claim is best exemplified in the Walker Brook Valley where all three peaks survey the Giant and Rocky Peak Ridge and the Dix Range. And while looking at these craggy summits, you get to climb around the most wonderful rock piles in the Adirondacks.

The taller of the Humps is but 2800 feet, but there are so many rocky knobs on this loop that you will climb approximately 2600 feet in a seven-hour circuit. If approached from a campsite high in Walker Brook Valley, you shorten the climb by 900 feet and the circuit by over two hours.

Section 11 details the climb along the brook and the point at which you begin your bushwhack, heading northwest about 320°. Within 100 yards you cross Walker Brook, the slopes of Camels Hump drop steeply to the brook. You have only to struggle up for ten minutes before the woods become delightfully open. You are climbing a nose covered with red pine. These slopes were logged for softwood in 1912. Within twenty minutes you are on open rock at about the 2100-foot level with views of Nippletop.

Continue climbing, generally toward magnetic north, but finding the easiest route between open patches. There is a band of birch at about 2400 feet, and above that a small band of balsam and spruce with big cedars. The latter is only 100 yards deep and ends on top the cliffs that range across the eastern side of this eastern hump, which is called Camel Mountain on the USGS. There is a beautiful view of Owl Pate and Lake Champlain. You can easily reach this point with an hour's bushwhack.

The true summit of this eastern hump is at 2740 feet and ten minutes north of the cliff top. From it you see Niagara Mountain, Sunrise, the tower on Boreas, and Giant and Rocky Peak Ridge mountains. To reach the western peak denoted as Camels Hump on the USGS, pick your way down the slopes nearly 200 feet into the draw between the humps. The first bit of climbing up the western hump is rough, but quickly opens up. There are ledges, so angle around them to the south, then climb back north along their tops to this 2800-foot peak. Time between peaks is about twenty-five minutes. Views overlooking a pair of smaller humps on the northern flanks of Camel Mountain are spectacular and dominated by the rocky slopes of Wyman and the Dixes.

At this point, you can return the way you climbed, or continue making a loop that takes you over the lower rock knobs of Camels Hump that seem to enclose the western end of Walker Brook Valley to the lower slopes of Niagara Mountain. Note that if you decide to go on, you have to climb part way up Niagara in order to avoid these cliffs.

The descent along the crescent of Camels Hump's southwestern flanks is a series of open rock patches. The first of these below the summit gives you an extraordinary view back north to the cliffs that line the western side of the western hump. Sometimes the walk between patches is easy, sometimes there is a real scramble over ledges or through the dense pine and balsam. Each open patch has a different view—and as you reach the knob at the 2400-foot level, almost into the col, you look down on Niagara Brook and back to both sets of cliffs on Camels Hump. From here you also see the series of open patches which ring Niagara Mountain's western flanks.

A narrow vein of rock, whose lowest point is 2200 feet, connects Camels Hump with Niagara. It is faced with cliffs on both east and west sides, rising 500 feet above the Niagara Brook Valley and 200 feet above Walker Brook Valley. It will take you about an hour to descend from Camels Hump and cross the ridge to the lower slopes of Niagara; as you begin to climb again, you are quickly rewarded with splendid views. A ten-minute walk brings you to the next patch—stay close to the western slopes, but far enough back from them to make easy climbing. There is a great opening at 2500 feet, and from it, a bushwhack east will bring you to Walker Brook; but walk at least to the next ledges at 2600 feet for the best views of the cliffs that drop to Niagara Brook.

The northwestern flank of Niagara Mountain is a narrow ridge; cross it from either of the western outlooks, heading east for the return. Contour down, heading generally east. It is steep, but there are few ledges that

Niagara Looking over Camels Hump to Giant

you have to find your way around. Less than thirty minutes brings you to Walker Brook, which is in a steep draw. Cross it and continue east above it. At about 1900 feet, cross the brook again where it has taken a more level route. You should shortly pick up the path that follows the brook. Alternatively, stay on the south side and watch for the path that leads up toward the draw between Niagara and Nippletop. It is an easy bush-whack to navigate because the contours draw you naturally down between the two streams. It should take no more than an hour to return to the path along Walker Brook, another hour to cross the Schroon River.

13 Nippletop Mountain
Bushwhack

Nippletop is deceptive; there are at least two nipples on its summit range, which extends over a third of a mile. There is a relatively direct way to reach the southern and higher peak. There is a chain of open spots which range up the northern peak suggesting a circuit with many views; but this route has one severe drawback—nearly a half mile band along the lower slopes is covered with a thicket of small beech sprouts so dense that at times it seems impenetrable.

The easy way first: from the blazed intersection high in Walker Brook Valley, section 11, take the left fork, which has a heading of 200° that changes shortly to 220°. The path stays on the west side of the stream that drains the saddle between Niagara and Nippletop for the first half mile. It is heavily marked with old blazes, but every once in a while you will lose it totally. Sometimes it appears to have the width of an old tote road; other times it disappears.

At the 1950-foot level, the valley has become very narrow and the path crosses to the eastern side. You have been walking about fifteen minutes from the blazed intersection at this point. In another ten minutes, at about 2100 feet, the east bank has become so steep that the path crosses back to the west side, but shortly becomes hard to find. It is sort of a "now you see it now you don't" situation for about ten minutes, until at 2200 feet the path crosses to the east bank again. Here it rises steeply and is again hard to follow. Note that at no time has it strayed more than 100 feet from the stream. Within ten minutes, you pass a huge rock below which the stream seems to form. Just beyond this point you reach the more level saddle between the hills. Notice that all along on the east side there are rock ledges and cliffs.

You reach the marshy area that is the headwaters of the brook an hour from the blazed intersection, and five minutes later, still walking through the walled valley, you reach the top of the col, which lies at 2400 feet. This is the first point at which the cliffs to the east look low enough to climb, so head up the ledges here. There are still some steep places, and it takes no more than five minutes to reach the first open ledge from which you can see the lower open ledge on Niagara and Camels Hump. Your course is a scramble just a little south of east.

At 2700 feet, you meet a large, irregular rock outcrop with cedar clinging to its slopes. This northwest face of Nippletop must stay wet throughout the year, for sheep laurel thrives in pockets of sphagnum moss. Patches of trailing arbutus also cling to the mountainside. It is so steep that you feel as if you were climbing the stairs of the Empire State Building. Less than half an hour from the col you come out through a cedar grove to open rock at the 2950-foot level. You can finally view the southern summit from this point below and west of the two summits.

Head east through the draw between the summits to the rocks below the southern summit, which is ringed by cliffs. There seems to be only one easy route on the final leg of the climb of this 3000-foot summit and even this is a bit of a scramble. The summit not only has the spectacular cover view across the northern part of the mountain to Camels Hump and Wyman with Giant and Rocky Peak Ridge in the background, it also sweeps a panorama from the mountains beside Lake Champlain through Schroon Lake to Hoffman Mountain, which rises above the beaver ponds and marshes along Niagara Brook. To the west lie Sunrise and the Boreas Mountains, with Marcy, Redfield, and Allen in the distance. McComb, Hough, Dix, East Dix, and Wyman complete the 360° skyline.

You can return to the draw between the two summits and much more easily wind your way up the northern ridge; first to a large square boulder, then up and down through clefts to the 2980-foot peak. To return, either go back to the draw and retrace your steps or head north along the nose, enjoying a last few outcrops with views. The northern route ends in the beech thickets. It is possible to descend to the west into the draw from the northern summit by first going north to a lower outcrop, then heading west. The entire western face of Nippletop is ringed with cliffs.

14 Niagara Mountain
Bushwhack

The outcrops on the three mountains that surround Walker Brook Valley are a string of pearls—a chain of vantage points with ever-shifting focus.

There might be some who would attempt all three in a daylong marathon, but it is preferable to split the trip and savor the summits. You can make a circuit on Niagara, or combine it with trips to either of its neighbors. Niagara rises to 3015 feet and its rock outcrops ring the mountain's southern and western slopes. And, like its neighbors, Niagara has two summits.

For a counterclockwise circuit, you can walk up Walker Brook Valley, climbing to 2300 feet before heading west to the western ridge line. This would put you at the 2600-foot outcrop that ended the Camels Hump loop. From here, wind south along the top of the steep western face, enjoying the two other openings that lie beneath the summit. These openings continue below the summit to the south, but you should cross over to the eastern knob and follow it down.

It is easiest to plan a climb of Niagara after you have examined it from Nippletop, noting that there is a low outcrop, then a long, gentle ridge that leads north to the lower, eastern summit. There is considerably more open rock on the western summit, and if you are ascending Niagara from the col between it and Nippletop, you might find it desirable to contour directly up to it. The route is west up from the col, then northwest from the first outcrop toward that summit.

15 West Mill Brook, Old Far, Bear, and Buck Mountains
Bushwhack, hiking or snowshoeing

Old Far is one of the lowest peaks (2300 feet plus) that lie near the west side of the Northway. As with other mountains in the area, it has several rock outcrops that provide a nice view, especially to the north and south. It can be reached from Walker Brook to the south, but the preferred access is from the West Mill Brook Valley to the north.

To reach West Mill Brook, take Exit 29 from the Northway going east to North Hudson. In 0.35 mile, turn left, north, on NY 9; in 4.7 miles you cross the Schroon River. After passing Greenough Road, at 5.25 miles on NY 9 you will see a large wooden post with a crosspost (but no sign) on the left. Turn left here, west down a dirt road. A notice on a tree reads "Public easement across private land. Do not leave this road. Respect adjacent private property." There is a red DEC trail marker on a tree.

Drive down the road for 0.15 mile to a brook, which you can ford in dry weather, and drive on through a gravel pit. If the brook is too high, park on the right and ford the stream on foot. There is a 36-foot public access right-of-way and easement signs on both sides of the road. After several

Camels Hump to Bald Pate

hundred yards through the gravel pit area, the road goes uphill in a draw with trees on either side. If the season is wet, do not go up the hill. Leave your car beside the road on the gravel and walk from this point. The road goes under the Northway in 300 yards and forks. The left fork is clearly marked as private property; the right fork is public but wet and muddy after a rain and may be passable only with a four-wheel-drive vehicle. You can make it with a passenger car in a dry summer. There are red trail markers along the road.

At the end of this road, less than a ten-minute walk from the gravel pit, you reach the Forest Preserve boundary line. There is a large grassy clearing, big enough for six or seven cars, and a camping place with a fire ring. Just beyond that there is a metal barrier across a tote road. As you walk around the barrier, West Mill Brook falls gently over round rocks on your right. It is a clear, attractive stream that looks as if there might be fish in it. A five-minute walk beyond the first barrier, there is another metal gate and a sign reading "State Land Wilderness Area." You are now entering the Dix Mountain Wilderness Area with its popular but trailless peaks that are usually climbed from the north or west.

The old logging road you are following continues to climb gradually; the brook drops over large boulders into clear, deep pools. Less than a fifteen-minute walk from the clearing, the wide, well-made, old road levels off. Three minutes later you will see a small clearing among hemlock and maple trees, a potential camping spot though there is no fire ring. A path goes to the right along the brook, but the main path goes straight across a small tributary. The way here is level. In a rainy August, chanterelle mushrooms flourish in the forest duff.

The road bends uphill to the left under huge white pine trees, crosses another small brook, then a muddy area. As you have noticed so far, this route makes a fine cross-country ski or snowshoe trail. Cross a third small brook, and swing right and then left around a knoll. After thirty minutes, slightly over a mile from the clearing and the first gate, you climb a hill and come out on a level hogback, still on the good tote road. There is a small stream on the left of the hogback, but the main brook is on the right.

After hiking ten minutes more, you notice the path starts to climb again; it is heading 310° magnetic and remains easy to follow. Two large erratics can be seen twenty feet off to the left. Soon the path comes back near West Mill Brook and you drop down to cross a large tributary and in another twenty feet, another smaller tributary. After these two crossings, the path starts uphill again and immediately forks. Take the left fork uphill. Climbing, you go through a grassy area; look for long beech fern and New York fern growing along the path, which now swings more to the west.

It takes the better part of an hour to cover the approximately 1.5 miles from the Northway to an opening with the brook close by on the right. There is some old tar paper on the ground and a large dead beech with pileated woodpecker holes in it. Heading toward magnetic south is a blazed path. (The path you have been following along West Mill Brook could be used to bushwhack up the north side of Camels Hump, but it is better to go up from Walker Brook.)

Take the path south and you will shortly see the remains of an old hunting camp with broken frying pan, stove, and tar paper. The path continues south up the west side of the small brook. In about 100 yards, you come to a steep hemlock-covered area that lies at about 1400 feet elevation. Water cascades over beautiful moss-covered rocks; it is a small stream in a steep ravine and the effect is absolutely stunning. You continue to climb; forty minutes after starting south, you climb through a beech thicket at about 1500 feet elevation. Cross the brook, then leave it after about an hour's walk south, as it veers off to the west.

Nippletop to Niagara Brook and Hoffman Mountain

At the point you leave the brook, head southeast through a beautiful hemlock grove. Continue up the hemlock ridge for twenty-five minutes and ahead you will see open rock, which lies on the west side of Old Far Mountain. In another ten minutes, two and a half hours from the start, you are out on open rock looking south to the valley between Nippletop and Niagara. Camels Hump is on the right. Work your way up through cedar and blueberries. There is no opening to see Little Far or Jug Mountain to the east; but near the top the view north is impressive. Bear and Buck mountains are rocky bluffs on the other side of West Mill Brook Valley. Farther on to the north is Wyman and East Dix and in the distance Rocky Peak Ridge ranges high above your 2300-foot vantage point.

It is pleasant to make a loop of this walk, so start down due east. It is steep, but the hemlock woods are open and easy going with many mushrooms and marginal shield fern underfoot. After a five-minute descent, you reach a beech and striped maple thicket but there is no way to avoid it. Swing left, northeast, until you are heading 20° magnetic. In fifteen minutes you are down to 1650 feet with an open hemlock ridge on the left. You will cross a small brook, but the stream valley is too dense to follow down, so keep to the ridge. After descending from the top for thirty minutes, you will be mostly out of the beech thicket into open hemlock and hard maple at 1600 feet. Soon you will hear West Mill Brook ahead; forty-five minutes from the summit, you are back to the path, just up from the spot where there was a double tributary.

To climb the rocky crags to the north of West Mill Valley, you will want to start from the same point where you headed south to go up Old Far. Take a bearing of 300° magnetic, heading under the open cliffs of Buck Mountain toward the summit of Bear Mountain. After an hour's climb, angle right up the steep slopes that lead to the saddle between them at 1800 feet. You can find a way up the rock face of either mountain, with the easiest routes from the north sides.

The trip to all three peaks can be made in a day, so perhaps you will want to climb the two northern slopes first, coming back to the valley near the double brook crossing. That way the return is only a pleasant thirty-minute walk back to the clearing, 300 yards from the Northway. In five more minutes you are back at your car.

If you prefer to stay along a path, you will find the trip along the mountain stream delightful. There are only one or two blowdowns so the route through the valley makes an excellent cross-country ski trail. There are few bushwhacks that are any easier and that lead to such fantastic views of the Dix Range.

16 Shingletree Pond
Trail, hiking, skiing, nature trip
1.1 miles, ½ hour, relatively level

It almost seems as if they built the Northway on top of Shingletree Pond, an acid teardrop full of pitcher plants and sundew. Fallen spruce and hemlock stretch out into its shallows, providing home for cranberries, bog rosemary, and the lovely rose pogonia orchid. That should be enough inducement to tempt you to make the short walk under the Northway sometime in early July.

Start at Courtney Pond on NY 9, section 3, at the parking area near the north end of the pond. The red-marked trail crosses the inlet stream in a wet and ferny area, then heads southwest along the pond. Climbing gently for 0.4 mile—the trail joins a logging road on private land that has been logged recently. The route turns right, downhill but still southwest, away from the active logging road, under the Northway and around the south end of Shingletree Pond.

17 Lindsay Brook
Bushwhack, hiking, hunting

The Lindsay Brook Valley does not have an easy-to-follow old logging road along a clear, tumbling brook as do those found in the two valleys to the south. Rather, the trip presents an opportunity to see if you can find the beginning of an unmarked path, and once on it, if you can spy the old tree blazes leading to an abandoned hunter's camp. This trip is for the woodswise—a "hunter's choice."

The beginning of the path is easy enough. It starts south of Sharp Bridge on NY 9 where it crosses the Schroon River, the same beginning as for Gui Pond, section 4. In twenty minutes on that trail you reach a six-foot tall, elliptical culvert under the Northway. A sign says "Notice—No trail maintained beyond this point. Do you have compass, maps, matches? NYS Conservation Department." If you are so equipped, walk through the culvert. On the far side a tree has fallen across the path knocking down some of the chain-link fence. Make your way around the tree and continue straight about 100 feet to the foot of a hill. Turn right, walking parallel to the Northway, about 20° magnetic.

A ten-minute walk past the culvert, your route will be blocked by a hill and a large rock on the left. Go up the draw around the rock onto a ridge overlooking the brook, below on the right. Bushwhack along the ridge

bearing 340° until you drop down to the brook fifteen minutes from the underpass. The brook is filled with cobblestones, bare in low water. Bushwhack upstream, or, if you can cross, there is a fisherman's path along the northeast side.

About thirty minutes from the culvert, you come to a shallow section of the brook with a big dead pine on the northeast side and cedar trees on both sides of the brook—the old trail crosses the brook at this point heading northwest or 320°. It is hard to identify and you may miss it as you walk up the brook. If you walk for forty minutes past the culvert, you will have passed the trail, so bushwhack west up the steep slope until you pick it up. It is well up on the hill, perhaps 300 yards away from the brook. The path runs at 320° magnetic and through this section there are frequent blazes on trees. Northeast, across the brook valley, there is an impressive, but unnamed, open rock hill.

Continue along the obvious blazed footpath—not a tote road—through an attractive maple, ash, and white birch forest. Occasionally there is red paint on a tree as a marker. One hour after leaving the culvert you cross a tributary of Lindsay Brook. Blowdowns make it easy to lose the path, so look carefully for old blazes and red paint daubs. Fifteen minutes later you will see and hear the brook down a steep hill to the right. Soon afterwards, look for silver tape and yellow surveyor's tape around trees. Shortly after this stretch, the path crosses straight through a wet area you detour around. After this, there are more yellow blazes and bands of rust-colored paint on trees—an interesting melange from annual hunters' forays. In an hour and a half, less than 2 miles from the Northway, you should reach the brook again. The path is very hard to find, but continue up the north side of the brook and you will reach a dilapidated hunter's camp. It is a pretty spot with the small brook watering some of the largest cedars that you will ever see in the Adirondacks.

The trail out is not much easier to find than it was coming in. If you cross the brook here and go straight at 140°, you will hit an old road that takes you to the Northway, but there is no way to enter the woods at this point. So follow down the brook until you hear the Northway traffic and then bushwhack up over the ridge to the culvert. It should take twenty-five minutes from the crossing to the culvert, another twenty minutes to reach your car.

Both valleys to the south lead you to delightfully scenic bushwhacks to rocky peaks. This valley does not do so. It could be used as an access to Wyman and Bear mountains, but the distances are greater and the route more elusive than using West Mill Brook.

Pitcher Plants at Shingletree Pond

18 Makomis Mountain
Path, hiking, snowshoeing, views

This trip under the Northway takes you on a one-hour and ten-minute trek to a small 1662-foot peak. It is an easy climb of 630 feet, and the view of the Dix and Giant Ranges is impressive for such a small effort. The path has an interesting assortment of wildflowers and mushrooms in spring. It is a nice winter trip on snowshoes but too steep and narrow for cross-country skis.

You reach the beginning of the path by turning east from Northway Interchange 30 onto NY 9, heading southeast. Within 100 yards take County Route 6 left toward Mineville, Port Henry, and the Champlain Bridge. Go over a small bridge and at 0.2 mile from its beginning the road turns right. The start of the path is at this turn on the left side of the road, just to the left of the roadside arrow. The path, which runs a little west of north, is easy to follow and leads you shortly through a tall culvert under the Northway. On the other side you start uphill; in ten minutes the path forks with a large rock outcrop ahead. Take the left fork, which contours around the hill. It is easy to follow, but there are no blazes or trail markers, so winter travel will be more difficult.

After forty-five minutes, you come to a large rock ledge. There is no special overlook, but there, as well as during the climb, you have glimpses of hills to the east as you look back. The path continues at 340° magnetic and you see south and southwest except in summer when leaves close off distant landscapes. In late April, you will enjoy broader views as well as the trillium and other spring flowers that line the path.

You reach the summit and the old fire-observer's cabin at 1.4 miles, after an hour and ten minutes. Only the cement piers of the fire tower remain. The view from the porch of the cabin toward the Dix Range is impressive; if you make the trip in early spring, you will see its extensive slides outlined in snow. East Dix and Spotted Mountain are at 260° magnetic; beyond them the Great Range and many of the High Peaks are displayed. A short walk down the summit to the west will open up a view of Giant and Rock Peak Ridge to the right at 330° magnetic.

The path to the left leads to private lands, so return the way you came. The return takes but fifty minutes.

Mineville to Lincoln Pond

THE REGION FROM Mineville north to Lincoln Pond and Westport is characterized by low mountains, scattered ponds, tote roads, and open woods. Today it is frequented by sportsmen, snowmobilers, and cross-country skiers. A century ago it was the northern edge of an area that included the largest and most productive iron mines in New York. Within its boundaries dozens of mining prospects were explored and millions of cords of wood were reduced to charcoal for the blast furnaces.

Along its western edge, the Lincoln Pond Road from Elizabethtown to Mineville provides points of access around the piles of mine tailings that rise like small conical mountains at Fisher Hill just north of Mineville. The road also gives access to Russett, Tanaher, Mill, and Lincoln ponds. The Northway bends across the north, dipping close to Westport on Lake Champlain. The western boundary of the region is the fault scarp that drops eastward to County Route 44, Stevenson Road, and the D&H tracks in the Lake Champlain Valley.

The region extends to Westport, a lakeside community on the shores of North West Bay, which was one of the most popular gateways to the Adirondacks when transportation thrived along Lake Champlain. William Gilliland created the Town of Bessboro from one of his original land grants in 1765 and named it after his daughter Elizabeth. The name was changed to Westport in 1815; by then it had become the eastern terminus of the road from the Saranacs, through North Elba, Keene, and Elizabethtown. While lumbering and mining were Westport's principal occupations, for a while there was a small spa with a medicinal mineral spring.

Today the village has a popular sailing marina and golf course, and is a growing residential community. In winter cross-country skiing is popular and the Westport Country Club permits skiing on the rolling hills of the golf course, near the center of the village.

Nichols Pond Tract

Almost all of the land from Mineville to Lincoln Pond is private, with the exception of part of the western boundary. The private lands on the edges are posted by landowners, including the LTV Corporation, the new owner of some of the mines. A network of town roads and logging roads

View from Belfry Tower Showing Tailings from Iron Mines

serves snowmobilers, of whom there are not many, making it possible for cross-country skiers to share, and appreciate the way the machines open the trails.

The heart of the area is International Paper Company's Nichols Pond Tract, which is open to the public. IP permits hiking and cross-country skiing, but prohibits camping, all-terrain vehicles, and (currently) snowmobiles. Unpaved roads lead to seventy-seven-acre Nichols Pond where, in summer, you can canoe, fish for trout that are stocked annually, or picnic along the cool shores. Numerous songbirds nest in the open hardwoods and are easy to see as you walk along the logging roads.

In winter the dense network of logging roads that crisscrosses the area offers excellent cross-country skiing. Although only those with more interesting destinations are described, there are many other tracks to follow. Best of all, this winter wonderland is just a few miles east of Northway Exit 31.

The Iron Mines

Iron was discovered at Cheever north of Port Henry on the shores of Lake Champlain prior to the Revolution. Later ore beds in the Mineville area were being worked by the late 1830s and the major mines were opened before 1848. The ore was smelted in blast furnaces near Moriah Center, at Fletcherville, section 25, and at Port Henry. According to *The History of Port Henry, N.Y.* by Charles B. Warner and C. Eleanor Mall, two companies evolved to dominate the production. The Port Henry Iron Ore Company was organized in 1864, and Witherbee, Sherman Co. consolidated many smaller holdings in 1900. The furnaces at Port Henry continued to operate into the 1930s until the cost of transporting coal by rail and the introduction of the taconite ores from Minnesota made competition uneconomical.

The region described is actually north of the main mining area, thus it does not contain the major mines. Nevertheless, there are many fenced pits, mostly filled with water. These are dangerous; cross-country skiers and hikers should not venture near them.

19 Belfry Mountain Tower
Short trail, spectacular views
0.3 mile, 10 minutes, 61-meter (200-foot) vertical rise

Outside Mineville, where you least expect it because there are no dominant peaks, is a special little hill called Belfry Mountain. From its operational fire observation tower there is a 360° view of the horizon. The observation platform on top the tower is not always open, but you can climb its first three levels to see the panorama. The towns of Mineville and Witherbee, with their conical piles of tailings, lie to the southeast, with Lake Champlain beyond. The Green Mountains of Vermont spread across the entire eastern horizon. Directly west the high peaks of the Dix Range lift their rocky profiles. To the northwest the slopes of Giant and Rocky Peak Ridge tower skyward, ready to be explored.

The trail to the tower is too short to be called a hike but the view from the fire tower summit is too wonderful to miss. To reach the trailhead from the Northway, take exit 30, NY 9 south for 100 yards to a left turn onto Tracy Road to Mineville. That lovely stretch of road winds for 8 miles to Witherbee where you take your first left onto County Route 7C, headed toward Lincoln Pond and Elizabethtown. The trail to the tower is just beyond the height-of-land a little over a mile from town (you can see the tower on the left as you drive up the hill). A yellow metal gate on the left, west, of the road marks the beginning of the trail, which follows a truck road to the tower. You can easily reach it in ten minutes.

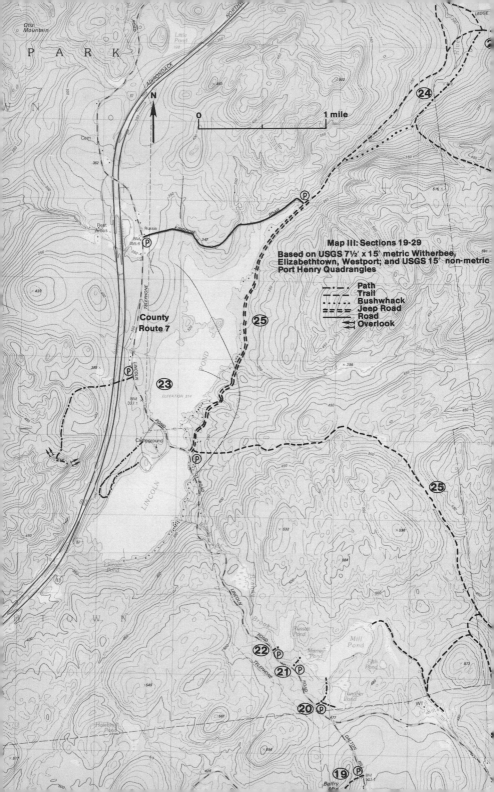

Map III: Sections 19-29

Based on USGS 7½' x 15' metric Witherbee, Elizabethtown, Westport; and USGS 15' non-metric Port Henry Quadrangles

Path
Trail
Bushwhack
Jeep Road
Road
Overlook

N

0   1 mile

County
Route 7

PARK

Otis
Mountain

Campground

20 Tanaher and Mill Ponds
Path, fishing

Two miles south of the causeway across Lincoln Pond and just north of the intersection of the roads from Witherbee and Mineville, there are four small ponds on the northeast side of the road, where bass, pike, and pickerel attract fishermen. The carries are short enough so that you can enjoy canoeing through the pickerel weed and water lilies that fill the shallow areas of all the ponds.

Going 0.5 mile north from the intersection (County Routes 6 and 7C) you see a small gravel road to the right. It forks in 200 yards. The way right leads another 200 yards to tiny Tanaher Pond. If you head north at the fork, a narrow footpath leads you over a crest and down to the outlet end of Mill Pond, the largest and prettiest of the group. You certainly want a canoe here, but there is a shorter route via Murrey Pond. The attractive stream connecting the two ponds is not canoeable.

21 Murrey and Mill Ponds
Path, fishing, canoeing

A wide, steep path no more than 300 yards long leads from the road, a quarter of a mile north of the route to Tanaher Pond, 0.7 mile from the intersection of the Witherbee and Mineville roads. The path drops fifty feet to water level where two boats are chained in this tiny pond. Put in here and paddle east to Mill Pond through the connecting open channel.

22 Russett Pond
Path, fishing, canoeing

Russett Pond is the closest to the road of the four ponds. A short, 100-yard path leads to it from a point 1 mile north of the intersection of the Witherbee and Mineville roads. The fishing is good here. Meadowsweet and meadow rue grace the shore; a path of sorts winds along it.

Mill Pond

23 Lincoln Pond Area
Camping, swimming, fishing, canoeing, hiking, cross-country skiing, short but spectacular bushwhack

Lincoln Pond is a large 467-acre body of water (really a lake) 6 miles south of Elizabethtown on County Route 7. A small (fifteen-site) DEC campground has an excellent beach, and there are many activities to attract those with various outdoor interests. Camping is regulated along the entire western shoreline of the pond. That shoreline and a small section to the west of the Northway are Forest Preserve land. Access to the water and paths is easy and distances are not great.

If you are interested in fishing, the pond is stocked with hybrid muskelunge (alias norlunge or tiger musky). Northern pike and pickerel are also there, so anglers can enjoy the thrill of hooking one of these large fighting game fish. There is a free boat launching place (power boats are permitted) with a spot to leave your car, just 0.1 mile north of the campground entrance.

You can have a lakeside picnic on the point near the launching site thirty feet from where you park your car. Another water access, for canoes or boats you can carry, is at the north end of the lake. A gravel seasonal road (not plowed in winter), called Kingdom Road, leads to the dam at the north end of the pond; it goes east from County Route 7, 1.75 miles north of the campground entrance or 0.55 mile after you cross the Northway going south from Elizabethtown. There are camping spots on the right as you approach the water at the end of the road. Put in a canoe and paddle around the shore in this secluded neck of the pond, which is the outlet to Black River, a tributary of the Boquet.

If you wish to camp in the area with access to an excellent sand beach, the DEC campground is open from mid-May to Labor Day. A prime tent/trailer site on the water is $8.50 per night, and other sites are available for $7.00. There is a bath house available for day use at the beach.

If you are staying at the campground or visit after it has closed for the season, there is a short walk along the shore of the pond. Beginners can try their cross-country skis here in winter. From the road entrance, it is a ten-minute walk to the beach. Just before you enter the beach area there is a small trail to the right. It is a level path along the shore of the pond, going southwest. In ten minutes you come to a nice point for swimming or picnicking. In fifteen minutes, the path leaves the lake and appears to end, but if you continue for thirty yards you will reach an old logging road that goes slightly uphill to the northwest. Follow it up several hundred yards toward the Northway (you will hear traffic) and you will notice a "deer culvert." This culvert provides access to the west side of the Northway but there seems to be no trail on the other side. You continue on the logging road that runs parallel to the shore path for a while and then ends. Go straight through open woods and you will come out on the road to the beach, an easy thirty-minute loop.

There is another pleasant hike that can be made from the campground or by parking your car off County Route 7. Go 0.2 mile north of the campground entrance and turn left, west, on a dirt road that leads to an opening where brush is dumped. In fifty feet there is a faint road to the left—only two car tracks through grass and low brush. You can drive in 0.3 mile on this rough track, but there is limited clearance, so it is better to leave your car up the hill where brush is dumped and walk in the 0.3 mile. At the end of the rough track there is an opening where cars can turn around. A path goes off to the left at 200°—almost south—on a wide old logging road. The altitude here is 1130 feet, 100 feet above the level of Lincoln Pond. The path swings west towards the Northway and in two minutes you come to a clearing. You will see a fence to the right; go toward it and you will see the walk-through deer culvert that goes under the Northway. At the end of the second culvert there is a small wooden bridge over a little brook on the right. Cross the brook and go up hill for twenty feet to an old logging road. Walk up the road, which goes uphill gradually to the left at 320° magnetic. There are a few blowdowns on the old road but it would still make a pleasant cross-country skiing trip. It goes through an open hardwood forest with a lot of beech. On each side of the road the forest floor is covered with running pine, *Lycopodium complanatum*.

Less than twenty minutes after leaving the clearing (thirty minutes from the car on County Route 7) the road forks. Take the left fork. The right fork goes west only a few hundred yards before it reaches the Forest Preserve Boundary and the private lands of the Beaver Meadow Hunting Club.

Several minutes farther on along the left fork, the road forks again. If you go straight, you again reach the No Trespassing signs of the hunting club, so go left, south, at 180° magnetic. In about three minutes, this road ends in a beech grove about ten yards from the Forest Preserve boundary. Notice the claw marks way up the trunk of several of the large beech trees— black bear climb them to reach the beech nuts.

From this point, go south along the Forest Preserve boundary, which is clearly marked by yellow paint blazes on trees. Bushwhack up a rock slope, which comes out on a large rocky outcrop. Reindeer lichen, several types of mosses and thin grasses create an abstract palette of greens and tans in the moist cracks of the anorthosite rock. Look northwest for a very special view of Bald Peak, Rocky Peak Ridge, and the slides and summit of Giant Mountain. You get an unusual perspective of the three peaks from this spot and an appreciation of the long climb up Giant from the east, sections 32 and 41.

Continue east to the top of this unnamed hill, which is 1686 feet high. Marginal shield fern grows throughout the summit in clumps among the sweetfern, a low shrub with woody stems and a fern-like foliage. If you crush the leaves and twigs, you will smell the aromatic oils that give it its name.

Keep walking east toward an opening and you will have a spectacular view of Lincoln Pond, spread out 650 feet below. The swimming beach is like a bull's eye in the panorama. It takes less than an hour from County Route 7 to reach this impressive peak, and you will be well-rewarded by the two overlooks and the several varieties of nonflowering plants seen on this walk. Retrace your steps and you will be back to the Northway underpass in thirty minutes.

24 Black River Road
Hiking, fishing, cross-country skiing, optional bushwhack
2.3 miles, 1 hour, relatively level

The Black River is the picturesque tributary of the Boquet River, which drains Lincoln Pond. The downstream portions are stocked with landlocked salmon. From Lincoln Pond it flows generally north for about 7 miles before emptying into the Boquet just east of the Northway and 2.7 miles north of Exit 31. You get an unusual view of the Black River as the Northway crosses it on a high bridge 1.6 miles south of Exit 31. This excursion explores the steep upstream section of the valley of the Black River south of the Northway crossing. North of the crossing, the Black River enters a flat-bottomed valley of pastureland, where it meanders through an extensive marsh before entering the Boquet.

Black River Road is not heavily traveled and not plowed in winter, so it is perfect for skiing. An attractive alternative during the spring or summer is a walk along the right bank of the river. This section describes a downhill trip from Lincoln Pond to the Megsville Road.

To park on the Megsville Road, leave the Northway at Exit 31 and travel west toward Elizabethtown on NY 9N. You cross the Black River at 1.1 miles, just upstream from its meander section. Brainerd Forge Road is on the right, north, at 1.3 miles, and you turn left, south, at 1.3 miles on Megsville Road. The Northway bridge is at 2.4 miles and at 3 miles the unimproved Black River Road is a right turn. There is room to park here or just east across the Black River.

The southern access is via Kingdom Road, see section 23. Kingdom Road winds and turns eastward, crosses an arm of Lincoln Pond, and reaches the dam 1.4 miles from County Route 7.

Today the 730-acre Lincoln Pond is formed by a 15-foot-high slab and buttress dam that was constructed at the turn of the century to provide electric power for the iron mines at Mineville. This more than doubled the size of Lincoln Pond. A small dam existed here in earlier years and Winslow Watson's 1869 history describes the site as Kingdom Forge, owned by the Essex and Lake Champlain Ore and Iron Co. (the same company that owned Valley Forge in Elizabethtown). The enterprise was started with two forge fires a half mile farther downstream by Henry R. Noble as early as 1825. The remains of Kingdom Forge can be seen along the left, northwest, bank of the Black River just below the Lincoln Pond dam.

There is a Dead End sign on Kingdom Road at the Lincoln Pond dam. Continue past the sign and follow Kingdom Road as it drops sharply to cross the Black River on pieces of old penstock. Immediately after crossing the river, turn left and you will be heading north on Black River Road. The road on the right leads south to camps on the east side of Lincoln Pond. During the winter it can be skied down to where Lincoln Pond Road crosses Lincoln Pond on the causeway that divides the pond in two. This road is the connector in the long ski trip of section 25.

After turning left onto Black River Road, you will find the unpaved road stays level and high up on the right bank of the river. At 0.5 mile, the road drops moderately to cross the river on a bridge. Just before this drop a trail enters on the right, from the east; it joins up with the trails that climb to Nichols Pond from Phunyea Hollow, and can serve as an alternate ski route for the loop described in section 25.

Along this first half mile of Black River Road the concrete supports for iron penstocks can be found in the woods between the road and the river. Occasionally pieces of this iron penstock have been incorporated into the road as culverts and those traveling the river farther downstream will find many large pieces of penstock that have broken loose in the flood waters.

Evidence of this early forge can be found if you explore carefully upstream from the bridge along the right bank of the river.

Just before crossing the bridge, you will see the remains of an early road on the right. It continues along the right bank of the river, though at present it is so overgrown that walking it must be considered a bushwhack, requiring map and compass. If you choose the old right bank road, be sure to revisit the river frequently in its upper stretches when you hear the sound of rushing water. You will be rewarded with views of several beautiful flumes and small waterfalls that have formed where water has eroded fractures and small black dikes in the more resistant, coarsely crystalline, green syenite rocks that form this "wild and narrow pass." (*NYS Museum Bulletin* 138) The bushwhack along the river is generally northeast for 0.7 mile to a tributary, then more northerly for another 0.7 mile where a change of direction to due north for 0.3 mile brings you to Megsville Road. Travel the 2.3 miles back along Black River Road to Kingdom Road and your car.

In summer you can make the bushwhack and return via the Black River Road. Those who are skiing will likely stay on the road after it crosses the Black River. The road generally contours, with some ups but more downs, along the left bank through a mixed deciduous and coniferous forest. It is possible to make at least one side excursion to the southeast through the open forest to see some of the flumes, but be careful.

The steep slopes to the left, northwest, form Tunnel Mountain (not named on the USGS map,) which has a summit elevation of 502 meters (1647 feet). Near the summit of Tunnel Mountain there is an old iron mine that gives the mountain its name and the remains of several additional prospects can be found at the foot of the mountain along its eastern end.

Gradually the road begins to descend, and at about 1.3 miles the Patten Flats Trail enters on the right. This trail can be used to reach Nichols Pond, Hoisington School, or Ledge Hill Road, sections 28 and 29. By staying left you reach the Megsville Road pickup at 2.3 miles.

The area along Megsville Road near the Northway crossing is the site of Megsville itself. In the 1870s, it was the location of the Kingdom Iron Ore Company of Lake Champlain. Early in this century, the Kingdom power plant of the Wadhams and Westport Electric Light Company was located a short distance upstream from the Northway Bridge. The abandoned building still stands on the right bank of the river just upstream from the old iron bridge. The broken pieces of penstock that you saw earlier in the trip carried water from Lincoln Pond to this power plant.

25 Fletcherville
Cross-country skiing, hiking, exploring

A short ski or hiking trip that begins near the ghost town of historic Fletcherville makes for an exciting adventure back in time. You can add to it a long loop from the same southern access and circle through the Nichols Pond Tract to make a full-day, 16-mile ski trek. This section details both the two-hour exploring trip and the all-day trek.

Fletcherville was the site of a blast furnace that began operation in August 1865 as an enterprise owned by Friend P. Fletcher of Bridport, Vermont, and Silas H. and Jonathan G. Witherbee, uncle and nephew, of Moriah. The furnace and the town around it operated until Fletcher's death in 1874. It is interesting to note that this furnace had one of the earliest chemical laboratories ever attached to a blast furnace.

To begin this trip, drive north on Lincoln Pond Road, County Route 7, from the intersection with the road to Witherbee, County Route 6, for 0.4 mile and turn right, northeast on Bartlett Pond Road. At 0.7 mile, turn left onto Spring Road, which has various local names: Cook Shaft Road, Davis Road, North Pond Road, and Mountain Spring Road. At 1.3 miles a road enters on the left and you are at the limit of winter plowing. Park here.

Ski north on Spring Road, which bends right at 0.3 mile and crosses a tributary of Bartlett Brook. This is Fletcherville and just across Bartlett Brook on the left, west, side of Spring Road a strange mound of rock and earth marks the site of the blast furnace. When it was new in 1865, it was forty-two feet high, constructed of quarried granite held together with bolted iron tie rods that can still be seen. A bridge connected the top of the furnace with the hill to the north to allow the furnace to be filled or charged with charcoal, roasted iron ore, and a limestone or marble flux.

Across the road, stone foundations mark one of the earliest industrial chemical laboratories in the country. Over a dozen stone foundations can be located in nearby woods—the last remains of a hamlet that had its own school and several houses and boarding houses. The depression of 1873 and the death of one of the owners of the foundry brought an end to Fletcherville.

Continue past the blast furnace for a short distance to the benchmark (418.3 meters) where a marked snowmobile trail enters on the left. Turn sharply left on this snowmobile trail and head southwest to where it crosses under the power lines. The rock wall on your right once formed a backdrop for a string of ten kilns constructed of brick. Each kiln held sixty-five cords of wood each time it was fired. The blast furnace is down below to the left and you can see the foundations of the charging bridge.

Your route continues under the power lines as the snowmobile route turns gradually to the northwest following the left bank of Bartlett Brook. The U-shaped stone structures on the left are the old roasting kilns. About 0.2 mile beyond the power lines, the trail forks to the left.

The route straight ahead goes north, past the head of Bartlett Brook and passes a red outhouse installed for snowmobilers. Gradually it climbs northwest to a height-of-land and descends to Molly Burns Swamp. In the swamp, the route turns left, west, and descends to an unnamed brook to join the road along the east side of Lincoln Pond, just north of the causeway. By leaving a vehicle at the east end of the causeway over Lincoln Pond, it is possible to make a one-way trip of 5 miles from Fletcherville.

To make a longer loop, continue skiing north along the road on the east side of Lincoln Pond to the dam at its outlet. From here you can ski the Black River Road, section 24, or head out to County Route 7 on Kingdom Road, if you have spotted cars at either trailhead. Alternatively, by using the Patten Flats and Phunyea Hollow Snowmobile Trails, section 28, ski to Nichols Pond where you can ski south and reach Spring Road, which takes you back to Fletcherville, completing the 16-mile loop. This is an extremely long and arduous trip and should be done only after you become acquainted with the northern segments.

For a shorter loop and more exploring, turn left from the snowmobile trail to Lincoln Pond. After crossing Bartlett Brook, the road climbs a short distance before turning abruptly south. On the right as you make the turn, you can see the foundations that once supported the hauling derrick of the Sherman Mine. The mine, now filled with water, is just across the road. Here and at frequent intervals in your travels in this country, you will see the red on white signs of IP Timberlands. The signs say "Danger, Do Not Enter, Unsafe Areas, Open Pits, Old Mine Works" and they mean it. IP allows skiers to use the old tote roads but will not tolerate trespass in these unsafe areas. Please heed the warnings.

The Sherman Mine was one of several that supplied ore to Fletcherville. After the blast furnace was closed down, the Sherman Mine continued intermittently until 1921. A spur of the Lake Champlain and Moriah Railroad was extended north past the Smith Hill Mine (see below) to Sherman Mine. Your route bends left at the Sherman Mine and follows this railroad grade south.

A short distance south of the Sherman Mine, a snowmobile trail enters sharply on the right. By following this trail for 1 mile to the west and southwest you can cross the northwest flank of the 573-meter hill to Fisher Hill. At Fisher Hill you come to Burhart Road, the Fisher Mine area, and the Lincoln Pond Road with the east end of Mill Pond, section 21. If you do this side trip, be sure to stay on the roads. The area west of Burhart Road over to Tanaher Pond has many old mines from the Burt Lot, and it is not a safe area for wandering around.

Continue south past the side trail to Fisher Hill for 0.7 mile on the old railroad grade. The platform for the haul derrick for the Smith Hill Mine is on the left of the trail. The Smith Hill Mine is immediately on the right of the railroad grade surrounded by a chain-link fence. *Do not go inside the fence under any circumstances.* The mine is dry and consists of a deep, nearly vertical shaft that leads to an ore bed that was mined on a very steep angle to the west. Because no bedrock is exposed near the surface, the mine had to be discovered by using a magnetic dip needle. The sand around the mine shaft is constantly caving in, making the entire area inside the fence dangerous.

Continue past the Smith Hill Mine for a short distance and take the next left, again crossing under the power lines. You will shortly reach your car parked on Spring Road.

The loop to Fletcherville and back by way of the mines is 2.5 miles and without side trips will only take about an hour, depending on conditions. One-way trips with two vehicles can be made as noted, and to Lincoln Pond Road via Russett Pond, section 22. With two vehicles, you can also ski to Nichols Pond and down to the eastern approach, section 27. The favorite trip, however, is the 16-mile loop from Fletcherville to Molly Burns Swamp, Lincoln Pond, Freedom, Black River Road, Patten Flats, Nobles Hill, Phunyea Hollow, Nichols Pond, and back on Spring Road. Allow a full day for this one as there is a lot of climbing and few trail signs. Sometimes Spring Road is plowed for logging, so check it first.

26 The Pinnacle

Hiking, cross-country skiing, picnicking, scenic overlook

A short hike or cross-country ski trip from the Fish and Game Club west of Westport brings you to a splendid overlook of Lake Champlain and the Green Mountains of Vermont. The Pinnacle and most of the trail leading up to it is on International Paper Company land, but day use is permitted. The 2.5-mile round trip has a climb of 75 meters (247 feet).

To reach the Fish and Game Club, where the trip begins, go west on Washington Street in downtown Westport, cross the railroad tracks and turn right on Mountain Spring Road. From the turn go 1.1 miles to a fork, then left to the Club at 2 miles. The trip starts by the club sign and a smaller sign reading "Bessboro Ski-ters." Go downhill, southwest, past a sign saying "Pinnacle Trail 1.3 miles." In three minutes of skiing, longer hiking, the old road forks. Go right over a little brook and continue south. After nearly ten minutes' skiing, the Pinnacle Trail goes off to the right, west, (there is no sign here) and begins to climb gradually, then more steeply. You climb through a pretty hemlock, pine, and hardwood forest—and it gets steeper, requiring some herringbone steps even with waxless skis. Less than half an hour from the start, as you level off at 800 feet elevation, there is a clear road to the right, east. This open road has barbed wire on the right and a cabin in the woods to the left. A gradual climb of five minutes gets you to the overlook.

For a short hike, the 180° view is magnificent. You can look northeast down on Westport, North West Bay, Split Rock Mountain and Lake Champlain stretching toward Canada. Across the lake to the east are the Green Mountains of Vermont. The remains of a beautiful stone fireplace and chimney and the charred cellar hole of a cabin stand on the bluff. It is a nice place for a relaxed lunch.

Leave the Pinnacle by the same trail, skiing west. At the T at the end of the first slope, turn right, north, to continue the loop back to your car. In eight minutes you have skied down an intermediate hill to another T. It is marked the Stacy Brook Trail and an arrow indicates that if you go left, you will reach the Nichols Pond Road. Go right, around the small pond, and in three minutes you complete the loop. The whole trip takes under an hour on skis, longer on foot.

If snowmobiles have opened the way you can make a much longer circle trip in this area, and reach another overlook. Starting as for the Pinnacle, go straight ahead after ten minutes where the Pinnacle Road turned right. This is the Delaney Trail and it heads southeast down a steep hill and then southerly in front of a summer home. Continue south at a lower level than the Pinnacle. Snowmobilers then head west up seasonal McConnley Road, south of Stockwell Mountain, and then north on what they call the Upper Poker Run Trail. This will take you back to the Pinnacle exit route and down to your car. The trip is about three hours on skis, and is good only if it is opened by snowmobiles since a number of old rolling roads make the route hard to follow. The longer trail climbs to 1300 feet in one spot and should be attempted only by intermediate skiers.

27 Ski Trekking to Nichols Pond
Cross-country skiing
9 miles, 4½ hours, 870-foot vertical rise

This seasonal road from the east into the Nichols Pond recreation area provides a wide cross-country ski track through an attractive hardwood forest. The loop described includes skiing along the pond. There are no signs of logging in this stretch and the view of snow-capped Giant and Rocky Peak Ridge on a sunny day is memorable.

Follow directions for the Pinnacle, section 26, to the fork 0.4 mile before the Fish and Game Club. The seasonal highway called Spring Road on the metric map goes uphill to the right from that fork. There is no parking at the intersection, and the steep snowbanks make you leave your car on the wide road.

The trip starts at 208 meters (682 feet) and begins climbing right away. You need the right wax or waxless skis for this climb. In twenty minutes you are at 900 feet; the road levels somewhat and turns more to the west with Stacy Brook on your left. At 1 mile you cross the brook, but stay near it and after an hour's climb you begin to leave the brook near a fork in the road. At 1.6 miles (one hour), the right fork called the Nichols Pond Trail goes more directly to Nichols Pond, but there may be no track along it. If you go left you reach an open meadow with a hunter's camp in about twenty minutes. The clearing provides a sweeping view of Giant and other snowy peaks to the west. It is a good place to have lunch and savor this Rocky Mountain-like beauty.

Continue past the clearing and in twenty-five minutes you reach the logging road from Fletcherville, section 25, which goes north, right, to Nichols Pond. This road is plowed in some years to provide access for logging trucks. If it is, you can ski up on the banks most of the way, reaching Nichols Pond at 4.5 miles, forty-five minutes from the turn, about three hours and a quarter from your car, including lunch.

The pond, which you can reach by car from April through November, is very pretty with white birch and an island in the center. Although there are several camps around the pond, they are not visible unless you go around to the north side. It is a destination point for some snowmobilers and a number of trails fan out from here.

The pond is at 465 meters (1550 feet) and the trip back to your car is rapid. You can take the left fork 0.6 mile from the pond and rejoin Spring Road 1 mile beyond. For the trip downhill, you need a good snowplow and stem christie, and even then you can expect to fall in the steep sections. It takes a little over an hour to get back—less if you take the more direct route along Stacy Brook.

28 Phunyea Hollow Telemarking
Cross-country skiing for the experienced skier, hiking

You cannot find the words Phunyea Hollow (also written Phunney Hollow by local snowmobilers) on the USGS map, but it is one of the best expert ski trails around. You climb about 1050 feet in a little less than 3 miles and the last section is steep enough for climbing skins, although you can herringbone it. The old lumber road is clear enough and wide enough for some tight telemark turns but it can be skied with a good snowplow and some stem christies.

The beginning of the trip is at a sandpit (marked on the topo map) on McMahon Road. From the fork on Mountain Spring Road, see section 26, go right for 2.15 miles; the spot is 0.15 mile south of Ledge Hill Road. Climb out of the sandpit to the southwest on a wide lumber road with Hoisington Mountain on your left, south. After less than ten minutes of moderate climbing, you come to a level stretch and swing more to the west. It is a pretty area—hemlock and hardwood—with no recent signs of logging although you are on IP land the entire time.

In just over twenty minutes, there is a scenic brook on your left and very extensive signs of deer, perhaps indicative of a winter deer yard. Shortly beyond the road forks and signs indicate "Harpers Mountain, Phunyea Hollow, Nichols Pond" to the left, "Patten Flats, Nobles Notch, Nichols Pond" to the right. Keep to the right, because the fork is not an open trail.

You cross a flat area with white pine, then, twelve minutes from the first fork, reach another fork. The left is marked "Nichols Pond via Nobles, Mineville via North Pond." At this point you have climbed 300 feet in about 1.3 miles. The route right, marked "Lincoln Pond via Patten Flats, Kingdom Dam, and Mineville via Lincoln Pond," goes north of Nobles Hill and is described in section 29.

Go left, southwest, getting a run down a small hill, and then swing westerly in a gradual climb. You are on the north slope of a deep valley, with the brook far below on your left and sharp rocky hills towering above you. After you pass the peak of Nobles Hill on your right and reach the headwaters of the brook, you cut sharp south up a steep hill and then con-

Howard Pond

tour uphill quite steeply to the southeast. After an hour and a half into the trip, you really begin to climb going southwest. There are splendid views through the forest of the valley north and of Lake Champlain to the east. At the point where the trail swings to the southeast, there is a route (unmarked) that cuts over to the Power Line Trail; this is another way over to Kingdom Road along the Black River, section 24.

You keep climbing, wishing for skins on your skis if you do not have them, and come out into a staging area for loggers. In the two-hour climb so far, you have gained 1050 feet. Up over the final hill and down two hundred yards you will reach the western side of the northern tip of Nichols Pond. Logging activity has opened the area so much it is hard to find the route, but you can return to McMahon Road by the old Tram Road. Go east around the northern tip of the pond and opposite the eastern tip look for an open route to the east, around the south slope of Harpers Mountain. The Tram Road is the steepest descent to McMahon Road and comes out 0.65 mile east of the Y. The middle section is steeper than Phunyea and only for experts.

Nichols Pond is quite pretty, a mile long with two islands. It was named after John Nichols who settled near the pond in the first decade of the nineteenth century. There were two iron mines north of the pond and charcoal kilns in the area. Iron was carried out on the tram way and the ruins of the separator were still visible in 1902 when they were described by Caroline Halstead Royce in her history *Bessboro*. In the Hoisington Cemetery an old marker records the death of Benjamin Nichols, age 46, in 1817. Nichols' nearest neighbors to the south were the Harpers—thus Harper Mountain to the east of the pond.

Starting back down from the pond, (it is best if you have mountaineering skis and can carve a turn) you can run the top part easily. Within ten minutes you reach the road going off to the power line, at about 1500 feet elevation. Bear sharp right down a steep grade going southeast. The road is about ten feet wide so you can weave across it, doing telemark turns as you drop very rapidly. The steepest part ends after twenty minutes from the top and you can relax and enjoy some great runs. In forty minutes you reach the spot where a left leads to Patten Flats and Kingdom Dam Road. From here back to your car is delightful skiing, all downhill, all fairly gradual.

29 Nobles Hill
Intermediate cross-country skiing, hiking

A shorter and easier route west begins at the sandpit and follows the beginning of the Phunyea Hollow route, section 28. Go right at the second fork, west, following the sign to Lincoln Pond via Patten Flats and Kingdom Dam. The road stays on the level for about fifteen minutes from the fork, winding north of Nobles Hill. It then falls from 1000 feet to 700 feet through open hardwoods. At Patten Flats the route forks, with the right fork going out north to Ledge Hill Road and the left fork going up Black River to the dam at the outlet of Lincoln Pond. You can either retrace your steps or make a long one-way trek by combining these trips and leaving a car at the beginning of Kingdom Road on County Route 7, the Lincoln Pond Road, section 23.

New Russia Area

THE FIRST RIVULETS of the Boquet River, which graces the narrow New Russia Valley, flow high on the northern slopes of the Dix Range. Its North Fork begins near Hunters Pass and tumbles down steep wooded gorges before it joins the cascading South Fork near the intersections of NY 9 and 73, northeast of Northway Exit 30. This clear, sparkling stream continues its rapid descent—it has fallen 3200 feet from its source already—over large rocks and cobbles until it drops over Split Rock Falls. Between the confluence of the forks and the falls it is swelled by Slide Brook, rushing down from Rocky Peak Ridge. Below the falls, Coughlin and Stevens brooks also come in from the west. Suddenly, the character of this swift mountain stream changes—during the twelve miles from the falls to Elizabethtown it drops only 120 feet. Here the Boquet meanders over a bed of sand and pebbles in a meadow valley, its flow increased only by Roaring Brook, which joins it below New Russia. The towering peaks to the west and the lower mountains to the east remind you, in Jamieson's words, of a "vale in Switzerland." The early settlers had a name for it that still appears on topographic maps: Pleasant Valley.

The name of the river (pronounced "Bo-KET"—not the way the French would say it) is not clear. One view is that it was named for the French Jesuit lay brother, Charles Boquet, who fought Mohawk Indians on the shores of Lake Champlain. Another possibility is that explorers may have called it *bacquet*, the French word for trough. In any event, the name dates from the mid-1700s, when French influence dominated the shores of Lake Champlain. Historians have now agreed, however, that the correct spelling is Boquet, the form used by this guide, even though the USGS still spells it Bouquet.

In the New Russia Valley, the river is classified as a Recreational River under the 1972 Wild, Scenic, and Recreational Rivers System Act. It is popular with fishermen and canoeists. It is stocked with rainbow, speckled, and brown trout and there are several access sites for fishermen. One is 1.3 miles north of Split Rock Falls at the start of the trail to Mt. Gilligan; another is 3.5 miles north of the falls. Canoeing is possible only in April and May or after a long rainy period; Paul Jamieson has an excellent description of the canoe route in his *Adirondack Canoe Waters—North Flow*.

The valley was settled by pioneers moving south from Elizabethtown in the 1780s. A steep drop on the Boquet near the center of town was the site of an 1870 forge. Iron was mined in nearby hills (one is called Iron Mountain) when the area thrived, but the pits were abandoned in 1882.

A small private ski slope operates at Otis Hill in the northern part of the valley. You will enjoy visiting this quiet valley with its majestic peaks which tower four thousand feet above the lowland fields. Start your hikes with Mt. Gilligan and Bald Peak and work up to the "Giant of Pleasant Valley," described in section 41.

30 Split Rock Falls
Scenic spot, picnic area

The sharpest drop in the Boquet River comes just before it levels out in the valley of New Russia. There is a small parking place beside NY 9 as you come down the hill, 2.3 miles north of the intersection of NY 9 and 73. As you drive north, the river is on your left and you cross over it just before coming to the parking lot. The falls are to the east, practically beside the road.

The water of the Boquet drops over precipitous angular rocks into deep pools, filling the narrow gorge with mist. In all the several cataracts fall over 100 feet. It is difficult to photograph because of the trees and lack of access downstream, but it is an impressive site, particularly during snow melt in the spring, when it is awe inspiring.

31 Mt Gilligan
Trail, hiking, views
1.2 miles, 1¼ hours, 770-foot vertical rise

The perch from the open rock slab just below the wooded summit of Mt Gilligan gives you a commanding view southeast from Pleasant Valley along the valley of the Boquet River to the slide on East Dix. On the climb a series of vantages look out to Bald Peak and Rocky Peak Ridge. This is a small mountain, nestled below giants, and the easy climb is all reward.

There is a parking area for fishermen beside the Boquet River, 1.3 miles north of Split Rock Falls, 3.6 miles north of the intersection of NY 9 and 73 at the turnoff for Beaver Meadow Road. Park here and walk across the bridge; the Boquet is here a pretty, shallow, cobbled stream.

A sign near the bridge says this is the Sunrise Trail (the mountain was formerly called Sunrise) to Mt Gilligan and the trail is marked with orange

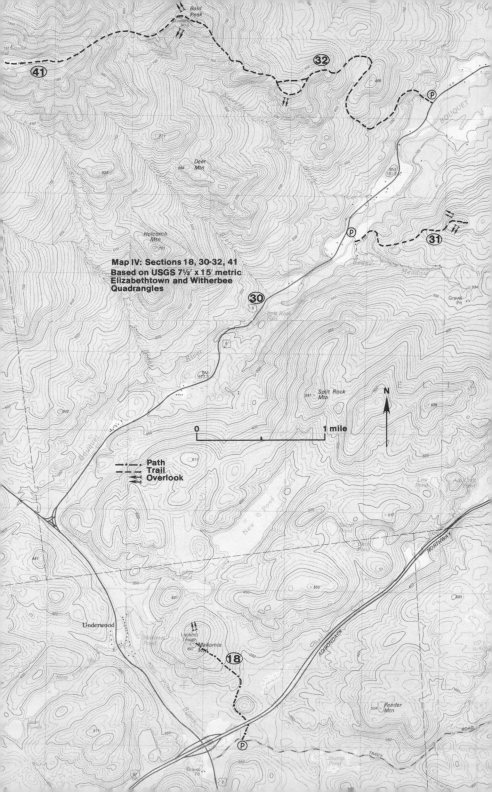

Map IV: Sections 18, 30-32, 41
Based on USGS 7½' x 15' metric
Elizabethtown and Witherbee
Quadrangles

(41)
(32)
(31)
(30)
(18)

Bald
Peak

Deer
Mtn

Holcomb
Mtn

Split Rock
Mtn

BOUQUET

Gravel
Pit

New Pond

Lou
Pond

Underwood

Lookout Tower
Makomis
Mtn

Peeder
Mtn

NORTHWAY

ADIRONDACK

TRACY ROAD

Stump
Pond

Gravel
Pit

N

0   1 mile

Path
Trail
Overlook

ADK disks. You cross the bridge and in 100 yards leave the road to head north on the trail, which starts out on the level through a hardwood forest with Christmas and oak ferns beside it. At 0.1 mile, you start to climb, zigzagging under a large rock ledge. Ten minutes and 0.3 mile from the beginning, you reach an open rock area atop the ledge. The view is northwest toward Rocky Peak Ridge with Holcomb and Deer mountains in the foreground.

You continue climbing generally north of east through the woods, where unusually large ironwood is mixed with tall hemlock and red pine. A stairs of rocks and roots leads to a second overlook, reached after twenty minutes. This one has views to the south and Split Rock Mountain. A third overlook, at 0.6 miles shows Bald Peak and Rocky Peak Ridge. The trail now follows a narrow rock ridge, then descends into a small draw to cross at 0.8 mile an old woods road that is being used by dirt bikes. Maidenhair fern can be found in this draw.

Two more overlooks lie between here and the final one below the summit. You climb steadily along the rocky path to reach the first, where red paint directs you northeast across the open rock. The ascent is now more gradual. You pass an arrow that directs you a few feet from the trail to an overlook. The trail becomes steep again as it begins the climb up the last knob and red arrows again direct you around the ledges.

You cross a patch of blueberries and rusty woodsia fern to reach the final overlook at 1.2 miles with its exquisite view of the Boquet Valley, both north and south.

Even with a picnic it is hard to stretch this walk (the descent requires no more than forty minutes), but if you want to stretch your legs, walk up Beaver Meadow Road. The roadsides are privately owned, but you can appreciate the beautiful hemlock gorge surrounding Beaver Meadow Brook from the road itself.

32 Bald Peak
Marked trail, hiking, birding
3.7 miles, 4½ hours round trip, 2400-foot vertical rise

As you gaze west from the overlooks of Mt Gilligan across the upper Boquet Valley, you see the massive slopes of the Giant Mountain Wilderness Area. To the northwest there is a rocky summit almost 2000 feet higher than Mt Gilligan. That is the destination of this climb. It is intermediate in difficulty and a good choice before tackling Giant.

Dix Range from Mt Gilligan

The trailhead is located on NY 9, 4.8 miles north of the intersection of NY 9 and 73, or 1.3 miles south of the road to Lincoln Pond in New Russia. The DEC sign indicates this is the East Trail to Giant Mountain, but the distances for Blueberry Cobbles (1.66 miles) and Bald Mountain (3.52 miles) are incorrect. A large parking lot shows the popularity of this route, which was cut to the top of Giant mountain in the mid-1960s, hence does not appear on the 15-minute USGS series 1955 map. (It does appear on the 1978 metric series used in this guide.)

The trail with sporadic yellow markers starts out at 190 meters (623 feet) and you go briefly northwest, then southwest, climbing gradually on old logging roads. Along the route you immediately notice many different ferns, among them maidenhair, Christmas, marginal shield, and spinulose wood-fern. This section is excellent for birding in the spring, when it also has numerous wildflowers.

In less than twenty minutes, at 0.7 mile, you will contour over to a small stream that you follow for several more minutes. You climb northwest through a nice hardwood grove of white birch and maple with a mixture of poplar, hemlock, and pine. After climbing for a half hour, there is a path to the right, slightly uphill, which ends in the woods and seems to go nowhere significant. In forty minutes you cross a noticeable old logging road running east to west; the trail is going north at this point.

After fifty minutes, at 1.5 miles, there is a spring on the right which may have water in summer. If so, it is the last water you will find on this hike, however, it is not reliable, so it is better to start with full canteens.

The trail now hairpins and takes a southeasterly direction. In less than an hour's climb, at 1.7 miles, a path to the left goes to a lookout south into the valley. The point is at about 520 meters, 1700 feet. You continue northward and reach a sign at 1.8 miles indicating a view to the right. From this overlook you can see your destination above and, looking up the Boquet Valley, the small town of New Russia. One of the joys of this hike is the frequent views of the barren rugged summit, ever closer, as you wind up the mountain.

The main trail with yellow disks is easy to follow through the woods, which here consist of good-size oak and red pine mixed with hemlock. After climbing one hour and ten minutes, at 1.9 miles, you walk over to an open rock ledge for a splendid view of Bald Peak somewhat to the right, with Rocky Peak Ridge just to the left of it, almost straight ahead. In five more minutes, just short of 2 miles, you come to a sign reading "Scenic Trail over Blueberry Cobbles" and the yellow-marked trail goes left toward it. To the right, a red-marked trail has a sign that says "Short-Cut Trail 0.23 miles."

A five-minute walk from the fork along the yellow trail takes you to the cobbles with its beautiful view south. You are at 610 meters, 2000 feet, and as you follow the yellow arrows around the open rock, the open peak of Bald rises one thousand feet above you. That rocky goal stimulates the adrenaline, producing the second wind you need for the rest of the hike. There is a marvelous view of Hough and the peaks going up to Dix, to the southwest, as you go along the cobble. Soon after, you drop down steeply into Mason Notch, where at 2.5 miles, an hour and a half of hiking if you do not pause too long for views and the famous blueberries, you pass the cutoff trail coming in on the right.

After crossing the col of Mason Notch, you climb northwest toward a small knob locally known as Mason Mountain. There is an extensive patch of maidenhair on its slopes and in May you can admire Dutchman's-breeches in profusion.

After a very brief descent, at 3 miles you begin the last steep ascent of Bald Mountain. As you climb, the range of High Peaks emerge in the distance looking toward 230° magnetic. Macomb is the highest (in the middle); Hough is on the right; South Dix is below Macomb; and East Dix is on the left. Looking at 220° magnetic you can see Nippletop, Niagara, and Camels Hump, described in the "Under the Northway" chapter.

The trail reaches open rock at 3.2 miles, two hours from the parking lot, and the way is now marked by cairns and occasional yellow paint daubs on rocks. Nice views continue to the south, occasionally you see glimpses of the summit. After climbing ten minutes more, the distinct ridge between Bald Peak and Rocky Peak becomes obvious; marking it, clearly, is a large boulder, which sticks up like a shark fin. The trail angles northwest over open rock. Below the summit there is a view of Green Mountain to the northwest across the valley of Roaring Brook; its south-facing rock cliffs stand out clearly. Due north the sharp prow of Owl Head shows clearly on the skyline.

The summit of Bald Peak at 925 meters, 3060 feet, is reached at 3.7 miles after a climb of two hours and thirty-five minutes. The violet-blue flowers of harebell and white cinquefoil bloom in crevices in the rock, even in fall. To the east you can see Lake Champlain and to the southwest the Dix Range. You may find, however, the most impressive view is to the west where Rocky Peak Ridge and the slides and summit of Giant loom and beckon. That climb from the peak you are on takes you to two peaks over 4000 feet and is described in section 41.

If you choose to return to your car to complete this hike, the trip back will seem effortless. If you take the red short-cut trail, it should take only a little more than one and a half hours.

Giant Mountain
Wilderness Area

THE ADIRONDACKS are old mountains with a long and complex history that includes a significant period of mountain building about a billion years ago. The rocks of the High Peaks, including the bulk of the Giant Mountain Range, were formed during this period that geologists call the Grenville Orogeny. Subsequently, the Adirondack dome has continued to rise at a slow rate while natural processes have worked to wear down the rising dome. The continental ice sheets that invaded the area several times in the last million years scoured and eroded the anorthosite bedrock of the High Peaks area. As the ice melted back, it left debris, which formed small hills, dammed valleys, and peppered the countryside with large glacial erratics that had been carried from distant places. The effects of these geological actions are especially evident in the 22,104 acre Giant Mountain Wilderness Area, the largest contiguous public land mass in this book.

Reports suggest that a British party from Sir Jeffrey Amherst's army may have climbed Giant in the 1750s. The standard reference for first ascents in the High Peaks is Russell Carson's *Peaks and People of the Adirondacks*. Carson believes the first ascent of the mountain was probably by Charles Broadhead, who ran a surveying line near the summit in 1797. Carson credits the first ascent, after it was called Giant, to Old Man Phelps, George and Levi Lamb in July 1854. Phelps and his son cut the first trail to the summit by way of Hopkins and Green mountains in 1866. Colvin set up a triangulation station on the top in 1873 and a trail was cut from Elizabethtown the following year. A decade later there was a good trail from New Russia; and the Roaring Brook Trail from St. Huberts was cut by Orlando Beede and Alfred Reed about 1873 or 1874.

People were obviously attracted to the mountain in early days. The area still offers a wealth of experiences and challenges: high exposed peaks, ski-touring in the north, slide climbing in the southwest, overnight camping in the interior, beautiful waterfalls and clear streams, secluded ponds, and the longest hiking trails in the northeastern Adirondacks. Although some climbs are short, most are steep and require strong legs and proper footgear. The area includes Giant at 1410 meters (4627 feet) and Rocky Peak Ridge at 1336 meters (4420 feet). These are two of the fabled forty-six peaks

East Slides of Giant from High Bank

recognized by the Adirondack Forty-sixers whose list of peaks over 4000-feet tall was based on the 1892 USGS Survey.

The area is wild and rugged with steep cliffs and exposed rocks; indeed, the entire southeastern section is virtually inaccessible even today. Much of the area was burned in 1903 when fire swept over the south shoulder and all of Rocky Ridge before it was extinguished not far from the Nubble and only 100 yards from the Otis farm at the foot of Chapel Pond Hill. Harold Weston in *Freedom in the Wilds* also describes the 1913 fire, which swept across the valley from the south, passed the Nubble, and reached virgin timber before it was controlled. Rocky Peak Ridge is still bare, although stunted spruce, aspen, white birch, and balsam fir are beginning to fill in some upper slopes.

Perhaps the most remarkable feature of the cone of Giant is its slides. Bowl-shaped cirques were carved by glaciers on the eastern and southwestern slopes, which held thin soils precariously attached to poorly jointed bedrock. The eastern slides above the bed of the Roaring Brook, which flows toward St. Huberts, occurred in one mammoth surge. On June 29, 1963, heavy clouds dumped six inches of rain in this cirque in a very short time. The soil became water logged and slipped, its mass and speed increased as soil, rocks, and trees swept the mountainside. As it reached the lower slopes the mass slowed but the momentum swept it into the valley floor, completely blocking NY 73 with rubble ten to fifteen feet deep. Debris also eliminated the beautiful Roaring Brook Falls as the stream was redirected into Putnam Brook. Conservation officers quickly constructed dikes, which can still be seen upstream from the falls, to force the stream back into its channel, thus recreating the spectacular falls seen from NY 73. Time has covered much of the rubble, but the extensive exposed rock slides on Giant's slopes are described in section 38.

The Giant Wilderness Area can be entered from all four sides. The eastern boundary is the Pleasant Valley of the Boquet River described in the New Russia chapter. The elevation change on this longest east trail is 4000 feet, the largest elevation differential per horizontal mile of any Adirondack trail. The northern boundary is NY 9N running west from Elizabethtown. From NY 9N the north trail leads to a lean-to in the core of the area between Giant and Green mountains, and then to Giant's summit or to the west. Another trail leads off this road to the easily climbed Baxter Mountain, and a bushwhack goes up Knob Lock Mountain. The two southern trailheads are reached from NY 73, which goes northwest through the fault valley from Northway Exit 30. The Ridge Trail starts near Chapel Pond and the Roaring Brook Trail begins 1.5 miles farther northwest near Roaring Brook Falls. These two trails from the south join before reaching the summit of Giant and, since they are the shortest way up, both are heavily used. Between these two trails, about a mile in, is the largest of three ponds in the area—the Washbowl. There is a trail around the Washbowl and another trail goes over the Nubble, a spectacular lookout northwest of the Washbowl. The western trailheads are described in the Keene Valley chapter. All in all, this is the most extensive official trail system in this book.

33 Roaring Brook Trail to Giant Summit and Roaring Brook Lean-to
Hiking, camping
5.1 miles, 5 hours, 3300-foot vertical rise

The stated time for this climb is slow to emphasize the extra time needed when you are carrying a pack; and with a pack this is among the most strenuous climbs in this guide. It offers a chance to load your backpack with freeze-dried food, cooking gear, sleeping bag and pad, and carry it up 3300 feet in 3.6 miles to the summit, then down Giant's north side for 1.34 miles to a lean-to where you can spend the night. You can make a loop with one car by hiking out via Hopkins and the Mossy Cascade Trail, section 45, and back via the road to your car.

On clear days the views are exceptional; however, the summit of Giant in thick swirling mist has an ethereal quality, so don't let the weather deter you if the spirit beckons. Side paths from this trail also lead to the bottom and top of Roaring Brook Falls and to overlooks of the slide.

The trailhead is near St. Huberts, 0.5 mile south of the road to the Ausable Club, and about 1 mile north of Chapel Pond on NY 73. As you start from the large parking lot, a trailhead sign indicates "Giant Mtn. 3.6 miles, Washbowl 2.8 miles, Nubble 1.8 miles, Base Roaring Brook Falls 0.3 mile." Another sign 100 yards down the trail reads "Campers take heed. This is an endangered natural scenic area, particularly with Roaring Brook Falls. Preserve safety by not camping overnight" [in the vicinity of the falls].

The path to the bottom of the falls goes right at 0.1 mile and the trail to Giant, the Washbowl, and Nubble branches left. You start at 384 meters (1260 feet) and now the trail starts climbing through attractive white birch, tall maple, and hemlock. These north slopes of Giant were spared in the 1913 fire. There are ATIS orange trail markers indicating that this trail is maintained by the Adirondack Trail Improvement Society, a private group. Notice the rich dark green of Christmas fern, the lace thrice-cut

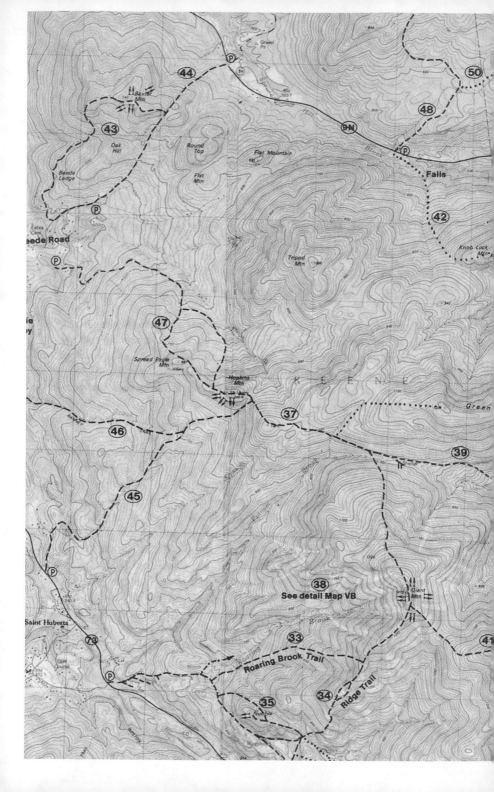

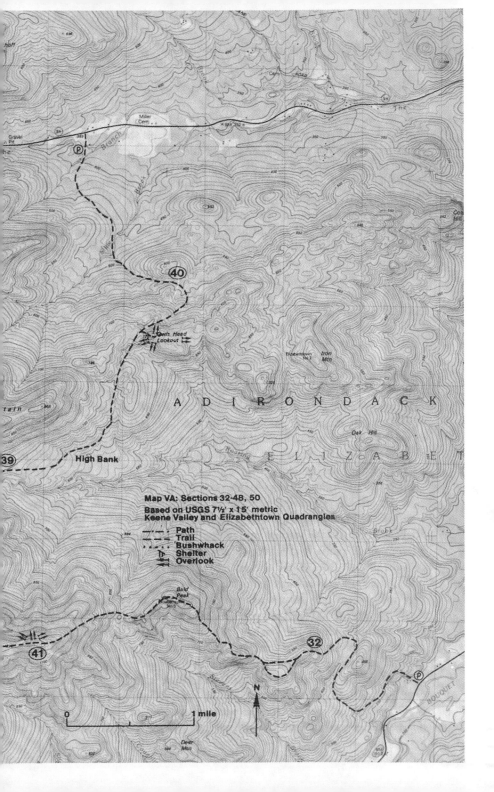

High Bank

Owls Head
Lookout

40

39

41

32

Map VA: Sections 32-48, 50
Based on USGS 7½' x 15' metric
Keene Valley and Elizabethtown Quadrangles

Path
Trail
Bushwhack
Shelter
Overlook

A D I R O N D A C K

E L I Z A B E T

N

0   1 mile

leaflets of spinulose woodfern, and the horseshoe-shaped flat fronds of the dainty maidenhair beside the trail.

After hiking twenty minutes, you will find the trail levels off and you can catch your breath. There is a very large rock on the left, one of many signs you will see of glacial action. The forest is outstanding; at the top of the rise, in a hemlock grove, a deep gully falls off to the right toward the falls. At 0.7 mile, after twenty minutes, the trail forks: Nubble-Washbowl-Giant to the left, the top of Roaring Brook Falls to the right. (If you go over to the top of the falls, there is an excellent view of the valley, but be especially careful as the rocks are wet with mist and very slippery. There have been countless accidents here, and several fatalities, so *do not approach the top of the falls*.)

From the intersection, the trail climbs steeply again for five minutes through a mixed forest of hardwoods and hemlocks carpeted with marginal shield fern. As the trail levels off, magnificent hemlocks, one of the finest groves anywhere, produce visions of the redwoods—in miniature.

After forty-five minutes a sign reading "Official Trail" points right and you soon (at 1 mile) cross Roaring Brook. Here a short path left takes you to the bottom of the slide. After crossing the brook, another sign (no chance of getting lost!) indicates Giant is 2.5 miles to the left, the Washbowl 0.9 mile, and Nubble 0.86 mile straight ahead. The trail to Giant goes uphill at 70° to 80° magnetic, parallel to the brook at first, but moving away as you climb. The woods are still pretty, but much smaller. In some places the trail deteriorates into root steps, but its covering of hemlock needles keeps it from being muddy.

Suddenly the forest changes—six to eight large spruce and many smaller ones are dead, reportedly the victim of the spruce bud worm. Other live spruce have blown over, no longer protected from the wind. Many trees are broken off and the scene is one of desolation. The trail is wet in places. Various small paths lead left toward Roaring Brook and provide a view of some of the slides. After one hour and twenty-five minutes, about 1.5 miles, the trail moves away from the ravine and rises steeply through a very rocky area. It is hard walking and in spring can be a watercourse. At 792 meters (2600 feet) large yellow birch are mixed with large spruce trees, many of which are dead.

After two hours, 2 miles, the trail swings around toward the east and at 3000 feet you come to a solid rock slab that you must climb over and around. Twenty-five minutes later, at 2.4 miles, a path right leads to an overlook south to Noonmark and the Dix Range. Following this the climb is steep, on solid rock—there are occasional views of peaks and valleys, but generally you are in a balsam, white birch, and spruce woods.

Just shy of three hours, at 2.7 miles, the trail goes sharp left, uphill. You climb roots steps to reach a moss-covered ledge with views to the west. At the 1170-meter level (3900 feet), after climbing for three and a quarter hours, you reach the intersection with the Ridge Trail to Giant, which comes in from the right. Signs indicate you have climbed 2.9 miles; it is 2.2 miles down to Chapel Pond via the Ridge Trail and the summit is 0.7 mile above.

The way is now more exposed. In five minutes you reach a huge rock on the left, one of the few shelters along the trail. Even if the ground is wet beneath the rock, the overhang could keep you dry in a rainstorm. The trail bears left through a thick balsam stand, going almost north. In ten minutes it turns right, east, climbing steeply. There is a rock bluff off to the right, with an overlook above a steep drop toward Rocky Peak Ridge. At just over 3.4 miles and elevation 1380 meters (4530 feet), the trail from Bald Peak and Rocky Peak Ridge comes in from the right. The sign indicating it is 7.2 miles to NY 9 is short; it is closer to 8 miles along the East Trail to New Russia.

The open anorthosite summit is 0.1 mile away, the route marked with yellow disks. In three hours and fifty minutes with a pack—or less without— you are there! There are views in every direction from the 1410-meter (4627-foot) summit. Major peaks and valleys of the Adirondacks lie before you with Lake Champlain and the Green Mountains of Vermont on the eastern horizon.

The trail on to the lean-to goes off to the north, down the steep north shoulder of the mountain. It passes through dense double balsam near the summit, by a fire ring and a place where someone has camped—improperly and illegally, because no camping is permitted above 3500 feet in the Forest Preserve. The trail is narrow, often on bedrock between dense overgrowth. Beyond the thick balsam there is an overlook to the north, then you start down a slippery, smooth rock trail. It is hard to make time with a pack as there are high rock steps to negotiate; fortunately there are conveniently placed trees to help. There is only one ancient trail marker, but the worn narrow path is easy to follow.

In less than an hour from the summit, at nearly 4.8 miles, you reach a trail junction at 940 meters (3080 feet). A sign with red trail markers points right, east, to the lean-to at 0.28 mile and Route 9 at 6 miles. The route south, the way you came, indicates Giant's summit is 1.34 miles away. The way left, west, points to the ATIS Hopkins Mountain Trail (no distance given).

Some trail work has improved the trail going right, east, to the Roaring Brook Lean-to as well as the lower part of the trail from Giant. Ten minutes after leaving the junction going east you come to a tributary of Roaring Brook (not the Roaring Brook that you followed on the east side of Giant). Here a sign points to the lean-to, which is to the right, south, 100 feet. This spot is 945 meters (3100 feet) and the lean-to faces east. Five hours after leaving your car, you take your pack and boots off, with a sense of accomplishment. It is a pretty spot with birch, fir, and a gurgling brook (the first water since leaving Roaring Brook) to lull you to sleep.

34 Ridge (Chapel Pond) Trail to Giant Summit
Hiking, scenic views
3 miles, 3 hours, 3050-foot vertical rise

This popular trail is the shortest way to the summit of Giant Mountain and passes the Washbowl and the path to the Nubble. There are some fine views of distant mountains and murky ponds as you look south and west from the open rock face which the trail traverses for much of its distance.

The trail begins on the north side of NY 73, 6.2 miles northwest of Northway Exit 30. Park off the road or 0.2 mile north in the Chapel Pond parking area. The trailhead sign gives distances to the Washbowl— 0.7 mile, Nubble—1.4 miles, St. Huberts via Roaring Brook—3.5 miles, as well as to the summit—3 miles.

The trail, marked with orange ATIS markers, starts out level and wet. In five minutes, however, you cross a brook and start climbing. In ten minutes, the trail moderates through open woods of white birch, maple, beech, and ash and swings right to 130° magnetic. In fifteen minutes, at 0.3 mile, you pass a spring off the trail to the right. Beyond the trail swings sharply left and uphill to begin a series of switchbacks. In twenty-five minutes, at 0.45 mile, you come to a brook, partially on the surface. The trail is rocky and generally uninteresting, without wildflowers, mushrooms, or ferns.

In less than forty minutes, you cross the outlet brook of the Giant's Washbowl and the trail goes directly up hill marked only with a hard-to-spot disk. There is an informal camping spot on the right in a grove.

At nearly 0.7 mile, the trail emerges at a rocky salient point, which provides a look at the inky depths of Chapel Pond below and the rock-climbing cliffs on the left. On weekends you can see and hear climbers scaling the sheer walls. Already you see Gothics, Armstrong, and Wolf Jaws, rising beyond the Ausable River fault.

From the overlook, the trail continues about 100 yards to the south end of the Washbowl and a junction. The left fork goes along the edge of the pond and down to Roaring Brook, section 35. The Ridge Trail goes along the east side and uphill through a large spruce grove. Short of 1 mile, about fifty minutes, you reach another fork. The way left past the Washbowl leads to Roaring Brook in 2.2 miles.

You go right; in three minutes there is a brook and immediately at 1 mile a path left to the Nubble, section 35. Turn right following orange ATIS markers to the northeast, up the ridge toward the summit of Giant. Climbing steeply through forests and then over open rock, you can look back at Round Mountain and the cliffs above Chapel Pond with Round Pond to its left. At one point, you look down into the deep dark waters of the Washbowl.

The trail continues on open rock with occasional small red spruce and tufts of deer grass and moss in the cracks. Pause to enjoy the views south to mountains in the Pharaoh Lake Wilderness and those that ring Lake George. The way is marked with yellow paint and cairns. Along this long climb over bare anorthosite you have a view of Dix, Nippletop, and Hunters Pass that looks like a gun sight.

Nearly an hour from the Washbowl, at 1.7 miles, the trail forks again. You can choose the easier route to the left, north, through a forested area, or the more exposed and steeper climb to the right. The routes rejoin at 1.9 miles. Along the narrow ridge beyond you have occasional views of the slides on Giant's cirque. The trail reaches the junction with the trail from Roaring Brook at 2.2 miles, after a climb of an hour and a half from the Washbowl. The summit is 0.7 mile ahead. You are at 1170 meters, around 3850 feet. The rest of the marked trail, which takes about thirty minutes is described in section 33.

35 Giant Washbowl and Nubble from Roaring Brook

Hiking, scenic views along a loop
4.75 miles, 3 hours, 1500-foot vertical rise

The Washbowl and Nubble can be reached by starting at Chapel Pond on the Ridge Trail, section 34, or by starting at Roaring Brook, section 33. The Ridge Trail reaches the east shore of the Washbowl in 0.7 mile and the Nubble in 1.4 miles from the east. The hike from Roaring Brook is longer but far more attractive and can include side trips to the falls and

to the rock dikes that put Roaring Brook back on its course over the falls after the 1963 washout. The hike to the Washbowl, a tiny pond that has been shrinking over the years, rises nearly 1000 feet but is relatively easy. You should not be deceived by the word nubble, however, and think of "nubbin" or a "small knob." It is a respectable sheer rock promontory, and you should be very careful to keep children away from the edge.

Directions to the parking lot for Roaring Brook Trail are in section 33. Ten minutes into your climb, look at the logs and other debris in the valley to your right, especially visible when the leaves are off the trees. These were deposited by the 1963 slide and flood.

You reach the turnoff path to the top of Roaring Brook Falls in twenty minutes. The stream flows fifty feet from the trail through a trough of solid rock before dropping over the lip of the falls. *The rocks at the top of the falls can be slippery and dangerous, so stay back.*

Continue on the Giant Trail for fifteen minutes from the top of the falls to a sign indicating the official trail to the right. There is a path to the left that leads out to the rock-strewn flood plain and a distant view of the slide; if you follow the flood plain up 200 yards or so you will see the rock dikes which keep Roaring Brook in its channel, instead of allowing it to flow into Putnam Brook. The 1963 deluge caused the diversion into Putnam Brook, but was reversed, and the falls restored, by the quick action of forest ranger John Hickey and District Ranger Bill Petty.

Back at the official trail, cross the brook and at 1.1 mile turn right at the fork toward the Washbowl 0.86 mile away or the Nubble 0.9 mile away. In five minutes, at 1.25 mile, after a steep hill, the trail forks. Go right up a rocky stream bed toward the Washbowl, passing a large rock with a polypody fern crown. The trail levels off at 1.6 miles with the towering cliffs of Nubble on your left, north. In half an hour from the brook, at 1.95 miles, you arrive at the Washbowl where the trail again forks, but both lead up to the Ridge Trail, one along the north side of the Washbowl, the other on the south rim. Go left, north, and you will pass huge cedars and a camping spot before the trail turns uphill and joins the Ridge Trail. Here a sign reads "Washbowl 0.1 mile, St. Huberts 2.2 miles via Roaring Brook, Chapel Pond 1.0 mile, Nubble."

Go uphill, north, on the marked Ridge Trail toward Giant Mountain for three minutes until you come to a sign at 2.25 miles indicating the Nubble is a left turn. The trail to the top of the Nubble, 260 feet above, goes off at 310° magnetic. You pass an overlook of Washbowl and in fifteen minutes, at 2.6 miles, after a level spot, the trail forks again. Go left

250 yards out onto and along the rocky overlook for tremendous views of Noonmark and the high peaks of Gothics and the two Wolf Jaws. Retracing your steps to the intersection at 2.9 miles, continue northwest and then west. The trail begins to drop rapidly. In twenty minutes, at 3.5 miles, you will reach the junction near Roaring Brook. Right takes you back 0.15 mile to the brook; retrace the lower part of the trail downhill to your car.

36 Dipper Pond
Bushwhack, marsh plants

The Dipper, which is also called the Fingerbowl by some people, is the smallest of the three ponds in the Giant Mountain Wilderness Area. If you look east of the Washbowl on most maps you will see this small pond nearby. Its closeness is deceiving, however, because there is no path to it and to reach it you have to hop over or skirt extensive blowdowns and penetrate seemingly impenetrable thickets. In summer, especially, it is very difficult to keep your bearings so do not try this without a map and compass.

There are two possible bearings off the Ridge Trail to reach the pond. The first starts about 100 yards from the Washbowl. After climbing from Chapel Pond, 0.7 mile, you keep on the Ridge Trail to Giant. The trail passes near the Washbowl and then turns right, east, past two yellow "no camping" disks. The trail then swings left, climbing through a nice red spruce grove. After you gain some altitude, in 100 yards or so, to your right and above you are two small hills with a col between them. Bushwhack toward the col with a 115° magnetic bearing up the hill. The slope is easy with little brush, so you are on the level of the col in less than ten minutes. Going down the other side, you immediately come to an impassable tangle of white birch blowdowns. Keep to the left side, high enough to avoid most of the tangle and continue heading at 115°. Within ten minutes from the col you reach a depression that slopes right and a small knoll dead ahead. Bear left, almost north, through a spruce thicket, and contour around the knoll to its east side. Then go downhill to the pond. It takes twenty minutes to go the 0.5 mile from the trail to the pond.

The upper end of the Dipper is swampy with alders; the shore of the pond is marshy, with a beautiful rim of leatherleaf. It is still as Harold Weston described, a snug little pond edged with luxurious cedar. Around on the north a large rock slab slopes into the water and is a nice place for a quiet picnic while you dip your feet. In season you will find many plants that like wet feet; in winter snowshoe rabbit and deer tracks are plentiful. At any time you can enjoy seclusion with little chance of meeting anyone.

You can return by a loop and thus explore the other (perhaps easier) way in. At the western, upper, end of the pond, follow a 300° magnetic compass bearing up the swampy valley, over and around more blowdowns. With that bearing you will angle up the hill on the left. Go over the ridge and down the other side, which falls steeply through a dense but passable balsam thicket. You should come out on the Ridge Trail, over 100 yards above where you left it, near the intersection marked with a sign "Washbowl 0.1 mile, St. Huberts 2.2 miles via Roaring Brook, Chapel Pond 1 mile."

The alternate way into the Dipper is from this intersection, bushwhacking up the hill on a bearing of 120° magnetic. It takes about fifty minutes to make the circuit from the trail to this secluded spot, but it is well worth it. Nowhere else in this 22,000-acre Wilderness Area will you find seclusion and the chance to see and hear the flowers and birds that prefer to live in a wetland community.

Once you find the Dipper, however, you can continue on to explore one of the Giant's best kept secrets: the waterfall on an unnamed stream that drains the valley between Giant and Rocky Peak Ridge and flows into Chapel Pond. The stream loops within 200 yards of the southeast corner of the Dipper. You can follow it downstream to the falls that cut through the steep flanks of the Giant. Bushwhackers sometimes use this stream as a guide to descend from the col between the Giant and Rocky Peak Ridge all the way to NY 73, a trek made difficult by formidable stands of small spruce and balsam.

37 Roaring Brook Lean-to to Hopkins Mountain
Hiking, camping
1.5 miles, 1½ hours, 300-foot vertical rise

Even though this section is an officially marked hiking trail, it is seldom used and is not very well maintained. It connects several trails from Keene Valley that go to the rocky overlook of Hopkins Mountain with the Roaring Brook Lean-to in the col on the north side of Giant. This is part of the route of the first trail up Giant, laid out by Orson Phelps from Keene Valley in 1866. You can use it for the return trip west from the summit of Giant and the lean-to.

Among this route's advantages are the fact that you are unlikely to meet anyone and that it enables you to tie a solitary trip to Green Mountain in with a climb of Giant. Green, by the way, has a wooded summit, but at 1207 meters (3960 feet) it is higher than three on the official list of forty-six peaks over 4000 feet.

The lean-to is the only shelter in the Giant Mountain Wilderness Area. It is reached either by descending from the north ridge of Giant, section 33, or by the trail from NY 9N, section 39.

Leaving the lean-to, follow the trail west for 0.28 mile to a marked junction. At this point, the trail up Giant goes south for 1.34 miles to the peak. The marked trail continues west for approximately 1.7 miles to Hopkins (there is no official mileage on the signpost). Within 100 yards you leave the height-of-land and cross a small stream flowing west, the beginning of Putnam Brook. You then contour around the lower slope of Green, going northwest, and climb steeply out of the col. There are blowdowns and the trail is overgrown with maple and balsam fir. For fifteen minutes you will find it hard to push through if you are carrying a pack. As the trail levels off, it becomes more open.

In twenty minutes, at 0.6 mile, you cross a stream coming down from Green Mountain, flowing southwest; it is a tributary of Putnam Brook. [Although not described as a separate trip in this guide, the top of Green Mountain can be reached by going up this streambed to 1050 meters (3445 feet) and then striking due east for the summit. Green Mountain has steep slopes or cliffs on all but this eastern approach.]

After crossing the brook, the trail climbs again. Thirty minutes after leaving the junction you are going west at 1000 meters (3280 feet); there are no trail markers and it is overgrown. After reaching a small crest at 0.9 mile, you drop into a wet, sphagnum bog. As you make your way through the swamp the first (new) ATIS trail markers appear. Continue climbing around the north side of a hill where the trail is clear with scrub balsam, woodfern, red-topped poisonous mushrooms, and lots of moss. After cresting the brow of the hill at 1.1 miles, you start down through dense balsam fir, overtopped with maple, and yellow and white birch. You must push through the balsam. If it is not cut back soon, the trail here will be impassable.

One hour and fifteen minutes after leaving the junction, the trail drops into the valley between Green and Hopkins. In the mud at the foot of the gully, was the print of a large cat, almost three inches across, large enough for a mountain lion. Perhaps you will be lucky enough to spot one. A few minutes later, look for the junction where the Mossy Cascade and Ranney Brook trails come in from St. Huberts, and another trail goes 0.2

mile right up to the summit of Hopkins, which is described in section 47 along with its other trails. The sign is high on a post and can easily be missed. These trails are all well marked and are described in the Keene Valley Hikes section.

38 The Slides on Giant Mountain
Slide climbs

For those who enjoy slide climbing, there is no area in the Adirondacks more easily accessible and consistently delightful and varied than the great cirque on the western side of Giant Mountain. From the parking lot on NY 73 below Roaring Brook Falls, you have only to follow Roaring Brook for 2.5 miles to arrive at the center of the cirque, and select from the half-dozen routes up to the summit ridge the one that is most appealing to you.

If you have never done any slide climbing, the best place to start is on the road around the golf course at the Ausable Club on the afternoon before your planned hike. Look from there at Giant, 4 miles away, and the principal three of six usual routes out of the cirque can easily be identified. From left to right, all ending immediately under the summit ridge of the mountain, are Bottle, Diagonal, and Eagle slides. If you immediately wonder whether these are really hiking routes up the mountain, take heart. Your instincts are functioning healthily, and serving you well. What they are telling you is that you should find someone already addicted to slide climbing to accompany you. Experience, either your own or that of another member of your party, is the best company to have along with you on any of these open slides.

In fact, in summer conditions, wet or dry, the slides do provide possible hiking routes to the summit ridge. (Ice and snow of course change this radically, so ascents in winter conditions are definitely technical, requiring special equipment.) Where slides are as steeply pitched as these, however, experienced judgment is useful in sorting out the walking routes from those that are beyond the realm of walking. It is possible to stray off route onto pitches that are dangerous unless you have basic rock climbing experience and technique. Furthermore, the route descriptions here assume that you are comfortable with finding your own way in off-trail hiking. There are of course no signs, and landmarks in the rubble on slides have a way of rapidly changing or vanishing. Sneakers or crepe soles are better than hard rubber Vibram soles for going up the steep friction pitches.

With all this in mind, however, before you leave the golf course, look once more at the Eagle, and identify the "feathers" extending separately

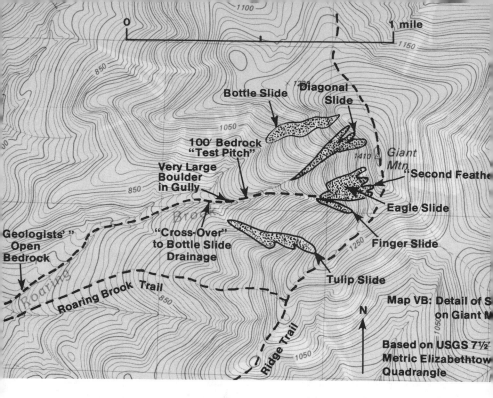

Based on USGS 7½'
Metric Elizabethtown
Quadrangle

up toward the summit ridge from the broadly spread wing. The standard route up this slide begins directly below the second feather from the right, and climbs straight up to and through it to the top of the ridge. This is the premier slide climb in the Adirondacks, though you may want to begin with one of the others. The description here takes you to the top of the Eagle, since all of the others can be thought of as routes branching off on the way there. If you take to slide climbing, you will want eventually to explore them all, but you are most likely to come back to the Eagle.

From the parking lot at the beginning of the Roaring Brook Trail, follow that trail for 1 mile until it crosses Roaring Brook, section 39. From here to the base of Eagle Slide, the brook itself is your route. The trail crosses in an area that extends for about half a mile along the brook, in which a very large amount of rubble swept out of the cirque in the 1963 slide came to rest. The main course of the brook here has shifted several times in the past dozen years, and the instability of the area almost guarantees that changes will continue. Keep generally to the left as you hike up the brook through here in order to avoid the potential confusion that can be caused by drainages entering the main brook from the right.

In low-water conditions, it is worthwhile on the way up to leave the marked trail to follow the brook from the top of Roaring Brook Falls, just over 0.5 mile from the parking area. There is a delightful section of flumes and ledges between the falls and the trail crossing. If for any reason, you end up returning from the cirque along the brook, it is easy to miss the place where the trail crosses, but you cannot miss the top of the falls. Simply go right fifty yards to pick up the trail back down.

As you hike up out of the rubble area, you will pass a barrier constructed to prevent Roaring Brook water from escaping into Putnam Brook drainage to the north, thus drying up the falls. Soon after, you reach a wide area of open bedrock over which the brook descends broadly through a series of mostly shallow pools. This spot is very close to the Roaring Brook Trail, up the bank to the right, but beyond this point the Roaring Brook Trail diverges to the east away from the course of the brook.

The brook continues northeast for 0.75 mile in a gully that becomes increasingly well defined. At several points through this section there are views of the Bottle Slide directly ahead. The gully then bends more to the east, providing early views of the Eagle Slide. At a jog back to the left, the stream that drains the Tulip Slide enters on the right. The Tulip is the easiest of the slides to hike, but not to find. As of this writing, the stream where it enters Roaring Brook is mossy and green, and must be followed through abundant vegetation for 0.25 mile before it opens out onto bare rock slabs. It ends on the ridge not far above the point where Roaring Brook Trail joins the Ridge Trail coming up from Chapel Pond.

You will also want to leave Roaring Brook in this vicinity if you want to visit the Bottle Slide. Clamber out of the gully to the left, and cross the narrow rubble bar into a parallel but less well-established drainage. Follow this northeasterly to the base of the slide. The Bottle is almost as steep as the Eagle but is narrower. The disadvantage of the Bottle is that there is not a graceful exit onto the ridge. From the top of the slide go to your right, crossing through the scrub below the forty-foot cliffs and above the top of the Diagonal Slide, and aggressively seek out a route up through the ledges. Further to the right the ascent to the ridge is less steep, but the thicket is much stickier. Take the trail on the ridge to the right to reach the summit.

Roaring Brook continues to bend more and more to the east, becoming steadily steeper, and soon reaches a house-sized boulder lying in the bottom of the gully. For twenty years after the massive slide of 1963, this block threatened hikers from a perch thirty feet higher on the left side of the gully, before finally breaking loose on a dry summer day to settle into its present location. There is copious additional unstable material on both sides of the main gully here, but especially on the south side. If you have been looking for the beginning of the route to the Tulip, you will be very unhappy if you look for it up the still-developing slide chutes entering from the south in this vicinity. Either hike back down the gully to find where you passed it, or accommodate fate by continuing on to the Finger or Eagle Slides, and return another day to explore the Tulip.

Beyond the boulder, the main gully continues its slow eastward bend, eventually reaching a 100-foot exposure of bedrock with a large rounded slab at its top on the left. This is a preview of coming attractions. You should be able to walk right up the middle of this pitch. If you feel you cannot, you are going to have trouble out on the Eagle, for it is steeper and much more exposed.

Immediately beyond this spot a major gully enters from the left. This drains the central part of the cirque. More of a climb than a walk, the Question Mark never opens out into a slide, but consists of a series of increasingly challenging slabs and benches leading directly to the summit of Giant. About one-third of the way from the Roaring Brook gully to the summit, the Diagonal Slide enters from the left. It takes some scouting to find a graceful way out of the vagaries of the Question Mark onto the Diagonal, but it is worth the effort. Exiting the top of the Diagonal is the same problem as exiting the Bottle. Bear right, but not too far.

Shortly beyond the Question Mark gully another enters, also from the left. This is the first drainage off the Eagle, and leads to its far left side. Pass by this, and also pass the next general area of gravel and rubble entering from the left. The main gully is now climbing very steeply, has become mostly talus rather than dirt, and is heading almost due east. As you continue, you will soon find yourself at the foot of a steep chute containing exposed reddish bedrock, over which you can look directly up across the Eagle Slide to the second feather, seen as a gap in the brush on the skyline. You have arrived.

Ahead here, up the main gully to the east, is the Finger Slide, a narrow strip of mostly open pitches broken by easy ledges. The Finger is significantly easier and proportionately less spectacular than the Eagle, and leads to the Roaring Brook Trail at the foot of the last steep rise below the summit ridge. For Eagle, turn and ascend the chute.

The first rule of the second feather route up the Eagle, already mentioned, is to climb straight up. You will have to negotiate three minor benches crossing the main part of the slide before you reach the feather. These benches and various cracks in the intervening expanses of bare rock will all conspire to push you to the left, out into the middle of the slide. Don't let them do it. If you zig left in your route picking, mentally note that you must zag back to the right again at the first opportunity. Any difficulties that you encounter on the route straight up are postponed only to be replaced by more severe ones if you allow yourself to be pushed too far out to the left. In addition, only if you stick to the straight up and narrow course will you be fairly sure of arriving at the second feather, which disappears behind the bulge of the central mass of rock once you are on the slide.

The second rule is to take your time and enjoy the drama of the geology unfolding around and behind you as you ascend through this open space. Remember, benches are for sitting.

At the bottom of the second feather is a fifteen-foot wall that must be climbed. It is not difficult if you don't rush it, and the exposure of the open slide has been left behind. Ten years ago this little cliff was only eleven feet high, but the foot traffic has beaten down the dirt base to improve the challenge, a process that is likely to continue. Similarly, the top of the feather has been extended almost two feet a year since 1963 as hikers have scrambled out into the summit brush. Angle to the right from the top to rejoin the trail to the summit, which is about 200 yards to the left.

Return to NY 73 on the Roaring Brook Trail, section 33. Or, if you have two cars, leave one at Chapel Pond for a more pleasant and scenic descent via the Ridge Trail, section 34.

39 North Trail via Owl Head to Roaring Brook Lean-to

Hiking, camping, ski-touring
6.2 miles, 3 hours, 1840-foot vertical rise

This northern approach probes the very core of the Giant Mountain Wilderness Area. It crosses Slide Brook, which feeds the Branch of the Boquet, and discovers the hidden valley of the eastern Roaring Brook before reaching the col between Giant and Green Mountain. It is relatively long, 5.8 miles directly to the lean-to, 6.2 miles if you add the detour to Owl Head, but the climb is gradual so you can go in and out in a day on foot or skis. Better yet, plan to spend the night in the lean-to and hike out over Hopkins, section 37 and one of the Keene Valley trails, or the summit of Giant, section 33. From the lookout of Owl Head on the way there are excellent views of the Green Mountains in Vermont, Hurricane to the north, and

all the commanding peaks in the Giant Wilderness Area. (In spite of the fact the new metric map calls this Owls Head, tradition makes it singular to differentiate it from other similarly named peaks.) Other vantage points along this trail show the extensive slides on the eastern cirque of Giant Mountain.

The trailhead is on NY 9N, 4.4 miles from NY 9 in Elizabethtown. There is a DEC signpost on the south side of the road that raises the excitement level with each notation: "Slide Brook 1.2 miles, Owl Head 2.7 miles, High Bank 4.2 miles, Giant Mtn. Lean-to 5.8 miles, Giant Mtn. 7.4 miles." In summer you drive in on a dirt road to a parking area and a trail register located at 389 meters (1276 feet.) From the roadway, look south toward the sharp promontory of Owl Head. From the parking lot, you see the vertical fractured rock cliffs of Pitchoff rising in the northwest.

The trail starts due south and later veers off southeast. Within fifty feet, you cross a small brook on a wooden bridge and in another 100 feet you leave the road, going left, following red DEC trail markers into the woods and across a smaller, sturdy bridge. You climb through a hemlock grove on well-traveled root steps and at 0.4 mile, within ten minutes, reach a Wilderness Area sign. Soon a deciduous forest emerges—very pretty—with large maple and ash, some beech and white birch. In fall the leaves are predominantly brown and rust, but include a spectrum from yellow to burnt umber. In twenty minutes you hear, then see, Slide Brook to your left; it is a scenic large stream tumbling over large boulders, draining the northern slopes of Green Mountain. At 1.2 miles, a stout two-foot wide bridge made of natural materials spans the stream—a good example of appropriate technology in trail construction.

After crossing the stream the trail zigs to the right, uphill, and then zags left, east, and ascends along a hogback. Rock steps, another example of good, natural trailwork, help span small watercourses. After hiking for thirty-five minutes, you find the trail is steeper and angular rocks create difficult footing. You cross several small tributaries, either on rock steps or on two logs, going east, up a small valley. It is an open forest, mostly white birch with little understory—an indication it was burned over in the past.

In forty-five minutes, at 1.8 miles, the trail swings south and crosses a wet area on a three-log bridge. Notice that the source of this small stream is a crack between two large rocks, with the water bubbling into a clear, cool pool. In fifty minutes the trail swings southwest and then west uphill before leveling off amidst maple, beech, and yellow birch. At 2.5 miles, after one hour and five minutes, you reach a junction sign indicating "Owl

Owl Head

Head Lookout 0.2 mile, Giant Mtn. Lean-to 3.1 miles, High Bank 1.7 miles, Giant Mtn. 4.9 miles, NY 9N 2.5 miles." You are at 725 meters (2378 feet) after climbing 1100 feet in that 2.5 miles.

A steep climb quickly brings you to the windy bluff of Owl Head. Orient yourself by the fire tower on Hurricane Mountain in the northwest, 330° magnetic; Pitchoff is nearer, below it. At 300° the rocky crag of Knob Lock Mountain rises. Ahead to the west-southwest the mountain mass is Green Mountain, to the left of it the Roaring Brook Valley (your destination), and, at 250° magnetic, the high crown of Giant Mountain. The slides on the eastern cirque show clearly. To the left of Giant looms Rocky Peak Ridge. Almost due south you see the shiny, wet, rocky patches on Bald Peak.

Return to the junction, 2.9 miles, and take the trail to the west toward the lean-to. It heads downhill briefly. As you circle around, stop and look back at the massive cliffs of the lookout towering above, eroding over time and yet permanent in this lifetime. As the trail levels off, you walk sprightly; the trees are healthy and there are no blowdowns. In the fall, after the leaves have turned, there is a clean leafy fragrance—the woodland equivalent of new-mown hay. After walking twenty minutes from Owl Head, the trail becomes wet in spots but is easily passable. A dense maple grove contrasts on the right with a ridge of rock going steeply up Green Mountain.

Forty minutes and 1.5 miles from Owl Head, you reach High Bank, a gravelly hillock whose soils seem strangely out of place. The hillside falls away to Roaring Brook; Rocky Peak Ridge towers above, and the eastern slides of Giant loom larger than at Owl Head. The cliffs of Green make a backdrop for the slender white birch. There is a fire ring at a campsite with scenery reminiscent of the Rockies. Ten minutes farther on, along the same gravel anomaly, there is another overlook. The most impressive aspect of this trail is the continuum of views of the high ridge to the south with the east slides of Giant growing ever closer, more distinct, and more awesome.

Along this section the white birch and maple seem especially large. Club moss grows in the rich duff and long beech and spinulose woodfern thrive. You climb gradually up the brook valley and, about an hour after leaving Owl Head, cross a stream flowing from Green Mountain; a few minutes later you cross another larger, very pretty stream. Now you climb more steeply uphill along a narrow trail and after walking for an hour and twenty minutes from Owl Head you cross another tributary descending from Green.

Green Mountain cuts off views of Giant, which is behind on the left. Jump rocks over another brook. Beyond the soil changes to a rich dark loam that holds moisture. There is some trailwork along here. An hour and a half after leaving Owl Head (nearly three from the trailhead) a sign marks the lean-to, off to the left, south. The Roaring Brook Lean-to nestles among spruce and balsam beside a small brook at about 940 meters (3080 feet). It is a pleasant place to camp.

From here there are three alternatives to follow. If you retrace your steps it will take somewhat over two hours to return to your car on NY 9N. From the lean-to, however, the trail continues west for 0.28 mile to a junction in the col. One route goes south, steeply up to the summit of Giant and then continues south down either the Ridge Trail, section 34, or the Roaring Brook Trail, section 33, (a different Roaring Brook than one you follow in the north.) You can also continue on to Hopkins Mountain, section 37, and from there into Keene Valley via trails in sections 45 and 46.

40 Owl Head Ski-Touring

Intermediate cross-country skiing, snowshoeing
2.7 miles, 1½ hours, 382-meter (1253-foot) vertical rise

When there is good snow cover, this is a great cross-country trail for the intermediate skier. The trail is generally wide. The way down is steep enough to require control by snowplow and stem christie, but the open woods provides a good slope to practice telemark turns. You can extend the trip by 3.2 miles by continuing to the lean-to in the col between Giant and Green mountains if you want, and even turn the trek into a winter camping trip.

The trail is the same route as the North Trail to Roaring Brook Lean-to in the col, section 39. Look for the DEC trailhead sign on the south side of NY 9N, 4.4 miles from NY 9 in Elizabethtown. Park on the shoulder of the road and go south across the wide wooden bridge and follow the red trail markers into the woods. The trail is somewhat narrow at the beginning but is skiable; after ten minutes it becomes wider and continues that way until you reach Slide Brook at 1.2 miles.

The bridge over Slide Brook is two feet wide and sturdy, so it is easy to cross. On your return there is a sharp right turn and trees above the bridge so it is better to run out on the turn and thus approach the bridge slowly. After twenty-five minutes, the trail moves up onto a hogback and is somewhat steep—it requires good wax or a herringbone to make it. After leaving the hogback, there is a beautiful section of trail, uphill beside a large rock with tinted icicles shining in the sunlight. There is a tree near the trail and it is tight skiing, so remember this spot on your return and zigzag through the woods around it.

Above this section, the trail is steep with large rocks that require a lot of snow for cover. You need a good snowplow coming down this section, or you can turn up into the hill and stop frequently. There are rocks or logs to help you cross small streams; look them over carefully as some can be run on skis and some must be stepped across slowly. After this section, which you reach in forty-five minutes, a more open forest begins. This is where you can have fun coming down; work out wide traverses, changing directions with stem christies, or, if you can, with telemark turns. There is little underbrush to catch your skis, so enjoy! In the upper sections there are a couple of tight turns before log bridges; it is prudent to run out on these turns rather than taking the narrow logs at speed.

You reach the trail sign below Owl Head in a little over an hour; the 0.2-mile path to the lookout is so steep you will have to remove your skis. The 360° views, described in the hiking trip, are spectacular. The wind blows constantly on the summit, however, so be prepared with a down jacket or an extra sweater if you plan to eat lunch there.

If you have time, ski on to High Bank or up the Roaring Brook Valley toward the lean-to. Above all, ski 100 feet to the west and look up at the cliffs of Owl Head; it is like a rocky balcony built to observe the slides of Giant and its mammoth stage.

If the snow is deep enough, skiing back is pure pleasure. The forest is sufficiently open to zigzag through the birches, using hills and gullies to control your speed. You will be back at your car in less than a half hour; some people in Elizabethtown do the trip on a long lunch break! With enough snow this is a unique skiing experience. With light snow cover, you can still enjoy the trail and the views from Owl Head by traveling on snowshoes.

41 Rocky Peak Ridge—East Trail to Giant Mountain

Hiking
10.6 miles, 8½ hours, 1525-meter (5000-foot) vertical rise

The longest but most rewarding trail to the summit of Giant is along the open crest of Rocky Peak Ridge. Nowhere else in the Adirondacks can

From Rocky Peak Ridge

you experience such vast openness, as you hike mile after mile among grand vistas. The beginning of this trail (it should be hiked from east to west for the most impressive views) is from the Boquet Valley by the trail up 3.7 miles to Bald Peak. There is limited water and no lean-to on the route so it is preferable to make a one-day through trip and end by walking down the Ridge Trail, section 34, 2.8 miles from the shoulder of Giant to a car left at Chapel Pond. This section describes the middle 4.1 miles of that 10.6-mile through trip, which with the 5000-foot vertical rise occupies a very long day. Nevertheless, it is the best way to appreciate the beauty and variety of this unique wilderness area.

The trail to Bald Peak, section 32, climbs 734 meters (2400 feet) in 3.7 miles and takes two and a half hours. From Bald Peak to the east the conical dome of Giant rises 1600 feet above you, the rock slides in its eastern cirque making it easy to identify. Closer and slightly left, two miles away as the crow flies, lies the bare, extended, jagged outline of Rocky Peak Ridge. Between you and this nearest peak an undulating, sinuous ridge forms your route. Bald Peak is often blustery, with no good place to get in the lee of the wind, so plan to eat further on.

The trail, marked by cairns, goes off the summit to the southwest. In five minutes, you drop to a protected spot; there is a fire ring and signs that people have camped—but it lacks a view. The trail continues mostly on bedrock through cedar, scrub white birch, and windblown red spruce and alder. This is an alpine environment, a major change from the red oak forest on the lower slopes.

After leaving Blueberry Cobbles on the climb up to Bald Peak, you have no doubt been tantalized by a large balanced rock, resembling a shark's fin, that sits atop the ridge. Now you approach this huge boulder and at 3.9 miles it is a good place for a snack. Rocks on each side of the trail shield you from the wind and let the sun warm you. Some hikers will try to scale the huge boulder; others can marvel at the sheer cliffs ahead. A camera is a must on this hike and you are certain to use it here.

One thing that makes this trail difficult physically is that several times you lose some of the altitude you have gained. The trail dropped a couple hundred feet after Blueberry Cobbles; here, descending steeply into Dickenson Notch, you drop 300 feet from the summit of Bald Peak. From this col at 4.15 miles, elevation 840 meters (2755 feet) you climb steeply west and southwest. An hour after leaving Bald—including time for a snack—you cross a small brook. In dry weather the brook can be completely dry. From a beautiful overlook at about 4.7 miles, you can gaze back at Bald above the valley. Climbing, you pass a large rock ledge that has huge flakes fractured off its face and water dripping from it. Beyond, two large balancing rocks stand beside the trail—one overhang is large enough to keep a person dry.

After walking an hour and a quarter past Bald Peak there is, at 5.1 miles, a view of Green Mountain to the north—the graveled High Bank can be seen in the Roaring Brook Valley below. Another overlook south from the ridge is a choice spot where campers have stopped. A few minutes later, you are on a rock knob with a view of Rocky Peak (not the Ridge) ahead. Here trail markers switch to cairns with occasional yellow paint on rocks and you scramble up through scrubby spruce to an outcrop at 5.4 miles. There are excellent views in all directions—see if you can pick out the fire towers on Hurricane, Belfry, and Pokamoonshine. The seasons are so severe here that bunchberry blooms even in late fall.

You continue hiking along the ridge through red spruce and balsam where the trail is slow going, damp, and muddy, and marked by cairns. At 5.7 miles, an hour and three-quarters from Bald Peak, you reach the highest point of Rocky Peak, 1228 meters (4028 feet).

Rocky outcrops and alpine-like scenery take you at 5.9 miles to the shore of Marie Louise Pond, which was occasionally visible as you walked along the ridge. The pond is the state's third highest body of water and was named after Mary Louise Hicks who first visited it in the late 1880s. Large rocks dot the surface of this shallow pond, which has salamanders in spring, and blueberries and cranberries along the shore in the fall. Look for Labrador tea among the cranberries at the damp outlet where the trail crosses. *The water is* **not** *safe to drink.*

The trip up Rocky Peak Ridge is especially fascinating and different. You zigzag through an open meadow, with gravelly soil covered with many varieties of moss and lichens and tufts of grass. If you step off the trail, it is spongy and you sink in, like tundra. The only trees are very small spruce, reestablishing themselves in this burned-over area. Many hours could be spent here with a moss and lichen book identifying these fragile alpine plants. On the slopes water erodes around heavy clumps of moss, leaving open patchy soil. Red crest and reindeer lichen are the most common of many species; rusty woodsia fern thrives in spots.

You reach Rocky Peak Ridge at 6.5 miles. The sign on the cairn, which is silhouetted against the sky and resembles the head of a cowboy looking east, indicates that it is 2.59 miles to Bald Peak. The sign underestimates, however. Because the Ridge Trail is so steep and tortuous and the views are so enticing, it takes two and a half hours to hike that distance. The cairn marks Rocky Peak Ridge, which, at 1336 meters (4383 feet), is the twenty-third highest in the roster of Adirondack mountain peaks.

As you drop down the west side of the peak, the view of Giant is fabulous, particularly the tremendous rock slides that scar both faces of that mountain.

You drop rapidly for 600 feet into a saddle at 7.3 miles before starting the climb up Giant. In the valley you cross a swampy area—if you follow the valley down for nearly 200 feet, there is water in the brook that some consider potable. The climb up the mountain starts through dense balsam; later the route is dominated by stunted mountain ash. Everything about you makes you sense the mass of the peak ahead. You climb steadily. About 400 feet above the saddle there is a side trail to the right that gives a panoramic view of the east slide. An hour and a quarter after leaving Rocky Peak Ridge, at 7.8 miles, you reach a junction with the trail from NY 73, the combined Roaring Brook and Ridge trails, which approach from the south. The summit is 0.1 miles up an easy climb, section 34, to the right. You can reach the top six and a half hours after leaving your car. The shortest descent from the intersection, 2.8 miles, is via the Ridge Trail to NY 73 at Chapel Pond.

42 Knob Lock Mountain
Bushwhack, hidden waterfall

Because this guide requires such a preponderance of bushwhacks in order to describe the majority of the region's superior destinations, it is fortunate that most are delightful and relatively easy. However, this one is not and is recommended only for those determined to bag another peak. It is essential to wear safety glasses because of the extensive spruce and balsam thickets through which you must wade. At the beginning, a short walk from the road, however, there is a beautiful, hidden waterfall and that may be all of the mountain you wish to explore on a hot, sultry day.

Leave your car in the informal parking spot opposite the beginning of the marked south trail to Hurricane Mountain. The trailhead is at the height-of-land on NY 9N, 3.5 miles from NY 9 at Elizabethtown and 6.6 miles from NY 73.

There are alternate ways to start this bushwhack. For the best look at the falls on an upper tributary of The Branch, go south into the woods for about fifty yards. When the upslope begins, contour around to the east, walking uphill from the road as it goes downhill toward Elizabethtown. In 200 yards you cross a small stream. In about 500 yards, after passing through a wonderful grove of cedars with trunks over a foot in diameter, you reach the brook with the falls. The water cascades over fractured rocks for 100 to 150 feet in a series of pools and sheer drops. It takes only ten minutes to walk to this secluded gem where lunch or solitude can be enjoyed.

If you want to continue to the top of Knob Lock Mountain, cross the brook at the top of the falls. Follow the brook up as best you can, working around ledges in a southerly direction until you reach a tributary coming in from the east—about half an hour's hike. Follow the tributary up to its source and from there take a compass bearing southeast up to the ridge. You go through successions of spruce and balsam thickets. After plowing up through these bands of green for 200 feet, you come to a band of dying white birch with a dense, short, new balsam understory. This is followed by a band of taller balsam and spruce, and then a band of dead spruce, ten to fifteen feet tall. The sharp dead spikes rip at your clothes and catch your hands and face; caution is needed to avoid a poke in the eye!

After pushing through this unyielding undergrowth for an hour and forty-five minutes, you reach a rock overlook and you can see the valley with Hurricane Mountain in the background. You are almost up to the ridge and you can see the summit above and to the east. You can make the ridge in two and a quarter hours, and it takes nearly another three-quarters of an hour to reach the rocky summit, which rises to 973 meters (3209 feet).

The summit view is impressive, but you have really earned it, and the worst is not over. Going down is almost as difficult as the climb since you cannot see your feet and are constantly tripping over hidden deadfalls. At times, the balsam is so thick you have the feeling you are swimming through a sea of green needles. Even pushing, it takes almost two hours to return to your car, but you do get a chance to enjoy the waterfall again.

Keene Valley Hikes

ST. HUBERTS and Keene Valley have been a focal point of hiking in the Adirondacks for so long that little introduction is necessary. While much attention has been on the Great Range to the west, nearby mountains like Hopkins, Spread Eagle, and Baxter have an extensive marked trail system that offers a variety of day hikes and connects with other trails leading into the interior of the Giant Wilderness Area for longer excursions. Hopkins is a relatively easy climb with three trails to choose from; try it at the height of blueberry season for a double treat.

Some of the famous names of the Adirondacks have hunted, fished, and guided in these peaks and valleys. Old Man Phelps, a famous guide of Keene Valley, took people up Mount Marcy in the mid-1800s and climbed Giant in 1854. St. Huberts, where the clear waters of the East Branch of the Ausable River flow down from Lower Ausable Lake, was the focal point for many climbers. By 1850, the area had become so popular with teachers, writers, and philosophers that Orlando and Smith Beede built the Beede House, a three-story hotel. These and other accounts are found in *Freedom in the Wilds* by Harold Weston.

In 1897, the Adirondack Trail Improvement Society (ATIS) was formed, open to all who wish to contribute cash or labor toward maintenance of trails in the St. Huberts and Keene Valley areas. This organization is still active and maintains many of the trails in this area.

The trailheads described in this section are located on the east side of the Ausable River and are reached from NY 73. The beginnings of all of them cross private land, but permission to do so has been traditionally granted by landowners. Normal courtesies and instructional signs should be carefully observed by hikers.

43 Baxter Mountain from Beede Road
Trail, hiking, spectacular views
3.5-mile loop, 3 hours, 1200-foot vertical rise

Painters and photographers have relished this small mountain to the east of Keene Valley for decades. The views are wonderful and the series of small summits along the ridge line of Baxter Mountain gives an ever-changing look at the High Peaks, the Hurricane Range, and Keene Valley. There are few hikes that take only half a day and yet give so much pleasure.

The trail starts from Beede Road, which is a right, east, fork from NY 73, 0.6 mile north of the heart of Keene Valley and the intersection with Johns Brook Road, with its sign pointing to the High Peaks. Beede Road crosses the East Branch of the Ausable then forks left at 0.3 mile to cross a second, smaller stream. At 0.4 mile, turn left again. At 1 mile, you reach an intersection with the sign "Baxter—Park Here." There is room for only a few cars at the side of the road. Beede Farm and the beginning of the trail is to the left, uphill; but parking is prohibited along that road.

Walk up the road to the farm, continuing straight ahead through the meadow until you spot the trail, uphill in an opening. The first part of the trail follows a wide tote road. There are very few trail markers along the way; the trail is maintained by ADK and you spot the first ADK disk 100 yards after you enter the woods. At 0.3 mile there is a fork; you take the left continuing on the tote road through a pretty forest of yellow birch, hemlock, and beech. In 200 yards there is a skid road to the left, you stay straight, following the markers and climbing a ridge line.

At 0.6 miles, after a fifteen-minute walk, the trail is a left fork at the intersection with another old logging road. The way now is steeper; the trail is a narrow footpath that is rougher and eroded. An intermittent stream joins the trail and accounts for the way it has been washed out. Yellow blazes replace trail markers here. After walking for thirty-five minutes you reach a large rock with a spring coming from it. The trail levels off, then climbs again to reach a marked intersection at 1.1 miles, a leisurely fifty-minute walk. The way right is the Spruce Hill Trail, section 44.

Take the left fork, which is marked with yellow blazes and leads steeply up for 200 yards through a notch and out to the first overlook. There are many paths here through the bearberry and blueberry patches leading to different overlooks that offer a panorama to the south and a view across Keene Valley.

Walk up to the uppermost overlook to discover the continuing trail heading west through the red pine forest. The trail to the southeast summit, at 1.4 miles, has several short, steep pitches. The main trail is marked with yellow paint, but there are numerous side paths to various outlooks; no matter this is such a popular mountain, there are enough vantages for a private picnic on even the most beautiful and crowded days.

From the southeast summit, continue northwest along the ridge line to the northwest summit, which looks due west at Porter and Cascade, with Big Slide to the left of Porter. You reach this 744-meter (2440-foot) summit at 1.6 miles in less than two hours, even with many stops to enjoy the distant mountain views. There is one more outlook, lower and to the west. You can either return from the northwestern summit or continue on to complete the loop.

The trail continues west, descending rapidly through piney woods to a sharp right turn that leads 0.2 mile to an open area with views of Giant, Spread Eagle, and Keene Valley. Continue west, reaching at just short of 2 miles the last overlook, perched atop tall ledges. The trail angles left, away from the overlook, and continues south on contour for 100 yards before dropping steeply over a pine-needle-covered, rocky base. Watch out, it is slippery! The trail goes due south and it feels like straight down. The trail quickly levels out in a charming hemlock grove that fills a small rock cirque. The steep pitches continue without markers for a twenty-minute walk in which you will descend 700 feet in less than 0.4 mile.

At 2.4 miles, you reach two cairns and three red-blazed trees. Go straight ahead, across the little freshet and up the ridge ahead. The trail contours along the ridge through a beautiful hemlock grove. The walking is easy now as the trail quickly joins an old wagon road that descends gently toward a residence. At three miles, just before the house, there is a marked left turn from the woods road to a path that circles away from the house and descends to its driveway. Walk down the driveway and the paved (unmarked, formerly Upham) road to Beede Road. Turn left and walk uphill 0.3 mile to your car.

There is no parking along the unmarked road and insufficient room along Beede Road, so park only as indicated. It is best to hike the trail in a counter-clockwise direction, as described here, because it is hard to find the way otherwise. Also, another house may be built near the end of the loop that may cause future rerouting.

44 Baxter Mountain from NY 9
Hiking, snowshoeing, spectacular views
1.1 miles, 1 hour, 235-meter (770-foot) vertical rise

This is one of the easiest hikes in this guide and the views from the double peaks of Baxter, section 43, are especially rewarding for such a small mountain.

This trail up Baxter starts on the *south* side of NY 9N, which is also called Spruce Hill Road. The informal, low trail sign is 2.0 miles east of NY 73 and 8.1 miles west of NY 9 in Elizabethtown. The trailhead is almost opposite (50 feet east) of the beginning of Hurricane road, which becomes East Hill Road as it approaches Keene.

The trail starts at 240° magnetic, or west-southwest, though you scarcely need a compass for this hike. The trailhead lies at 510 meters, 1673 feet. The trail climbs gradually through balsam and red spruce; there is pipsis-siwa beside the trail, which is attractive even after a light snow. In a few minutes, the trail becomes wider and there are ADK disks on trees, mak-ing it easy to follow on snowshoes in winter. After fifteen minutes, the forest becomes more mature, with white birch and beech and an open un-derstory. You climb a little more steeply, but since the entire trail is well-maintained, you will have good footing.

After forty minutes of climbing you reach a junction at 0.7 mile with the trail that comes in from Beede Farm and Keene Valley. Follow the directions as in section 43 to climb to the series of open rock summits as far as the tallest one at 1.1 miles. In winter you will find the climb out of the col short but steep, so you may have to take off your snowshoes and use crampons. The trip back from the eastern summit to NY 9N takes only twenty minutes. Since you can do the entire hike in an hour and a half, you will have time to walk across the summit ridge and picnic at one of the more remote overlooks. It is a good climb to start off with if you are out of shape.

45 Mossy Cascade Brook to Hopkins Mountain
Hiking, snowshoeing
3.2 miles, 2½ hours, 634-meter (2080-foot) vertical rise

This ATIS-marked trail is one of three ways to reach the bald dome of Hopkins Mountain from the Keene Valley area. It is the longest route but includes a scenic gem—a hemlock-shaded waterfall from which Mossy Cas-cade Brook gets its name.

The trailhead is on NY 73, immediately south of the bridge across the East Branch of the Ausable River, 0.5 mile north of the road to the Ausa-ble Club in St. Huberts and 2 miles south of the sign to Johns Brook Val-ley in Keene Valley. You must park across the road on the shoulder, but do not block the mail boxes. There is a small green sign, hard to see, be-yond the guardrail reading "Hopkins-Mossy Cascade." Step over the guardrail and down the bank to a small wooden bridge over a little brook flowing into the Ausable River.

Baxter Looking West to High Peaks

The beginning of the trail is a level old woods road running northerly, parallel to the clear gravelly river on your left, west. Notice the very large white pines along the route. In nine minutes, at 0.3 mile, you move away from the river and reach a dirt road with a red house on the left. The trail, marked by a green sign with an arrow and a double blaze, continues northerly up an actively used jeep road. This road forks as you go uphill, but the trail is obvious with another green arrow and double ATIS markers on a cedar tree. After hiking for fifteen minutes, at 0.5 mile, follow the trail as it turns left, north, and leaves the dirt road. The spot is marked by a green arrow, two ATIS markers, and some pink ties. The dirt road makes this section unattractive, but there are large interrupted and ostrich ferns to admire along the way.

You are now in a handsome woods, climbing with a vertical rock cliff on your left. In twenty minutes, at 0.75 mile, you reach a small sign directing you left to Mossy Cascade; the trail to Hopkins forks to the right. The beautiful, shady forest of hemlock and pine shelter chanterelle mushrooms in the moist duff in summer. Go left along the "billy goat" trail to the forty-foot-high waterfall. Some waterfalls emit a sense of power and force; Mossy Cascade is veil-like and dainty. You feel peace here, and want to stay—except that it is apt to be damp and chilly in the deep shade.

After the cascade diversion, the trail to Hopkins climbs steeply. The brook on the left, north, drops over large jagged rocks. Ten minutes above the waterfall, at 0.9 mile, the trail passes below a private lot with a cabin. Large trees have been cut in front. After crossing the brook, you pick up an ATIS marker; the trail goes off to the northeast (40° magnetic), still climbing through a hemlock grove. You gain altitude fairly constantly, up over a hogback, but it is a clear trail and easy walking. You level off in a grove of large hardwoods including red oak—1800 feet seems high for this species. Twenty minutes after crossing the brook you are at 2000 feet, out of the oak and into hemlock, birch, and ash.

In less than an hour after starting, just short of 1.5 miles, a sign indicates an outlook to the left. A High Peaks panorama spreads before you: Dix, Colvin, Wolf Jaw, Rooster Comb, Brother, Porter—to name a few. After leaving the overlook, the trail passes over a ridge with Christmas fern and leads into a slight depression. Notice the sizeable grove of hop hornbeam here and, later on, large beds of maidenhair fern. Continuing northeast, you climb again. Within ten minutes from the first overlook you reach a second at 1.7 miles. It faces south; moss and ferns make this a pleasant spot to rest and see the lower slopes of Giant. Ten minutes more and a third overlook at 1.9 miles reveals Wolf Jaw, Dix, the Gothics, and Brother with the slide on the right. You will appreciate having a map to help identify these and other peaks. At these rocky spots, in summer, you can find pale corydalis growing from the joints in the rocks. The whitish leaves of this delicate pale pink flower with yellow lips and a bulbous spur have an unpleasant odor when crushed.

Two hours after leaving the car, allowing plenty of time for stops at the overlooks, you reach an intersection. Here, at 2.3 miles, a heavily trodden trail goes downhill to the left, west, with a sign pointing to Keene Valley. It is the Ranney Brook Trail described in section 46. Now the trail levels off a bit, climbing but not as steeply, heading 60° magnetic. Half an hour later, at 3 miles, you reach a junction where the ATIS trail goes right to Giant Mountain via Green Mountain and the north spur, section 33. The trail to Hopkins goes left. A steep climb on old roots gets you up to Hopkins' summit in a few minutes.

The summit is impressive! It is an immense solid anorthosite rock, a very large area of which has no cracks or joints. Along the western edge, the rock is fractured and thin soil supports lush blueberries, three-toothed cinquefoil, and moss. The view of Keene Valley, up the Ausable River Valley, the High Peaks to the west, and Giant to the southeast, should not be missed.

The return goes quickly as footing is generally easy. You reach Ranney Brook Trail intersection in twenty minutes, the sign at the first outlook in fifty minutes, Mossy Cascade in one hour and a quarter, and your car in an hour and thirty-five minutes.

46 Ranney Brook to Hopkins Mountain
Hiking, snowshoeing
2.6 miles, 2 hours, 2140-foot vertical rise

This almost unmarked trail is the middle of the three trails from Keene Valley area to the summit of 3183-foot Hopkins Mountain. The mountain was named after a minister from Troy, New York, the Reverend Erastus Hopkins, who hiked in the region. While the climb, without stopping for overlooks, will take a little over two hours, the return takes but an hour and a quarter.

The beginning of the trail is at an iron bridge over the Ausable River with a sign: "H. N. Scott." The first part of the trail is over private land and there may be a chain across the bridge. There is no sign along the highway to mark this trail but there is a long-standing permission to hike this route. Respect the land and the owner's property. Park on the west, beside NY 73, a little to the north of the bridge. Do not drive across the bridge, which is 1.1 miles north of the Ausable Club in St. Huberts (0.6 mile north of the NY 73 bridge over the Ausable), and 1.5 miles south of Johns Brook Road in the center of Keene Valley. Walk east across the bridge and along a dirt road. Within 100 feet you cross another bridge with pipe railings. Just beyond look for a small sign on the right that reads "Hopkins-Giant." Turn right, east, into woods and follow the well-traveled woods road uphill. The brook valley is on your right. The trail climbs gently uphill and at 0.7 mile (twenty minutes' hiking time) crosses Ranney Brook. The trail continues up to the east-southeast with the brook on your left, north. In thirty minutes, you cross a yellow-blazed property line running north-south as you climb a little more steeply in an open maple grove. Somewhat steep areas intersperse with level sections.

You climb for an hour and a quarter, 1.8 miles, from the iron bridge to reach the intersection with the Mossy Cascade ATIS-marked trail coming in from the right, southwest. From here the trail to the summit follows the route described in the Mossy Cascade trip, section 45.

47 Phelps Brook to Hopkins and return via Spread Eagle Mountain Trail

Hiking, great views
4.6-mile loop, 4 hours, 1880-foot vertical rise

Two trails lead from the same point in Keene Valley to the summit of Hopkins Mountain. The western trail traverses the summit of Spread Eagle Mountain on the way. It is best to combine the trails into a circuit walk and while either direction has its advantages, this guide describes it in a clockwise direction.

The trail is well marked, well maintained, and easy to follow. The hardest part is finding the trailhead and winding through a maze of roads etched on the lower slopes of Spread Eagle Mountain. These were built to serve a proposed development that never materialized. Fortunately, there are adequate signs—it is questionable if in their absence directions would suffice to guide you through the number of turns.

Even though the trail is very steep in places, this is a mild, short day hike with unusual plants and geological forms to add to the famous views across Keene Valley to the High Peaks.

To reach the trailhead, turn right, east, on Beede Road, 0.6 mile north of the center of Keene Valley. Cross the Ausable River and Phelps Brook and bear right at 0.4 mile. (Left leads to Baxter, section 43.) The road narrows and winds steeply uphill past several driveways. At 0.9 mile there

Keene Valley and High Peaks from Baxter

is a driveway left and the road ahead is impassable for ordinary vehicles, even though a sign indicates parking is further along. There is very little room to park here, and you must be careful not to block the driveway.

Walk along the roadway for 0.1 mile to the purported parking area, where the trail turns sharply right. At 0.25 mile you see a sign for the two mountains and turn left now onto a narrow track, which climbs fairly steeply to intersect another dirt road. Turn left here at this intersection; at 0.6 mile a dirt track comes in from the right and you continue straight for 100 feet or so to an intersection. The road continues, but you turn right then quickly (in 250 feet) left onto another road.

You can hear Phelps Brook downhill on your left. The road follows the valley of the brook southeast and uphill, past a foundation, until at just over 1 mile you reach a marked fork in the trail. In about a half hour, you have already climbed 700 feet to reach the fork. To make the clockwise loop, turn left on the Hopkins Mountain Trail, which starts as a logging road through a tall, straight forest. The road is relatively level, but watch as it begins to dip, about a five-minute walk, 0.2 mile from the turn. Leaves are apt to conceal the trail sign. The trail, now a narrow path, forks right uphill and begins a high traverse. It is several minutes into this section before you finally reach state land.

On this steep and straight traverse you have occasional views through the trees toward Baxter Mountain. Heading generally south now, you cross several small or even intermittent streams; in a wet draw at 1.75 mile, look for silvery spleenwort as well as more common ferns. Go straight across the next draw; weeds and horse nettles can obscure the foot tread. Just short of 2 miles, forty minutes from the intersection, the trail turns right toward the steep slopes of Hopkins. Now the trail is a steep scramble. Watch for a few clumps of the rare Braun's holly fern beside the trail.

Within a few minutes of climbing you reach the spruce level—everything has changed, even the understory. The slopes are a hanging bog with mosses and ferns. Cedar clings to steep ledges. You clamber up over roots and ledges, gaining 500 feet in 0.2 mile to reach an intersection. The way left leads in 0.1 mile to Hopkins Summit. The trail emerges from the spruce just below the 3180-foot summit, after a two-hour climb. Take time to enjoy the marvelous anorthosite rock of the summit. This coarsely crystalline igneous rock, composed mostly of plagioclase feldspar with a little dark-colored minerals such as ferro-magnesium but with no quartz, is the basic rock of the High Peaks. Here the solid rock summit is surrounded by patches of blueberries. The views of Giant, the Dixes, St. Huberts, and the rest of the High Peaks are spectacular. The trail leading to Giant or Green Mountain or St. Huberts, sections 38, 45, and 46, begins from the top of the rock slide.

To return via Spread Eagle, return to the intersection just below the summit, at 2.4 miles, and turn left. A guideboard with mileages to Keene Valley points the way. The narrow footpath leads across the narrow wooded top of the spine that connects Hopkins and Spread Eagle, and it takes about thirty minutes to hike the .55 mile between the summits. There is a gentle descent at first, then the trail drops steeply into a hollow and out to an overlook on a large rock outcrop marked with a cairn. As you return into the woods, the descent is again steep, down into a col, sharply left and up another knob, along a ledge through blueberry bushes and out to the open rock of Spread Eagle. You walk for a couple of hundred yards along the ridge with open rock, blueberries, and fantastic views all the way.

As you start to descend to the north from Spread Eagle, there is yet another super view at 2.9 miles, this one to the north. You circle the north side of Spread Eagle's ledges, steeply down a staircase trail, so steep you will need to find handholds among the bordering trees. Ten minutes from the last view spot, at 3.1 miles, there is another outcrop with view, then a level traverse, and another steep section. The trail becomes less steep, but the rocky footing continues to make this a cautious descent all the way back to the logging road intersection, where you turned left to go to Hopkins earlier. You have come 3.6 miles and by turning left, and retracing your steps for 1 mile, you will reach the trailhead.

Hurricane Mountain Primitive Area

HURRICANE MOUNTAIN, 3694 feet in elevation, dominates a high range of irregular rocky outcrops. Rising from its summit is an abandoned fire tower, an obviously identifiable marker that can be seen from many places in the northeastern Adirondacks. This 13,449-acre parcel of state land is classified as Primitive, partly because of the fire tower.

Fire swept eastern parts of the Hurricane area in 1906 and 1908, burning soil down to bedrock, which is still exposed. The barren peak, which can be reached by three trails, provides a wonderful view of Giant and other summits to the south, the High Peaks to the southwest, and the Jay Range to the north.

The western section of this area, near East Hill Road outside Keene, is as pleasant as the eastern part is rugged. It is more congenial to peace and reflection, with attractive trails winding through hardwood and conifer forests that open to rock ledges with stunning overlooks. Two lean-tos nestle among trees for overnight camping. (A third is near Falls Brook on the eastern flank of Hurricane Mountain.)

The conical summit of Hurricane Mountain has been an important landmark since William Gilliland pressed westward from the shores of Lake Champlain. Elizabethtown, named after his wife, was founded in 1798. Falls Brook, which flows down the southeasterly slopes of Hurricane, joins The Branch of the Boquet, and these valleys were sources of trees for the prosperous lumbering business. An abandoned road—the "Old Military Road" was built from Elizabethtown to Wells Hill Road, which now forms the northern boundary of the area.

Hurricane Mountain played an important role in Verplanck Colvin's triangulation survey. Colvin climbed it in July 1873 and established a station on its summit, which was the key to connecting the interior triangles with Split Rock and Juniper Island lighthouses on Lake Champlain.

The beautiful valley of the Boquet and the surrounding hills of Elizabethtown attracted numerous painters to the area. In the 1860s Alexander Lawrie, a hiking artist, sketched scenes from the top of Giant, Hurricane, Wood Mountain, and Mount Tom. In the late 1800s another climbing artist, James N. Rosenberg, hiked and camped in the area. Rosenberg was so impressed that in 1923 the family bought land on Shanty Brook and came there every summer. He remarked once that Elizabethtown was his "favorite place in the world," and he and his family now lie in a peaceful cemetery on the slope of the mountain. Many of Rosenberg's paintings are local scenes, some of which can be seen at the Adirondack Center of the Essex County Historical Society in Elizabethtown. There is also a large relief map of the area at the Center.

A different kind of cultural group was formed near Keene. In 1889, Thomas Davidson, a philosopher, established the unique School for the Cultural Sciences on East Hill Road. Some of the country's leading philosophers and scholars, including John Dewey and William James, came to Glenmore in the summer to discuss, argue, and lecture—and to explore the nearby hills. When Davidson died in 1900, the school continued for ten years under the direction of S. Burns Weston. As you hike the trail to Gulf Brook, Lost Pond, and Weston Peak, you can feel satisfaction that scholars of a century ago saw this area much as it exists today—and that it is and will remain "forever wild."

In spite of the size of this Primitive Area, there are only three trailheads, not counting the bushwhack entrance to Ausable No. 4 from the north side. It provides a delightful variety of official trails, exciting bushwhacks, open peaks, cozy lean-tos, and bubbling streams (but only one pond) and it is guaranteed to lure you back for four-season adventures time after time.

48 South Trail to Hurricane Mountain
Hiking, birding, scenic views
2.6 miles, 2 hours, 604-meter (1982-foot) vertical rise

This is the easiest and most popular trail to the top of Hurricane Mountain. The time given for the climb assumes a fast hike on a cool day. The round trip, even with lunch on top, takes little more than four hours. If you like wildflowers and bird song, hike it in early June—but bring insect repellent; the black flies on top are ferocious.

The trailhead is on NY 9N, at the height-of-land 6.6 miles west of NY 9 in Elizabethtown and 3.5 miles east of NY 73. You can park on the wide shoulder or in the small parking area across the road where your car will be protected from the sun. There is a signpost on the north side of the road; the trail is marked with red DEC trail disks. The wide trail begins at 517 meters (1700 feet) and climbs steeply through pine and mixed hardwoods. Its surface is worn but well drained with limited erosion. Beside the trail, in spring, you see sarsaparilla, Canada mayflower, bunchberry, false Solomon's seal, and wintergreen at lower elevations. In the woods listen for oven bird, red-eyed vireo, and black-throated green and black-throated blue warblers.

In twenty minutes, at 0.7 mile, the trail crosses a swampy area on rough log bridges and then crosses a stream, the beginning of Spruce Hill Brook. Soon you are out of the wet area heading west on a beaten trail of stones and roots. A thick grove of balsam fir gives a fresh Christmas-y smell to the air. The way is obvious.

The trail swings to east of north. After climbing for just over an hour, at 1.9 miles, just beyond a steep pitch, you reach an overlook to the southeast. In this middle elevation grow foam flower, clintonia, white bunchberry, dwarf rattlesnake plantain, and twinflower. You continue steeply uphill in the same direction until at 2.5 miles you reach an intersection with a trail going north to Gulf Brook Lean-to and Crow Mountain Clearing, section 51. You turn right, up and out onto open rock.

The top of the mountain is barren—no plant life or trees have returned since the soil on the summit was burned. The skeleton of an unmanned fire tower seems forlorn and unattractive. You only appreciate this poor beacon from distant peaks when it serves to help you identify Hurricane as a base point in the skyline.

From a perch near the scrub at the edge of the rock, listen for the familiar song of the white-throated sparrow and the less common blackburnian and redpoll warblers. Let your eyes sweep around nearby peaks to the remote deep blue and purple landscape. It is exhilarating! The way back down can be walked in an hour and a half, with time for finding flowers you missed and hearing more birds marking their territory in the woods.

49 East Trail to Hurricane Mountain

Trail, hiking, camping, snowshoeing
1.3 miles, 1½ hours, 457-meter (1500-foot) vertical rise

The shortest and most direct route to the summit of Hurricane Mountain is along the trail from the east. To reach the trailhead, take a right, north, fork from NY 9, 2 miles west of Elizabethtown. It is called but not labeled Hurricane Road. The fork is immediately west of a bridge over The Branch.

The road climbs 1300 feet in 3.3 miles past private lands to a small parking area at the edge of the Forest Preserve. You will find the road well groomed and safe for all vehicles, except in extraordinary times like the

**Burpee
Road**

N

0   1 mile

Map VI: Sections 40, 42-44, 48-58, 62, 66-67
Based on USGS 7½' x 15' metric Lake Placid,
Lewis, Elizabethtown, and Keene Valley Quadrangles

Path
Trail
Bushwhack
Jeep Road
Road
Shelter
Overlook

summer of 1986, when one of those severe mountain thunderstorms dumped several inches of rain in a very short period, turning the road into a stream and exposing boulders and crevices that stopped all traffic.

Red trail markers direct you up the road from the parking area which lies at 2200 feet in elevation. In fifteen minutes you reach a clearing and descend to a lean-to beside Falls Brook. A path left immediately beyond the brook appears well traveled but ends after a ten-minute walk parallel to the brook. You head uphill on a clear but eroded trail, which has few markers. In five minutes you reach a small level place with a very small brook to cross; here the trail goes to the right and heads up steeply again near the brook. There are lots of blowdowns and the trail is filled with rocks, making it uneven and the climbing rough. White birch, balsam and hemlock border the trail.

For the next half hour you will alternately walk across short level patches and struggle up steep pitches edged by beautiful moss-covered rocks. The way continues steep and easy to follow until you reach open rock. As you emerge from the woods onto the rocks, note the beginning of the trail if you plan to retrace your steps. The trail's entrance into the woods to the north of the lower outcrop is not well marked. The way down is steep enough so that you will spend nearly as long on the descent as on the ascent.

You have only 100 yards more to go over small ledges to the fire tower summit. With views in all directions from the open rock, you will not mind that the tower is closed.

If you are making a loop trek using one of Hurricane's other trails as the first leg, note that you will need to walk east, descending along the open rock almost to tree line, then look for the path to the north, back from the open ledges, marked only by a small cairn.

50 Pitchoff Mountain
Bushwhack

It is easy to become confused over names in the Adirondacks as there are so many duplications. This Pitchoff Mountain is a small foothill south of Hurricane Mountain; another better-known and taller Pitchoff overlooks the Cascade Lakes east of North Elba. The vertical cliffs of this mountain stand out impressively as you near the height-of-land driving west from Elizabethtown and the rugged escarpment has been captured by many Adirondack artists. The mountain can be climbed from the east side by starting from a gravel pit down the road from the cliffs. The more common route, however, is the one described.

The beginning of the hike shares the well-traveled trail used to climb Hurricane from the south, section 48. Climb steeply for twenty-five minutes to the point where the trail levels off and you cross a wet area, at about 650 meters (2130 feet). The trail follows along a brook through the wet area. At the point where the trail angles off to the left away from the brook, leave it and bushwhack up beside the brook to the east.

Continue along the brook as closely as possible, although you pass through a dense balsam thicket and have to detour frequently. The brook peters out, and the woods open up at about 720 meters (2350 feet), and you continue east. After climbing for an hour and fifteen minutes you reach a level col and here you go southeast, 135° magnetic up the hill toward the top of the mountain, which you can only sense but cannot see. There is a lot of very dense balsam interspersed with alder thickets, so the going is slow.

Keeping the easterly direction, you reach the top in a little more than two hours, a climb of 328 meters (1076 feet). The top has a curious combination of very healthy "double" balsam mixed with decrepit-looking alders. The scenery is not spectacular, but in one opening there are views of Owl Head Lookout, and Knob Lock and Tripod mountains to the south. A steep open slope looking east toward Elizabethtown and the Boquet Valley makes a nice place to have lunch.

You can return to the Hurricane Trail by going southwest from the summit. Occasionally you glimpse the rocky profile of Hurricane with its fire tower to the right. There is no way to avoid the balsam and alder growth as you proceed gradually downhill. After walking for thirty minutes, you drop more steeply and soon cross a brook. Continue due west and in less than an hour from the top you are back at the trail somewhere in the wet area. Turn left, southwest, and in less than twenty minutes you are back at your car.

51 The Crows Loop
Hiking, scenic views
3 miles, 2 hours, 334-meter (1096-foot) vertical rise

Towering above East Hill, east of Keene, are two rocky crags that provide marvelous views after a steep but short climb. The loop can be hiked with one car by walking 1.3 miles between trailheads on an attractive dirt road. To find the upper trailhead at Crow Mountain Clearing, head east on East Hill Road from NY 73 in Keene for 2.1 miles to O'Toole Road. You can reach this spot from NY 9N by taking Hurricane Road (which becomes East Hill Road in the north) north for 4 miles. Turn east up O'Toole Road for 1.1 miles until it ends in a grassy old farm clearing with an apple tree. This is Crow Mountain Clearing and a guideboard indicates "Big Crow 1.05 km, elev. 853 m, Little Crow 1.71 km, elev. 774 m, Road 3.22 km."

If you wish to use two cars, leave one on East Hill Road at a solitary maple tree with ADK trail markers on the trunk, 0.25 mile north of the junction with O'Toole Road.

From Crow Mountain Clearing walk north through grass and bracken fern, past a sign marking the boundary of the Hurricane Mountain Primitive Area. A maroon ADK marker signals that you will not get lost. In five minutes there is a rocky and wet section and then the trail starts steeply uphill through a balsam forest, with white pine and poplar mixed in. Birds are plentiful and although the forest is too thick to see many, you will hear the calls of the hermit thrush and several species of warblers.

The marked trail rises steeply but views give you an excuse to pause for breath. Look back and enjoy the mass of Giant and the distant peaks of the Dix Range. In twenty minutes, at 0.5 mile, you reach a fork; Nun-da-ga-o Ridge, section 52, is to the right and Big Crow is 0.2 mile to the left. It only takes a thirty-minute walk from the clearing to reach the summit of Big Crow. With the exception of the Jay Range to the northeast, you have an open view all around. Dix is at 200° magnetic, Hurricane at 165°; and with a map and compass you can pick out over twenty other major peaks from this 2800-foot vantage point.

From the summit, go west toward Little Crow Mountain, which you see nearby. The trail, marked by cairns and paint blazes, drops off the bare rock, through scrub trees, around a rock ledge, and into the col between the two Crows. You climb through woods to the east summit of Little Crow and then continue across rock to the west summit. From here to East Hill Road takes about twenty minutes; it is less than a mile. You descend several steep stretches following markers, cairns, or paint blazes; the trail zigzags but is easy to follow. At several places as you wind south, you find views of a broad sweep of the High Peaks. Altogether, it takes little more than an hour and a half, with time to enjoy the views, to reach the road where you turn uphill for the 0.85 mile return to the clearing.

52 Nun-da-ga-o Ridge and Weston Mountain Loop

Path, hiking, scenic views, camping, cross-country skiing (portion)

In each book there are favorite hikes. The rugged and rocky ridge of Jay Mountain and the alpine-like east meadow of Rocky Peak Ridge are hard to beat, but this trip is a close third—and much easier. There is a path, which has become easier to follow in the past few years. Take your time and make sure you see the next blaze, cairn or tie before you lose the last one, and you will join those who prize this 5.65-mile loop along the ridge at just below the 920-meter (3000-foot) level.

The mountain ridge followed by this loop walk is called the Soda Range on the USGS maps. The description takes you from west to east, which seems more impressive, but the trip can be taken in reverse.

The path starts as a trail from the popular Crow Mountain Clearing described in section 51. It is the end of O'Toole Road, 1.1 miles uphill, east, from East Hill Road. You start north on the trail to Big Crow. If you look on the east side of the parking area you will see a small bridge—that is where you will come out.

Start up the Crow Trail, and after walking through an area with high bracken fern you will see a State Land Primitive Area sign and an ADK red trail marker. This is followed by a short, rocky, wet section and then you start steeply uphill through white pine, balsam fir, and poplar. In June and July you may hear a hermit thrush or a black-throated green warbler as well as other birds who find this a good place to nest. The cover opens quickly and you can rest and enjoy the views of Giant and other peaks to the south.

In twenty minutes, at 0.5 mile, the trail splits; a small sign indicates Nun-da-ga-o to the right. Here the marked trail ends and you must walk cautiously looking for cairns and blazes. After less than ten minutes of winding through woods, at 0.7 mile, you go over a rocky crag. From the top, the slides of Whiteface Mountain show clearly to the northwest. Go along the rock ridge, climbing slightly and angling towards the east.

Forty-five minutes from Crow Mountain Clearing, at 0.95 mile, there is an open ledge with a view of Hurricane (you can see the fire tower) a little east of south. Now you meander through pretty new-growth bal-

sam, with fancy woodferns on the forest floor, on the way to another rock overlook at 1.25 miles of Hurricane, Giant, and the panorama of peaks.

You continue walking along the ridge. About an hour and twenty minutes into the hike, there is a very large rock outcropping that runs back along the base of the ridge. Five minutes later, at 1.7 miles, you are on a higher bluff with another view of Whiteface and, as you pan to the east, other distant mountains in a sky of clear air, the Jay Mountain ridge, and then, at 80°, the twin humps of Saddleback. Duck again into the woods and then emerge on another ledge with a different scan. Well along on the ridge you have a fine view of the Dix Range. As you walk in and out of clearings it is like a slide show, with each scene slightly different. Anticipation of the view at the next opening increases the level of enjoyment and excitement.

Your pace is slow because of pauses for views and the time it takes to search about for the continuing path. Two and a quarter hours from the start, at 1.9 miles, the path seems to go off the last rocky promontory and turns down, southeast, into a valley. This is only a temporary descent, and the path soon swings back onto the rock, heading south along an exposed ledge. Note: a double orange tie (flag) on a tree indicates a change in the direction of the trail, though this impermanent mark may not be there when you walk through.

At 2.15 miles you are on a high point of the Nun-da-ga-o Ridge at 890 meters (2920 feet). You leave this ridge going south; at a large cairn the path goes down off the cliff—it is easy to miss the way as you don't expect it to go down so steeply. You drop 200 feet into a valley and then regain the altitude, heading southeast along the ridge through a pretty woods of white birch with woodferns. At 2.75 miles you drop into a valley and begin the 0.5-mile climb along the north ridge of Weston Mountain, named for Stephen Weston, a director of the Glenmore School.

The going is easy and the path is relatively obvious. You reach an opening at 3.25 miles just below the birch-covered summit of Weston. With pauses to enjoy the views, the walk so far takes over three hours, so this is a good spot for lunch. As you gaze northeast, the crescent ridge sweeps before you, above the wooded cirque. You can retrace your steps visually, locating each southern overlook along the path you have just walked. This is one reason to make the trip west to east; another is the stunning view of Lost Pond as you start down from Weston. It looks like a huge sapphire in a green vale.

Lost Pond from Weston Mountain

Fifteen minutes from the top, dropping steeply through the 0.45– mile descent, you are at the Biesmeyer Memorial Lean-to, at 3.7 miles. The sturdy log shelter was built by the Adirondack Mountain Club in honor of Walter Biesmeyer, founder of the Mountain House on East Hill Road and an organizer of ADK's Hurricane Mountain Chapter. The inscription reads "The peace of heart and mind he found in this wilderness will be forever shared by those who lift up their eyes into the hills." If you are camping, this beautiful spot near Lost Pond is the place to stop.

Leaving the lean-to, go around the western, right, side of the pond, far enough away from it to avoid the alders and a swampy area. The path follows down the west side of the outlet brook, going south, and is easy to follow since this section is used frequently.

Fifteen minutes from the lean-to, at 4.1 miles, you cross a tributary brook and a gorgeous clump of ostrich ferns. Ten minutes later you reach Gulf Brook and an old sign saying "STOP End Snowmobile Trail." There is a camping spot in an open area.

Gulf Brook flows roughly west, and you follow its right bank down on a wide, open woods road. Thirty minutes and 0.85 mile from the Biesmeyer Lean-to you come to the Gulf Brook Lean-to, at 4.55 miles. Across the brook from the lean-to you will see an ADK marker for the north trail to Hurricane Mountain, section 53.

To return to your car, continue on the woods road to the northwest. In July, shinleaf nods beside the trail; it is a good area for spring wildflowers. Ten minutes from the lean-to, look for a large split erratic. The path out is practically level; it would be a short and easy cross-country ski trip into the Gulf Brook Lean-to and back. You walk the 1.1 mile out from that lean-to in twenty-five minutes. It takes less than an hour from the Biesmeyer Lean-to. The entire trip takes six hours, including a stop for lunch. If you do not have that much time, you can reverse the route and go only to Lost Pond and perhaps add a brisk climb up Weston. But be sure to come back to enjoy this delightful primitive path along the top of this wild, forested amphitheatre.

53 North Trail (Gulf Brook) to Hurricane Mountain

Trail, hiking, camping, snowshoeing
3 miles, 2½ hours, 547-meter (1500-foot) vertical rise

The longest, gentlest climb up Hurricane is from the north along Gulf Brook and its tributaries. Park at the trailhead for the Crows, section 51. The trail, with sporadic ADK markers, starts at the east side of the parking loop. It crosses a small stream then follows an old tote road southeast contouring along the hillside through tall, open forest. The trail gradually takes on an easterly direction and rises slightly to reach the Gulf Brook Lean-to at 1.1 miles after gaining less than 100 feet in elevation.

Gulf Brook Lean-to is located right above the brook. The trail to Hurricane crosses the brook just downstream from the lean-to and begins to follow a tributary of the brook that drains the saddle below Saddleback. In 100 yards you cross the tributary but continue following it. The trail is rocky and rough; the tributary has overflowed into it more than once.

Fifteen minutes from the lean-to, at 1.6 miles, you cross the brook again and leave it, heading into a wet, sloppy place. The broad, relatively level trail continues generally south to pick up a very small stream and cross it after another ten-minute walk. You are now in a very handsome and extensive stand of white birch with a lovely understory. Ten more minutes and you cross a babbling brook that falls over moss-covered rocks on the right.

The trail continues south with few markers; for the next half hour, you will be climbing steadily. Half a mile from the summit, the trail begins to curve to the southwest and just before you emerge on the open rock below the summit, at 2.9 miles, you reach a fork with the south trail. You quickly reach open rock; just above it is a cairn, note its place in relation to the beginning of the trail if you plan to retrace your steps.

54 Glen Road—Wells Hill Road Cross–Country Skiing

Cross-country skiing in winter, trail bike riding or walking in summer

5.8 miles, 2½ hours, 190-meter (623-foot) vertical rise

This seasonal road separates the Hurricane Mountain Primitive Area from the Jay Mountain Wilderness Area. It is drivable in a dry summer with a passenger car, and is great for a trail bike. It is prone to washouts, however, so that sometimes even a four-wheel-drive vehicle will have difficulty. In winter it is not plowed and makes an excellent cross-country route. The only drawback is that you must either ski it in both directions in one day or make a very long shuttle from Lewis to Jay using NY 9N between Elizabethtown and Keene.

For a one-way trip, it is best to ski east from Glen Road outside of Jay toward Lewis. Leave a pickup car on the Wells Hill Road at the point where Seventy Road turns north and Wells Hill Road becomes a dirt road. (See introduction to the next chapter for directions.) To reach the beginning of the road on the west, it is easiest to drive south from Lewis to Elizabethtown, west to NY 73, and north through Keene to Styles Brook Road, which leads uphill to the Glen Road. This is a one-hour drive.

You can drive as far as the road is plowed, so park where the plow turns around. Mileages are given from the intersection in the Glen. The road heads southeast, passing several seasonal homes. After a mile you can get glimpses of Saddleback Mountain, whose twin humps rise to the east. Coal Dirt Hill and the Soda Range of the Hurricane area are to your right. You reach a height-of-land, with state land on the north, after 2 miles and a vertical rise of 238 meters (780 feet). Here you pass between two small hills—Frenyea Mountain and Spruce Hill. The road levels off for 0.75 mile with an alder swamp thicket on your right, then crosses a brook. This area may be flooded enough to impede vehicular traffic in wet summers. About 0.3 mile after crossing the brook, a snowmobile trail forks right. This route leads to Burpee Road, west of Lewis, and is an alternate route for a ski trek another day.

The steep eastern side is frequently washed out in summer. The route downhill on Wells Hill Road parallels Spruce Mill Brook, which has several interesting cascades, and was once the site of a small mill where the former road crossed to the north side. Today the road stays on the south side and drops 315 meters (1033 feet) in about 3 miles, making it an easy and gradual run unless it is icy.

55 Conners Notch—Chase Mountain
Bushwhack, scenic views

If you stand on NY 9N where Hurricane Road leads off to Keene and look northeast, a deep V cuts the horizon. This is Conners Notch and the peak to the left is Chase Mountain, rising almost as high as Hurricane. Access from the south is blocked by private land, but this elusive notch and ledgy peak can be reached. The notch is a real classic: large boulders are scattered over the bottom, and in winter huge icicles drape from the cliffs. The flat rocky summit provides a different vantage point to view Hurricane and Giant.

The trip begins from Crow Mountain Clearing on the East Trail to Hurricane, sections 51 and 53. Hike to the Gulf Brook Lean-to, 1.1 miles, and cross the brook and start up the trail to Hurricane, which is marked with occasional ADK markers. About thirty minutes from the lean-to, after you have been going south in a relatively level section, the trail crosses a brook and then begins to climb steadily. At the point before the trail begins climbing, Conners Notch is to the right, southwest, on a bearing of 200° magnetic. When the trees are bare you can see the notch and Chase Mountain to the right of it, but it is more difficult to detect them in summer.

The 200° bearing takes you into the notch, which is easily identified by the steep cliffs of Chase Mountain on the right, northwest, side. If you like climbing around boulders, the trip through the notch is for you. Over the years large rectangles of rock have fallen from the cliff face, forming a massive jumble below. It is fun to climb over these blocks and explore the crevices for ferns and mosses that thrive in the moist depths. Notice that the bark of most white birch in the notch have been gnawed in spots— the food of porcupines who reside in these crevices. Their droppings are light grey here, in contrast to the dark scat of those who live on hard maple bark.

If you make the trip in early winter, before the snow is deep, you will be greeted by icicles hanging in long sheets from the cliffs of Chase, some over ten feet long. After exploring the notch, a climb up Chase is mandatory. As you come back out of the north going northeast, angle left, north, up the stepped wall of the mountain. You have to hoist yourself up in some places, but ascent on this side is possible. Scraggly white birch mixed with conifers hide views at first until you break into the open with a fascinating view of Hurricane from a new perspective. Higher up, the views of Giant to the south with more High Peaks to the right, capped by Mount Marcy, are magnificent. Somehow this 971-meter (3185-foot) summit produces scenes from angles that are especially photogenic.

Walk northwest along the flat summit when you leave. A thick band of balsam must be pushed through as you start down, but you are soon in open woods. An easterly bearing of about 70° magnetic will get you back to the trail from Gulf Brook at approximately the spot you left it.

56 Ausable No. 4
Bushwhack

This is a very rewarding but strenuous and difficult bushwhack in the southeast corner of the Hurricane Wilderness Area. The approach is basically a bushwhack in a southerly direction from the Wells Hill Road. The introduction to this chapter tells you how to reach the Glen Road, which turns into Wells Hill Road after it crosses Styles Brook. Continue east from Styles Brook on Wells Hill Road to the Jay Town line at 2.7 miles, where there is a sign marking the road into the Town of Lewis as being for seasonal use only. In wet seasons you park here. In dry seasons, it may be possible to continue to the trailhead. At 3.3 miles you cross a wet area and Spruce Mill Brook. Exactly 125 yards past this crossing and just before a tiny tributary of Spruce Mill Brook, there is room to park one vehicle perpendicularly to the road on the right. This is the beginning of the bushwhack to Ausable No. 4.

If you prefer to approach from Lewis, follow the directions as for Slip Mountain, section 62, to Wells Hill Road. Continue west past the turnoff for Slip Mountain for 3 miles to the trailhead. You first cross Spruce Mill Brook, and will find that the road is very rough and steep. From this direction, you may locate the beginning more easily if you drive past it to Spruce Mill Brook crossing and retrace your route for those 125 yards.

Set your altimeter for 705 meters (2312 feet), the starting elevation and head toward true south, 195° magnetic. You very quickly begin to climb at a moderate rate. Forty minutes of hiking through a fairly open maple, white birch, and spruce forest will bring you to an elevation of about 900 meters (2952 feet). You can look back and see Saddleback Mountain to the north through the trees. An hour after you start, you come out on an unnamed summit at elevation 975 meters (3200 feet). Although this summit is wooded there are good views from its east-facing ledge and it makes a good rest stop, since most of the climbing is now completed. The view is unobstructed from 85° to 215°, and you can easily identify Mount Mansfield and Camel's Hump in Vermont. Lake Champlain north of Split Rock is visible and so is Northwest Bay farther south. Lewis lies at 105° and Elizabethtown at 155°, while Limekiln Mountain dominates the valley below at an elevation of 891 meters (2922 feet) at 175° magnetic. By exploring to the west on this summit, you can get good views from true north through the east to 220°. This background view includes Saddleback, Whiteface, the Sentinel Range, and much of the High Peaks as far

Cliffs on Ausable No 4

south as Nippletop. In the middle ground to the west the Soda Range, section 52, can be identified.

Allowing half an hour for this first summit, continue now on a heading of 230° magnetic, dropping off the 975-meter (3200-foot) summit and bush-whacking through fairly open woods and over a flat unnamed summit. Thirty minutes later, or two hours from the trailhead, cross the wooded height identified with elevation 991 meters (3250 feet). Here, turn more southerly, toward 215° magnetic for fifteen minutes. At this point you must be care-ful to stay on the ridge to Ausable No. 4 and avoid straying off the 991-meter summit on the false ridge to the southeast. Your route then shifts right to 245° and you continue through open woods, keeping the steep side of the ridge to your left. As you hike along the ridge keeping the left, east, side in general view, your bearing will shift still more southerly until, after another thirty minutes, you are heading toward true south, 195° mag-netic at an elevation of 991 meters (3250 feet), with the steepest part of the ridge still on your left. Some meandering is necessary to avoid the small spruce thickets. Another fifteen minutes and you reach the open south-facing cliff of Ausable No. 4.

You are now at an elevation of 1022 meters (3352 feet), having bush-whacked for 2.1 miles and climbed 317 meters (1040 feet) in three hours. Frequently, a light breeze can be found at this exposed summit making it an ideal, bug-free lunch spot. Be sure to allow plenty of time to enjoy this cliff face. It extends from east to west for 90 meters (nearly 300 feet), providing open views for all but 40° centered around magnetic north. The cliff face has been mapped (*NYS Museum Bulletin 261*) as part of the syenite series with Marcy anorthosite appearing to the south below the cliff. A characteristic of this rock is its tendency to weather to a white color that obscures the lovely green found where it is quarried as ornamental stone by the Ausable Granite Company at Ausable Forks.

The return trip will only take a little over two hours, since the way should be familiar and more downhill. You retrace your route by bushwhacking due north, 15° magnetic, for fifteen minutes before gradually turning right to a bearing of 60°, keeping the steep part of the ridge on your right. Remember to head northerly over the 991-meter summit before following the ridge northeast back to the 975-meter summit. From the 975-meter summit it is easy to head due north, 15° magnetic, because Saddleback Mountain will loom directly ahead for quite a while as you descend to Wells Hill Road.

Jay Mountain Wilderness Area

A BARREN AREA of rocky bluffs, scrub-thick deep gullies, open vistas, and forested valleys lies south of Jay and northwest of Lewis. There are several bushwhacks that enter this little-used wilderness, one of which is from a newly acquired parcel of state land. This route may become a trail. Traversing Jay's sinuous ridges or climbing its steep peaks requires some of the most tortuous, unusual, challenging, and ultimately satisfying bushwhacks that you can encounter on an Adirondack day trip.

The duff on the rugged summits was deeply burned in various fires in 1906 and 1908, exposing unusual rock outcrops formed by the large mass of gabbro. Wind blows constantly on these heights, contributing to a sense of isolation and bleakness. A few wildflowers cling to mineralized soil and patches of thin sod have been rolled up by hard gusts. Some streams flow in the valleys and join the Ausable to the northwest or the Boquet to the east, but the peaks are dry and there are no ponds. However, this 7100-acre Wilderness is small and accessible, so its secrets are easily revealed.

By 1796 settlers had reached this area, and a primitive passage had been pushed westward from North West Bay (now Westport) to Mallory's Bush on the East Branch of the Ausable River. The narrow track went either through Bluff Mountain Notch, section 63, the current northern boundary of the area, or up Spruce Mill Brook to the flat uplands now called the Glen. Mallory's Bush prospered by cutting virgin forests, mining iron ore, and harnessing hydro power where the Ausable River cascaded over rock ledges. Early settlers, including the Storrs, Purmonts, and Mallorys, started an iron business and forge in 1798, built a dam above the "Falls" and sawmills, grist mills, tanneries, carding machines, and other industries below it, south of the current covered bridge. The town, named for John Jay, the Governor of New York State, was established in 1800.

Most industries were swept away by a flood in 1857 and many were never rebuilt, though the old covered bridge in Jay, the longest in the state, was built immediately afterwards. The famous J&J Rogers Iron Company bought the iron business in 1864 and ran several forges in Jay, using ore from Palmer and Arnold hills.

The Ausable River valley is now a farming and residential area; motels

Cairn on Jay Mountain, Whiteface in Background

cater to summer tourists. Fly fishing is popular and canoeists run the river in the spring, portaging around the falls. Alpine skiing at Whiteface is a short distance to the west and cross-country skiing is possible on several woods roads. In summer, swimmers slide down cascades and enjoy the pools above the covered bridge. The mountains, rising over 2900 feet above the valley, are a backdrop to the village green in Jay.

Access to the Jay Wilderness Area

The northeast boundary of the area is Seventy Road, which goes past Bluff Mountain and becomes the Lincoln Hill Road to Jay; it was used in the last century to haul charcoal and is kept open now by snowmobilers. The southern boundary is the dirt portion of the Wells Hill Road, which is sometimes called Spruce Mill Road or Glen Road. The Forest Preserve land is without trail signs or markers because, with a few exceptions, state land is ringed by private farms and forests. Some landowners, particularly Ward Lumber Company, permit access to state land across their property. It is very important, however, that users be careful to leave no litter, pick no wildflowers, and deface no trees, or the land will be posted.

Access points on the east are from Wells Hill Road, sometimes called Spruce Mill Road, which heads west from NY 9 north of Lewis. From

Northway Exit 32 head west. Within 1 mile, before you reach NY 9, Slip and Saddleback—the highest peaks in the Jay Range—loom ahead. Go straight across NY 9 at the intersection 1.7 miles from the Northway and you are on Wells Hill Road. In 2 miles this paved road goes right, north, and becomes the Seventy Road, which leads to the entrance of the wollastonite mine and to climbs up Bluff, Beech Ridge, and Death mountains. Wells Hill Road becomes a dirt road and continues straight, west, at the 2-mile mark toward the Glen and passes jump-off points for Slip and Saddleback mountains.

Access points from the west are all from NY 9N. Most trip directions begin at the Jay covered bridge from which the Glen Road leads south via Nugent Road to the northern bushwhacks up Jay, US, and Arnold mountains. If you continue south on Glen Road/Trumbulls Corners Road/Luke Glen Road for 4.45 miles you reach the new western route to the Jay Range. Continue south on the Luke Glen Road through the mowed farmland of the Glen to where you cross a one-lane bridge at 5.6 miles from the covered bridge in Jay. Continuing east, uphill 2 miles more on a gravel road takes you to the southwest route up Saddleback Mountain. This road continues east to become the Wells Hill Road. You can also reach the Glen by taking Styles Brook Road east off NY 9N north of Keene, or Trumbull Corners Road to the East of Upper Jay.

57 Jay Summits from the West
Bushwhack, future trail, hiking, scenic views

The state has recently acquired a strip of land which connects Luke Glen Road with the public land that surrounds Jay's summits. This new route is the best way to climb the 3600-foot chain of summits known as Jay Mountain. The previous route via Merriam Swamp is now posted.

To reach the beginning of the hike, cross south over the covered bridge in Jay and turn right on the other side onto Glen Road (County Route 22). At 3.7 miles turn left onto Trumbulls Corners Road and at 4.4 miles bear left at the Y onto Luke Glen Road. Just past the Y on the left (east) look for a Forest Preserve sign and a yellow blaze on a white birch. Park off the road on the west.

This route will take you to the western rock outcrops of the Jay Range but it is a serious bushwhack. While climbing the mountain via this route is fairly straightforward, returning to this narrow strip of state land is a real challenge. The bushwhack is sufficiently difficult that you will be hard pressed to walk the entire range and return in one very long day.

Allow three and a quarter hours for the climb to the west summit, two hours for the return, assuming you can find the shortest most direct descent. Do *not* attempt it unless you have a topographic map (the new metric map for Lewis is more detailed than the earlier series), a compass, and an altimeter.

At the yellow blaze there is a corner post and a path heading a little north of east, almost toward magnetic north up the mountain along an old boundary line, which now marks the southern boundary of the new state parcel. You start at an altitude just over 450 meters, about 1500 feet. The boundary generally parallels a brook, which is off to your left, north. After a few minutes you are walking through a red pine plantation.

After a 400-foot climb of about 0.5 mile in half an hour, you reach the edge of the newly acquired parcel. Yellow blazes go off to your left, following the north-south line of that parcel. Straight ahead is a very old property line marked with dull red paint daubs that continues up the mountain in the same direction you have been following. The marks are not always easy to see, but it is worthwhile searching about for them for this is the most direct route to the western summit.

This course takes you through a fairly open woods, across a shelf, then steeply up a knoll of red pine—the needles make it very slippery. At the 2400-foot level, you descend into a depression, climb again to cross a knob that stands out on Jay's western flank, then descend back below the 2400-foot level into a boggy swale. The terrain forces you to vary from the compass heading, so watch that you compensate for deviations from it. The forest gradually becomes thicker as you climb to the end of the blazed line. That end point with its witness trees is so concealed in deep forest that it is almost impossible to find on the way down.

Continue bushwhacking now on the same compass course. The way is very steep. After another section of larger trees you reach open rock about forty minutes from the swale. Scramble up from open patch to open patch for another half hour to the first overlook. Whiteface is obvious to the west and the High Peaks dot the horizon all the way around to the Dixes; Hurricane blocks views directly south.

Walking between open patches generally south and east on the ridge, you reach West Jay Peak at 1028 meters (3373 feet) in under twenty minutes. It is marked Jay Mountain on the metric map and from it there are views of the farmlands of Glen Road, the Styles Brook Valley, Clements Mountain to the west, and the Sentinel Range beyond.

From the western summit, pick a course of about 330° headed for the

last open rock that was your approach to the ridge. Retrace your steps down into the woods, then pick a compass course of magnetic west toward the end of the blazed line. If you miss it, stay on course and keep the small stream on your right. You should intersect the north-south segment of the new yellow blazes this way so you can return to your car all the way on state land.

58 Jay Summits
Paths and bushwhacks

A herd path of sorts connects West Jay Peak with the other two of Jay's three main summits. From the western summit to the eastern—and highest—summit, it is 1.1 miles, and the round trip from West Jay Peak will take from two to three hours.

Heading east from West Jay Peak, look for a path along the ridge. There is some open rock interspersed with grassy fields and small dense patches of scrub brush and stunted trees. Often it is not easy to find the path through them, so you may have to search about for it. Scout ahead, leaving one of your party back on the path. It takes about thirty-five minutes to traverse the 0.4 miles from the western summit to Grassy Notch.

Grassy Notch is a small cleft in the ridge, where the path from Merriam Swamp ended. It is grassy, but filling with scrub white birch and alder. The path east is full of delightful scrambles and changing vistas. All the summits are marked by tall, elegantly constructed ceremonial rock cairns that appear as solitary hikers when viewed from a distance. Smaller cairns mark the easiest route along the rock. Only the first scramble to the east of Grassy Notch will be at all difficult.

From the notch, head east along the narrow footpath, working north behind the first knob. In the first 100 feet, it may be necessary to scout for the path, leaving one of your party in the notch until you are sure you locate it. The path leads you up the steep slope through a passage below an overhanging rock. It makes this circuitous route in order to avoid the steep slope of crumbly scree on the southwest side of the knob. You emerge at the next lookout atop the ridge, which is composed of coarsely crystalline rock known as Jay Mountain Gabbro. It can tear your hands as you grab it for holds on some of the short climbs along the ridge; and the pebble-filled beds of weathered gabbro make unsure footing.

The ridge is almost devoid of trees. Follow cairns east, then up a steep section to reach the first of the two middle summits. The garnet-rich anorthosite rocks here are fractured in rectangular shapes. Six-foot tall cairns mark both the middle summits. It takes about twenty minutes to walk between the two. The views to the north and east from both are memorable, with barren peaks dotting the horizon. To the south you see Saddleback, sections 66 and 67, and farther on, the full sweep of the Hurricane Primitive Area unfolds. At your feet, white cinquefoil clings to the mineralized windswept soil. In spots, sod and layers of moss have been rolled back by gale-force winds. You are atop high cliffs whose height you can appreciate only as you move further east.

A large black basalt dike traverses east-west across the col between the middle and eastern summit of Jay. It is a wild, inhospitable environment—unique in the Adirondacks—but there is an allure to this bleak place. There is one real scramble on the western side of the col, but thirty minutes after leaving the eastern middle summit, you stand on the easternmost and highest of Jay's summits at 1140 meters (3740 feet), where another tall rock cairn monument marks this moon-like landscape.

From the eastern summit, views range across Lake Champlain to the mountains of Vermont. As you turn about to retrace your steps, the distant slides on Whiteface form a backdrop to the changing summit ridge. Between the middle summit cairns you have a spectacular view along the cliffs that range below them. .

On the return, as you approach Grassy Notch, remember to head down the north side of the knob, do not venture down the scree. From West Jay Peak, return as indicated in section 57.

59 Western Summit of Jay down Kelly Basin
Bushwhack

From the most western open rock on Jay's ridge, described above, there is an alternate way to descend. If you leave a car on the north side of the mountain, you can go down the western ridge into Kelly Basin to an isolated area via a somewhat difficult bushwhack.

To place a car on the north side of Jay Mountain, drive south from the covered bridge in the hamlet of Jay via Glen Road 1.4 miles to Nugent Road, a left fork. Go 1.5 miles east on Nugent, passing two roads to the right, to a Jeep road going uphill to the right, south, just before a yellow iron gate, which may be open. Leave the car at the foot of the Jeep road. This is Ward Lumber Company land, but you will pass a sign indicating hiking (not camping) is permitted.

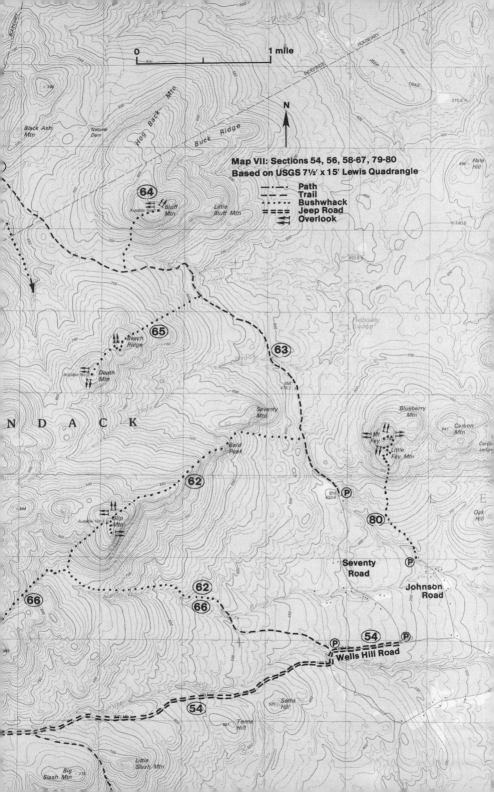

Map VII: Sections 54, 56, 58-67, 79-80
Based on USGS 7½' x 15' Lewis Quadrangle

Path
Trail
Bushwhack
Jeep Road
Overlook

From the western open rock patch described in section 57, head northeasterly (30° magnetic) to a lower, open ridge, which you can spot ahead. There is no path; you make your way around rocks and through scrub growth. Blueberries grow profusely on this northern exposure.

Continue down the ridge on a 30° bearing for as long as you can stay on rock (to about 850 meters, 2790 feet) and 1.2 miles from the notch. Then bear left downhill about 290° magnetic. You should be heading somewhat north of the visible peak of Big Lawler Mountain. When you leave rock you will run into a massive area of white birch blowdowns. Since you are in a valley, it is likely that an ice storm weighted the branches down enough to cause the trees to tip over and pull their roots from the shallow soil. Make your way downhill around the birch as best you can.

An hour and a half after leaving Grassy Notch, you should reach a small brook in the valley. Follow it north or northeast, 30°, and in an hour and fifty minutes, at 2.8 miles, you reach a larger brook on a jeep road. Follow this down for 1 mile to your car. The altitude of your parking place is 370 meters (1214 feet) so you have dropped 658 meters from the west peak. This is for people who love bushwhacks. There are no tremendous views after you leave Jay's western ridge, but the route gives real satisfaction for orienteering achievement. Those who made this trip were not surprised to see a black bear that ran off when it heard them—the Jay town landfill is near the end of the trip.

60 US and Arnold Mountain Loop
Bushwhack

This is probably the most difficult bushwhack in this guide. It traverses rocky terrain, interspersed with spruce and birch thickets, and crosses steep-sided valleys. It is easy to get lost; a compass, altimeter, and map are essential. It is an especially scenic trip, however, with majestic views as you wind across the sinuous spine of US Mountain. Pick a sunny clear July day and allow plenty of time, seven and a half to eight hours. The vertical height you attain is only 500 meters (1640 feet), but the numerous gorges you traverse on the long ridge add perhaps a thousand difficult feet to the climb.

The loop can be done with one car left at the foot of the Jeep road 1.5 miles east on Nugent Road, as described for the descent down Kelly Basin, section 59. Park and hike east on Nugent Road and then quickly turn south on a Jeep road, starting at 370 meters (1214 feet). In fifteen minutes the road forks; go left, ford the brook and in twenty-five minutes,

US Mountain Looking Toward Arnold Mountain

at 1 mile, you will come to a small, brown hunting camp—"Pissonya Lodge," at 490 meters elevation. From the spike horns and eight-point racks tacked under the gable, you can see how successful the hunters were. Walk by the latrine to an old logging road running 160° magnetic, along a brook down the bank to the left. In twelve minutes from the camp, at about 1.3 miles, the tote road ends and you climb along the bank high above the brook, heading 165°–170° magnetic through a white birch and poplar forest. You drop down the hill toward the brook and pick up another old tote road running uphill at 140° magnetic. The old road levels off and you continue to follow it, although detours around blowdowns are frequent.

Thirty minutes past the camp there is an attractive waterfall with a refreshing pool at the bottom. Water flowing over ledges of anorthosite create the falls and plunges into the pool and flume below, which are worn into the softer Grenville marble. The two pale green pools at the base of the flumes make this an exceptionally beautiful spot.

Above the falls, the old road crosses the stream and continues at 150° with the stream to your right, west. At 2000 feet, about an hour from the camp, the road rises steeply, going 160° and crossing to the left bank of the stream again. Here the tote road is eroded and swings to 120° magnetic. At 2500 feet, fifteen minutes later, and just below a white birch grove, the road seems to fork. Go 130° through the grove and you will pick up the road, which has swung around, now running east. At the point where it starts downhill, 1.3 miles from the cabin, above the white

Burned Summit of US Mountain with Glacial Erratics

birch grove, leave it and go 140° up onto a rock overlook.

From the top of this overlook at 854 meters (2800 feet) you can see Big Lawler Mountain across the valley with Whiteface in the distance. Continue to make your way up the rock through scrub until you reach the height of the ridge. You are now on the southern peak of the double summit of US Mountain at an elevation of 870 meters (2855 feet). From its eastern side there are views of Bluff, Death, and Beech Ridge mountains—with the distant outline of Camels Hump in Vermont. There is a deep notch to the south and the wooded ridge beyond hides the summits of Jay. You will need to pause a minute to get your bearings; it takes over two hours to reach this spot from the hunting camp.

US Mountain has a series of summits, a row of rock outcrops separated by wooded gorges. To start to traverse them, bushwhack north off the ridge through open scrub white birch and low brush. You soon reach steep ledges and must bear left to drop down into a 150-foot gorge and up the other side to another summit. The top of this summit has been burned bare on the west side. A huge split rock and many other glacial stones give an unusual foreground to a beautiful view of Whiteface and the MacKenzie Range.

From the split rock, you can go east across the summit to an eastern overlook, where cinquefoil thrives in the poor soil. Retracing steps to the split rock, leave this area at 70° magnetic, through a heavy spruce thicket and a wooded valley. At the next opening, there is another view of Death Mountain and Beech Ridge, and the distant Green Mountains. Leaving this view spot, go north into and out of valleys—a difficult series of ups and downs—and then into a deep valley just south of Arnold Mountain. You can see the bare west side of Arnold Mountain as your objective ahead. It looks steep and difficult, but takes only ten minutes to climb and is surprisingly easy.

The top of Arnold is also rocky, with more scrub spruce and stunted white birch. The dainty blue harebell seems out of place in this stark environment. Allowing time for photos and lunch, it takes about three hours to traverse up and down from the south ridge of US Mountain to Arnold.

You leave Arnold on the north, then go down the northwest face headed for Hardwood Hill at 340°, but it is not always possible to maintain that course. If you have to deviate, bear left. You will come out somewhere on the Jeep road, below another hunter's camp, near the end of end of the extension of Nugent Road, which is here just a logging road. You should reach your car about two hours from the top of Arnold.

61 Grassy Notch via Gelina Basin
Bushwhack

The Jay summits can be reached from the north by a relatively easy bushwhack that begins on Ward Lumber Company land. The beginning of the trip is the same as for section 60 to US and Arnold Mountain. You park in the same place, hike up to the hunting camp, and then up to the top of the waterfall at 1900 feet. Above the falls you should follow the main brook south for ten minutes and then slightly west of south—190° magnetic—staying with the brook. Be sure you are following the main part of the brook as the eastern tributary will take you up US Mountain.

Continue on a 190° course for about twenty minutes. At about one hour and fifteen minutes from the camp you will enter a white birch stand at elevation 760 meters (2500 feet). The northwestern tip of Jay will be uphill to the right and you will be in a valley where the sides are getting steeper. That is about all the clues you will have to the fact you are in a place with such a lovely name as Gelina Basin.

From here, take a compass bearing of 165° to avoid the steepest part of the mountain and the open rock area to your left. You may even be able to pick up a hunter's path that will take you to Grassy Notch and the summits of Jay, described in section 58.

Grassy Notch is at 1000 meters (3280 feet) and the climb from your car should take less than two hours. If you have two cars you can leave one on the north side, hike up the new route from the west, and descend via Gelina Basin. A path from the notch quickly disappears, so take a heading of 345° magnetic toward the brook valley, then follow it down to the falls and the hunter's camp and out.

62 Slip Mountain—Northeast Ridge and Bald Mountain Loop
Bushwhack

Slip Mountain was surveyed as Ausable No. 3 with a contour elevation of 1010 meters (3313 feet) on the new metric series maps. That makes it the third highest peak in the Jay Mountain Wilderness Area after Saddleback and the several summits on the great ridge of Jay Mountain. The summit is a moderate bushwhack if you choose to retrace your route after enjoying its very rewarding views. This description of a loop trip over Slip and down its northeast ridge, over Bald Peak, and east to the Seventy Road is a difficult bushwhack that requires both stamina and orienteering skills.

To spot a car at the end of the bushwhack, drive to the intersection of NY 9 and the Wells Hill Road in the hamlet of Lewis, as described in the introduction to this chapter. Head west from the intersection, and at 2 miles the main road turns sharply right. This is the beginning of the Seventy Road, which heads north, while the Wells Hill Road continues unpaved on the left. Go north on the paved Seventy Road to the end of pavement at the entrance to the NYCO wollastonite mine at 3.9 miles and bear right, staying on the unpaved portion of Seventy Road. Pass the "Seasonal Use—Limited Highway" sign and continue beyond several trailers that are used as hunting camps at 4.2 miles. Leave your car here for the end of the trip.

To find the best spot to begin the bushwhack, return south on Seventy Road to Wells Hill Road, 2.2 miles from your parking spot. Turn right and head west on the narrow West Hill Road for 0.5 mile where you park at the "One-Lane Bridge" sign that indicates you are approaching Spruce Mill Brook around the bend to the left. Signs indicate a side road to several camps on the right, north. The hike begins along this northern road, starting at an elevation of 410 meters (1345 feet) on unposted, private land. Within two minutes from Wells Hill Road, take the left fork heading west. After passing a series of log landings in a white birch forest, the camp road becomes more overgrown and passes a turnoff on the left at fifteen minutes. Five minutes later, you reach an overgrown intersection, but you continue west taking the left fork.

As you pass the remains of an old camp on the right, you will begin to hear Derby Brook off to the north. Thirty minutes into the trip, about 0.9 mile, you reach a very overgrown fork in the road. You take the right fork north down to Derby Brook where it is flowing east. Cross the brook and search around on the north side for the old tote road that runs along its left bank. Follow that tote road, and one hour into the hike the road has become less distinct, although you can still hear Derby Brook to the left. Through the trees to the north, you begin to see the eastern cliffs of Slip Mountain. Eventually, the trace of the tote road disappears altogether and you continue to bushwhack uphill to the east.

At an elevation of 750 meters (2460 feet), you enter the basin on the southwest side of Slip Mountain and at one and three-quarters hours into the trip you reach the main drainage off the southwest side of Slip Mountain. At this point, after 2.4 miles, you turn to a bearing of 25° magnetic and head up the moderate slope of Slip Mountain in a white birch forest broken only by one-inch-diameter spruce trees. You begin to see Saddleback Mountain in the distance behind you to the southwest, while at your feet you may see the plentiful white flowers of the three-toothed cinquefoil. After two and a half hours of hiking, about 2.9 miles, you reach the first of the three or four bare outcrops near the summit of Slip and you can begin exploring the many views. One of these outcrops, just west of the summit has the telltale drill hole of the Ausable No. 3 survey station. From here a magnificent panorama includes Bluff Mountain or Ausable No. 1 (at 355°) and Death or Ausable No. 2 and Beech Ridge at 345°. Continuing west to almost south you see the summit of Jay with US Mountain behind, Saddleback, Hurricane with its fire tower and the High Peaks behind, and Giant with Rocky Peak Ridge to its left. A ten minute bushwhack, a little south of east, will bring you to the top of the nearly sheer cliffs on the east side of Slip. From this vantage be careful as you look directly down on the wollastonite mine and east to Mt Fay and Fay Bog. Further east the length of Lake Champlain, from the Four Brothers Islands north of Willsboro Point, south to Northwest Bay at Westport is interrupted only by the prominence of the Split Rock Mountains.

For those who have chosen a moderate hike without the necessity of a vehicle drop, this is the place to begin retracing your steps. The bearing off the Ausable No. 2 survey point to the basin southwest of Slip is 205° magnetic, and the return trip to your car on Wells Hill Road will take an hour and a half.

The direct bearing to Bald Mountain from the top of the cliffs on the east side of Slip Mountain is 40°. However, because of an embayment in the steep cliffs of Slip Mountain, you have to leave the summit of Slip on a bearing of 20°. In hiking the northeast ridge of Slip on this bearing *it is essential that you be careful to stay to the west of the cliffs that make up part of this ridge.* About fifteen minutes after leaving the summit of Slip, head more easterly, to 55°, until you reach the cliffs on the east side. Continue a more gradual descent at a bearing of 25°, keeping the cliffs on your right. Less than thirty minutes after leaving the summit you will reach a poorly defined col between Slip Mountain and Bald Peak. By heading east at the col, it is possible to get out on a rocky knob that gives an impressive view to the southwest up the sheer cliffs of the east side of Slip. From this knob, a bearing of 55° takes you up the open ledges of Bald Peak, about 4 miles into the trip. These ledges continue to give good views to the south of Slip and across the Hurricane Primitive Area down to Giant Mountain. About an hour after leaving the Slip summit, you cross over the broad summit of Bald Mountain bearing 15° at an elevation of 700 meters (2300 feet), with rocky outcrops scattered in a white birch forest. Continue the gradual descent from Bald Peak on a bearing of 15° magnetic until you are one and a half hours from the summit of Slip and reach a small drainage heading east. At this point change your heading to the east 65°, and continue through the open woods for an hour until you reach the Seventy Road. Turn right and head south on Seventy Road for about 0.5 mile to the car you left there.

63 Seventy Road Traverse
Hiking, cross-country skiing
5.4 miles, 4 hours, 220-meter (722-foot) vertical rise

The Seventy Road traverse is an easy low-elevation hike or a moderate cross-country ski trip, depending on snow conditions. Without side trips the traverse can be completed in under four hours, leaving time to make the additional bushwhack to Bluff Mountain along the way, section 64. Gray's Atlas of 1876 shows this road as the major connecting link between Lewis and Jay when it was a more important transportation route.

For skiing all the way through, the preferred direction of travel is from north to south, but this involves a long car shuttle. The southern part of the route is frequently done using one car, so the skier heads north and retraces his route to get the downhill run to the south. The description gives the through trip, but you can easily adapt it to your needs.

Leave the pickup vehicle at the same location for the Slip Mountain trip, section 62. Return to the intersection of Wells Hill Road and NY 9 (mileages are given from this point) and head north for 5 miles to cross the North Branch of the Boquet River. Turn left across the bridge and head northwest on Trout Pond Road. At 13.2 miles Trout Pond Road makes a T intersection with Green Street and you turn left, southwest, onto Green

Street. Go past Grove Road at 16.1 miles, past Black Mountain Road on the left, to a fork in the road at 18.5 miles. Here Stickney Bridge Road goes right, north, and you continue left, still on Green Street. At this point there is a spectacular panoramic view to the west across the agricultural lands of the East Branch Ausable River to Whiteface, the Sentinel, Pitchoff, and Cascade mountains. Continue on Green Street, past Santo Road on the left at 18.8 miles, to an intersection at 19.7 miles, where you turn left, southeast, onto Hazen Road. At 20.3 miles you pass Murcray Road on the left. Lincoln Hill Road enters on the left, southeast, at 22.9 miles. It is unpaved and marked with a "Dead End" sign. (It is easy to miss Lincoln Hill Road as Hazen Road turns right to head northwest toward Jay.)

Follow Lincoln Hill Road as it climbs to the southeast for 1.5 miles until grass begins to appear between the wheel tracks and you come to a grassy area on the left where you can park. In winter you probably cannot drive this far and will have to search for a place to park safely at the side of the road.

You begin by heading southeast along Lincoln Hill Road as it gradually climbs. Stay left at the first fork, the right leads to a camp. Shortly you can see Hardwood Hill, elevation 689 meters (2260 feet) off to the right. The road is quite attractive and deeply entrenched between ancient stone walls. Posted signs appear on the right and you reach a barrier, which limits vehicular access. Since your beginning is dependent on the season, mileages start from this barrier, which is at least 0.2 mile from a parking spot. You quickly pass a tote road on the left. You go right and almost immediately, at 0.1 mile, cross McNalley Brook flowing southwest.

The forest of white birch and spruce thickets is typical of the second growth that develops after a major fire. The conflagration of 1908 struck here. The road climbs steadily following the valley of Number Five Brook. Twenty minutes from McNalley Brook you pass an old tote road on the right and a couple of minutes later your route levels off. Five minutes later, at 1.6 miles, you cross Number Five Brook. After the brook, the road you are following has several names, including Lincoln Hill Road, the Seventy Road, and Number Five Road. Just past the brook you pass another tote road on the right, and in another five minutes you begin to see Arnold Mountain through the trees to the right, southwest. The road climbs again, still bearing southeast, but becomes more overgrown and may even require some searching about to stay on course. The road becomes more distinct again, levels off, and swings easterly in a white birch and striped maple forest.

Fifty minutes from McNalley Brook you begin to see Beech Ridge and Death mountains to the southeast. Very soon you see the gap in the trees to the right that indicates the presence of two small beaver ponds. Here, at 2.5 miles, you can bushwhack south to the eastern edge of the ponds for a good view of Arnold Mountain to the southwest. About three minutes past the ponds, at 2.6 miles, you are in the broad, flat col between Bluff and Beech Ridge mountains. The road is flat, seasonally wet and somewhat eroded by all-terrain vehicles.

The southeastern end of this broad col just before you begin to descend on the other side is the place to begin the bushwhack to Bluff Mountain, section 64. A small cairn by the road marks someone's favorite starting point.

Past the col, the road begins to drop gently and for skiers this is the beginning of a three-mile downhill run to Hale Brook. Fifteen minutes past the col, after a sharp bend in the trail, at 3.1 miles, you reach a trail intersection with primitive signs ("Old Brich Mill," sic) to the left, Lewis to the right, and Jay back the way you have traveled. At the intersection you can see Bluff Mountain through the trees on a bearing of 355° and the steep cliffs of Little Bluff Mountain at 30° magnetic. According to the 1876 Atlas, J&J Rogers Co. of Ausable Forks had one of their many charcoal kilns here at the foot of the cliffs of Little Bluff Mountain. It made charcoal for their iron-making forges. The left route is favored by snowmobiles in the winter and leads into the posted, private road network of the Hale Brook Division, then generally eastward for 4 miles to the Fairview Cemetery 0.8 miles west of NY 9 on Hale Hill Road, 4 miles north of Lewis.

Your route is to the right following the Lewis sign to the southeast. In six minutes you will pass a large four-foot-high boulder on the left. This is the start of the bushwhack to Beech Ridge and Death Mountain. As you continue, two more tote roads soon enter on the left and are shortcuts over to the road to Fairview Cemetery. The road heads gently downhill, angles right, and at 4.1 miles, thirty minutes from the intersection with signs, crosses Hale Brook. Off to the right, southwest of the road beyond Hale Brook, there were more charcoal kilns.

In fifteen minutes you reach Fay Bog on the left. Here at 4.8 miles, a short bushwhack provides a lovely view of Mt Fay, described in section 80. Soon you cross the drainage into Fay Bog and you see a Forest Preserve Primitive Area sign on the left. The posted signs for the NYCO wollastonite mine, which is now just over the ridge to your right, west, appear as the road turns more southerly.

After crossing an intermittent stream that flows southeast, you reach your pickup vehicle, one hour past the intersection with the signs and 5.4 miles from the barrier. It will take an hour to drive the 27 miles to retrieve the second vehicle at the start.

Bluff Mountain Summit

64 Bluff Mountain
Bushwhack

Bluff Mountain is a rewarding but steep bushwhack from the Seventy Road. The start of the bushwhack is described in section 63 and is reached after a one-and-three-quarter-hour hike from the Jay end or a one-and-a quarter hour hike from the Lewis end. Allow three hours for the bushwhack from the Seventy Road to the summit and return. When combined with the Seventy Road traverse this makes a full day trip.

From the eastern end of the col between Bluff and Beech Ridge at an elevation of 675 meters (2214 feet) you bushwhack northeasterly on a bearing of 35° magnetic. The area of open hardwoods drops into the headwaters of one of the tributaries of Hale Brook, and in fifteen minutes you are at the base of the cliffs of Bluff Mountain.

The ascent involves circling to the left, northwest, and climbing along the base of the cliffs. By staying in the woods and working your way to the left, you can avoid the exposed cliffs. It is more fun to scramble up the steeper areas and shorter cliffs adjacent to the woods. This way your rest stops on the climb are enhanced by views of Mt Fay and Lake Champlain to the southeast, as well as Beech Ridge and Death mountains to the south.

By the time you approach the actual summit your route will have shifted to the right to 80°. It takes an hour and a half to climb to the summit at 895 meters (2936 feet), if you have been careful not to take chances on the open cliffs.

The summit is broad and flat and distinguished by a couple of large, balanced rocks. The drill hole marking Ausable No. 1 survey station is easy to find since someone has carefully constructed a ring of small stones around it. The edible thimbleberry, ancestor of the raspberry, fruits abundantly in season. The rock of Bluff Mountain has been mapped as syenite, a coarsely-crystalline, feldspar-rich rock. The views northeast and west are especially impressive.

To return to the Seventy Road after exploring the summit and enjoying its views, simply retrace your steps being careful to keep well to the right of the cliffs as you descend. This brings you to the head of the draw around the tributary; cross it in a southerly direction to pick up the Seventy Road.

65 Death Mountain and Beech Ridge
Bushwhack

The name Death is intriguing and may refer to some early logging accident now forgotten. A local hunter advised exploring the Beechnut on Beech Ridge. This trip traverses both summits and begins from the Seventy Road. See section 63 for a description of the starting point, about an hour's hike northwest. You will probably have to backtrack six minutes from the intersection with the signs to find the four-foot boulder on the northeast side that marks the starting point.

From the boulder, at an elevation of 580 meters (1900 feet) you bushwhack on a bearing of 250° magnetic. You soon see Beech Ridge rising through the open forest of white and yellow birch and maple. The slope is gentle at first, then moderate and finally fairly steep. You cross one or two minor ledges in the steep section. An hour of steady bushwhacking on that bearing brings you to the broad, flat summit of Beech Ridge, 0.7 miles from the Seventy Road.

The summit is wooded with small white birch and some balsam. The white birch are particularly interesting in late fall when the leaves are down and the limbs seem entwined.

The views on Beech Ridge begin directly across the 836-meter (2742-foot) summit on the southeast side. From here Bluff Mountain can be seen at 23° magnetic. A few minutes of hiking south along the top of the west-facing cliffs of Beech Ridge brings you to the thumb-shaped rock promontory called the Beechnut. Hike around its west side and climb the slab rock on its south side. The view from the Beechnut is unobstructed for

300° from north through west, south, and east, although the mass of Death Mountain occupies 50° of the view to the southwest.

To continue the bushwhack to Death Mountain, you hike back north along the top of the west-facing cliffs of Beech Ridge until you are past the cliffs. Then it will take about five minutes to scramble down the 100 vertical feet into the first col between Death and Beech Ridge, on a bearing of 225° magnetic. Be careful to stay to the right of the cliffs on Beech Ridge. It only takes a couple of minutes to cross a low ridge to the second col. You now climb steeply on a bearing of 225° for fifteen minutes to the top of Death Mountain. The summit is wooded. Continue to the west side, where you are rewarded with unobstructed views to the west and south that extend from 145° to 335°. The drill hole marking the Ausable No. 2 survey station can be located at the south end of the summit at an elevation over 860 meters (2820 feet).

This summit opening to the west is a fifty-meter square expanse of bare rock with hundreds of loose rocks lying in disarray on the bedrock. Like the summit of Saddleback, this is an example of the intensity of the 1908 fire that was fanned by strong winds from the west. When the organic material in the soil burned away it exposed the rocks originally deposited during the recession of the melting glacial ice. A careful examination of the loose glacial material shows many blocks of cross-bedded sandstone, probably from the Potsdam Group of the Late Cambrian age. These pieces of sandstone are very much younger than the underlying garnet schists of the Precambrian age.

The views from the summit include Whiteface, the US Mountain ridge extending from Arnold at 320° to the main summit of Jay at 267°, Saddleback at 223°, Ausable in the distance at 215°, and Slip Mountain at 188°.

To return to the Seventy Road, you retrace your route across the wooded summit of Death and drop into the col between Death and Beech Ridge on a bearing of 55°. From the top of Beech Ridge it takes about thirty-five minutes, hiking downhill on a bearing of 70°, to reach the Seventy Road.

An alternative approach to Death Mountain can be made from Jay on Nugent Road, the end of the trip over the western summit of Jay described in section 59. Follow Nugent Road as far as practical and park. Hike east to Rocky Branch. There is a reasonable tote road along the Rocky Branch that runs up along the west flank of Death Mountain. From the tote road, forty minutes of bushwhacking to the southeast brings you out on the summit of Death Mountain.

66 Saddleback Mountain from Wells Hill Road, Lewis

Bushwhack

With an elevation of 1102 meters (3615 feet), Saddleback Mountain is the true high peak of the Jay Mountain Wilderness Area. Its views to the west show the High Peaks of the Adirondacks in an exceptional fashion. It also provides a unique opportunity to view the great Jay Ridge from the south. This bushwhack of Saddleback from the east is strenuous, and the opportunities to get off course—particularly on the descent—are substantial. *Thus it should only be attempted by those with stamina and good orienteering skills.*

To climb Saddleback from the east, park your vehicle on Wells Hill Road at the same spot described for the climb up Slip Mountain, section 62. This is just east of where the road crosses Spruce Mill Brook and 0.5 mile west of Seventy Road. The early part of the hike follows the route for climbing Slip Mountain to the point at an elevation of 750 meters (2460 feet) where you enter the basin on the southwest side of Slip.

Instead of turning north to climb Slip, work your way to the left to the edge of Derby Brook. In the basin Derby Brook is actually meandering generally southeastward for a short distance within a section of sandy banks. You can see Slip Mountain on a bearing of 25° magnetic. At the west end of the basin, Derby Brook will have turned so that it is flowing toward you from a bearing of 210°. Keep Derby Brook on your left and follow it upstream so you are heading 210°. After thirty minutes from the basin meanders, during which you have been climbing moderately to steeply in a white birch and poplar forest, you will find that the brook is causing you to bear left on a bearing of 195°. After an hour from the basin meanders, Derby Brook becomes a ponded trickle and you reach the wooded col between the unnamed eastern summit of Saddleback at 963 meters (3159 feet) to the east and the true summit of Saddleback to the northwest. The unnamed summit can be reached by bushwhacking due east for ten minutes with very little climbing. It is a flat, wooded area with scattered rock outcrops that do not provide views.

For the true summit of Saddleback, change course in the col to 305° and forty minutes of steep climbing brings you to that 1102-meter (3615-foot) peak. Saddleback has two summits, and its west side is a broad, open area that was burned bare by 1906 conflagration. This phenomena of bare areas on the west sides of summits is common in this Wilderness Area and clearly suggests that the flames were fanned by west winds. The view to the west is truly panoramic and is unobstructed for over 200°. You can easily identify Whiteface, Algonquin, Cascade and Porter, Colden, Big Slide, Marcy, Haystack, the peaks of the Great Range, Nippletop, the Dix Range, Giant, and Rocky Peak Ridge. By poking around to the northwest, crossing a short, steep col, you discover the northern promontory with its wonderful views of the sheer cliffs on the face of the Jay Ridge, as well as views of Bluff and Slip.

To return to the basin southeast of Slip, leave the Saddleback summit on a bearing of 125°, being careful not to follow the natural ridge trend that will tend to lead you on a bearing of 170° true and into the valley toward Frenyea Mountain. Once you reach the col, retrace your route down Derby Brook on a bearing of 30° true. The brook will bend right to 40° as you descend. An hour after leaving the summit of Saddleback you are back to the sandy meanders of Derby Brook. From here it is about an hour and ten minutes to your parked vehicle.

67 Saddleback Mountain from Glen Hill Road, Jay
Bushwhack

The western approach to Saddleback's summit is shorter and perhaps a bit easier. It takes about two hours to traverse the 2-plus miles to the summit, almost that much for the return, and a good hour to explore the peak. The trek begins on a newly acquired parcel of state land that avoids the previous route over private land.

Drive east on Glen Hill Road, 2 miles from the intersection Luke Glen Road and Styles Brook Road. It is a seasonal road and in poor condition—the last hill, in particular, has loose gravel and is tough for some cars. At the crest of the hill there is a Forest Preserve sign on the left and a yellow painted cairn. Park just beyond off the road on the right.

This is a bushwhack that *requires* a compass, and an altimeter is strongly recommended. There is no trail and no view of the summit from the road. The only way to reach it is to follow a compass bearing of 55° magnetic, which takes you to the open southwest face of the mountain.

You start at approximately 680 meters (2230 feet). A blazed lot line goes due east from the cairn up the steep slope of Frenyea Mountain. If you follow that line to the point where it gets too steep to continue easily, then take a bearing toward Saddleback of 50 degrees. It is actually easier to contour around the north side of Frenyea and use a 55° heading.

Jay Range from Saddleback

The woods are open and fairly easy for bushwhacking, although you climb steadily. At times there will be small ledges that you must climb up—but nothing severe. After an hour and a quarter, you should reach Saddleback's open, sloping rock face at roughly 900 meters (2950 feet). From here you continue very steeply climbing and scrambling up the open slopes of the knob that is the southern summit.

Plan to spend time exploring the saddle and hiking over to the northern end of this more or less flat-topped peak. This bushwhack takes you over open patches and through scrub-filled crevices. From the northern vantage you can enjoy the mountain's full 360° panorama with its views of Whiteface, Death, and Slip and the spectacular cliffs on Jay.

The route back is a reverse of the trip up. It is easy to follow your way back down the rock face and you should recognize some of the ledges you climbed on the way up. You can see Frenyea Mountain, the small hill to the southwest, and you want to head for its right (west) side. The bearing from where you leave the open rock face is about 230 to 235 degrees magnetic. Chances are you will not follow the identical route you took going up, but don't worry if it doesn't look familiar. Keep your compass reading on a fairly easy traverse, heading downhill. You will cross logging roads but these lead to private land. The return should take about an hour and three quarters.

The Shores of
Lake Champlain

THE 120-MILE LENGTH of Lake Champlain was the entry way for set-
tling the northeastern Adirondacks. From 1609, when Samuel de Champlain first viewed the high western peaks from the lake, this waterway was
the route by which the French (and later the English) moved south. It
was also the natural thoroughfare for some settlers in New England and
the Hudson Valley to move north and west. The names of mountain peaks,
rivers, and lakes—Chazy, Ausable, Boquet, Champlain—attest to the French
presence from Montreal to Lac du Sacrement (Lake George). One of the
early settlers from the south, William Gilliland, was a New York merchant
who was born in Ireland. He bought land between Split Rock and the
Boquet River in 1764. He is quoted as saying it was "a howling wilderness,
more than one hundred miles from any Christian settlement, except the
military posts at Ticonderoga and Crown Point." From Westport, which
Gilliland called Bessboro, he expanded west to Elizabethtown and north
to the Boquet. He bought cattle and encouraged families to settle. Although
his empire later collapsed, Gilliland helped open up these shores and the
pleasant farming valleys with their good soil and temperate climate.

Several military engagements were fought here during the Revolutionary War and the War of 1812. The Battle of Valcour is mentioned briefly
in section 73. Crown Point, section 68, and Fort Ticonderoga have interesting ruins to explore, and your visits can include a walk, picnic, or
a cross-country ski trip on the rather extensive and attractive grounds at
either historic site. After these wars, the lake became the key to growth
and commerce in the region. Lumber from the interior mountains west
of Elizabethtown and Lewis was shipped by boat to Montreal and Quebec,
with the heaviest trade between the years 1815 to 1820. Iron ore from
the smelters in New Russia, Jay, and later from Witherbee, Moriah, and
Mineville was shipped south from Westport and Port Henry. Stone for
buildings was quarried near the lakeshore and taken out on barges. When
the prime forests and the richest iron ore deposits were depleted, the lake
became less important commercially. In recent years, the railroad and the
Northway have superseded the lake as a carrier of commerce. Now the
lake is an important and growing recreational area that provides a wide
variety of activities to Adirondack residents and four-season visitors.

One of the most popular sports is sailing. The clear waters, secluded anchorages, and scenic mountain vistas are constantly increasing the number of boaters from the United States and Canada. Details of the water routes and anchorages are beyond the scope of this book, but the *Cruising Guide to Lake Champlain* (edited by Alan and Susan McKibben in 1986 and available from Lake Champlain Publishing Company, 176 Battery Street, Burlington, VT 05401) is excellent.

A popular winter sport is ice fishing. As soon as the lake freezes, shanties are towed out and lined up over favorite underwater banks in the deeper parts of the lake. Smelt, also called icefish or frost fish, are the prime catch, although lake trout are also landed on smelt bait. Shanties and rigs can be rented in Port Henry and other lakeshore towns, and people will show you how to fish. If you time your trip right, you may also be there for an Ice Fishing Festival or Winter Carnival, which is a lot of fun. There are many places where cross-country skiing from the lakeshore is enjoyable.

State-owned land on the shores of the lake is not plentiful. There are the Palisades east of Split Rock Mountain; Valcour and Schuyler islands; Crown Point, Ausable Marsh and Wickham Marsh game management areas; and Cumberland Head and Point au Roche State Parks. All are described in this chapter. There is also a new state park at Point au Roche. In addition, there are frequent boat-launching sites (free) along the shore, clearly marked if you drive the secondary roads that parallel the shore. Bulwagga Bay, Essex, Port Douglas, Port Henry, Westport, and other towns have public beaches, some with bath houses and rest rooms.

This brief sketch of a fast-growing summer area hardly touches the swimmable water, bathable beaches, relaxing vistas, and beautiful sunsets over dark mountains. The combination of light with distant mountain mass swells the spirit as it has done for centuries, and you will not want a vacation here to end.

68 Crown Point Ruins

Historic site, cross-country skiing
2.8 miles, 1½ hours, relatively level

Crown Point State Historic Site occupies a promontory stretching north into Lake Champlain. Bulwagga Bay lies to the west of the promontory, the bridge to Vermont spans the narrows, and the Crown Point Campground and boat-launching site lie to the east bordering Lake Champlain.

A visitors' center with a small museum is open in the summer months. You can walk around the ruins throughout the year, and in winter a cross-country ski trail leads through the fields and woods surrounding the site. You can stretch your legs along the trail the rest of the year.

North winds push snow and ice into the bay, making this a deep snow area. Even on a summer day, winds often sweep across the exposed point. The ruins were tucked behind tall earthworks for protection from invasion, but they are sheltered from the elements as well.

The site was first occupied in 1731 when the French built a fortification called Fort Saint Frederic, allowing France to control the Champlain Valley until the British waged battle for it from 1755 to 1759. In 1759, the British began construction of the fort, whose buildings and roads covered three square miles. The fort assured the peaceful settlement of the Champlain Valley until the Revolution. Then the fort was captured by the American troops in 1775, but recaptured by the British who controlled it until the end of the war, when the fort was surrendered intact. The ruins are really remarkable, and you will want to spend some time walking about them.

The ski trail begins 0.25 mile from the gate to the site on the west side of the access road. It heads west, forks right to circle north of the ruins, descends to Lake Champlain, then turns south on high ground above Bulwagga Bay. Straight ahead at 1.3 miles leads in 0.5 mile to the park boundary; a sharp right fork takes you back in 0.6 mile to the intersection near the beginning.

Walk this route for birds, field flowers, early spring blooms, mountain views, and history. Historical brochures and a map of the site are available from the visitors' center.

69 Split Rock Mountain
Champlain Palisades — Big Snake and Dam Rock Bays
Hiking, cross-country skiing, exploring

State land on Split Rock Mountain is classified Wild Forest, and it offers one of the most interesting moderate cross-country ski trips or hikes available in the northeastern Adirondacks. The shoreline views of Lake Champlain are unique and extraordinarily picturesque. Indeed, it is one of the few places along the Champlain shore in New York where you can still feel the sense of wilderness that Samuel de Champlain must have felt when he sailed past this area in 1609. The associated history and folklore of this

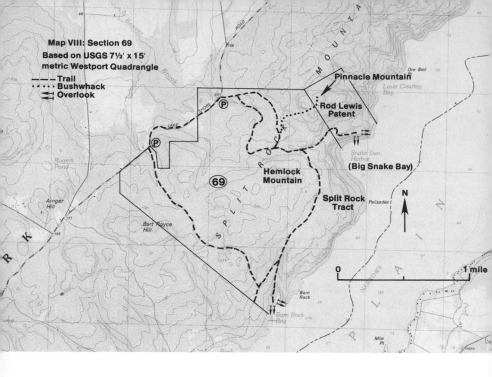

Map VIII: Section 69
Based on USGS 7½' x 15'
metric Westport Quadrangle
——— Trail
• • • • Bushwhack
⪤ Overlook

area include rattlesnakes, mining, monsters, and tragedy.

Split Rock Mountain is located on the west side of The Narrows of Lake Champlain and consists of two contiguous acquisition parcels. The smaller, about 895 acres, is known as the Rod Lewis Patent and is located on the northwest side of Big Snake Bay. It includes an 887-foot peak known as Pinnacle Mountain, a part of Split Rock Mountain that is not named on the 15-minute Port Henry topographic map. The tract was sold to the state for taxes in 1893.

The larger tract, 1260 acres, was purchased by the state in 1980. It includes almost all of the Lake Champlain shoreline for two miles from Big Snake Bay to a little south of Barn Rock Bay. The property is accessible by boat from Lake Champlain and from two locations on Essex County Route 22J, the Lake Shore Road. These two access points are used to make a wonderful clockwise loop trip from County Route 22J to Big Snake Bay overlook, then to Barn Rock Bay and back by a different trail to County Route 22J. The trip finishes with a 0.9-mile walk along County Route 22J that you can eliminate either by using two vehicles or by doing just a portion of the trip and retracing your route.

From Northway Exit 31, drive east for 4.1 miles on NY 9 to NY 22 in

Westport. Mileages to the trailheads are given from this intersection. Head north on NY 22, passing the State Boat Launching Site in Westport at 0.4 mile, and turn right, north, onto Essex County Route 22J, the Lake Shore Road and continue right again at 1 mile where Sherman Road enters on the left. Continue northeast to a Y intersection on the left at 3.1 miles where you go right. At 3.9 miles you pass an old blue trailer on the left and a Forest Preserve sign on the right. Almost immediately you cross a tributary of Beaver Brook. You will end the loop near a purplish farmhouse just across the brook at 4 miles. Park here and seek permission at the house if you intend to return through the pasture on the right.

To begin, drive northeast on County Route 22J to a dirt road at 4.8 miles. Park here. The dirt road is marked by a Forest Preserve sign and a private posted sign, but the road is on Forest Preserve land.

You start your hike (or ski trip) at 330 feet and head east along the dirt road, which is posted on the left. You climb slightly to an intersection where one fork heads east, the other south, but both rejoin about 0.6 mile along the one eastern fork, which is the shorter. The eastern fork climbs gradually with Beaver Brook well below on the right, then bends south as the gentle climb continues. After about fifteen minutes of skiing, longer if you are hiking, the road turns east and levels off at an elevation of about 500 feet, while the alternate route rejoins at a sharp angle on the right.

The longer route, about 1 mile to the rejoining point is considerably more interesting. From the northern intersection it drops sharply to cross Beaver Brook and then bends left and begins to climb, a short steep section followed by a more gradual rise. This is a particularly beautiful wooded road that winds and turns through a lovely pine and hemlock forest. The road generally contours around the north side of Hemlock Mountain, which is not named on the topographic map and has an elevation of 648 feet (not 346 as on the map).

Forty minutes of skiing on this route brings you to the eastern intersection. For those interested in a fairly strenuous bushwhack side trip to the summit of Pinnacle Mountain, 887 feet in elevation, this is a good place to start. The bearing is true north and you will need to contour around the base of the cliffs to the west side of Pinnacle and approach the summit from the west. Pinnacle has two summits and the lower, eastern, one gives exceptional views of Lake Champlain.

At the point where the trails rejoin you are on the height-of-land in the col between Pinnacle and Hemlock Mountains. From here the route continues easterly, about 115° magnetic and begins to descend slightly. You reach the intersection with a fork right to Barn Rock Bay in five minutes. You will take it later, but for now, take the left fork northeast into the Rod Lewis Tract at 65°. This road makes a long downhill for skiing, then levels out after 0.3 mile near a junction. The way straight drops steeply to the shore of Lake Champlain at Louis Clearing Bay, but just before the steepest section the road enters posted private land. You turn right and head south across a level stretch for two minutes to a low ridge.

The low ridge can easily be climbed on skis. Once on the ridge turn left and head easterly to enjoy this special place. The ridge trends west to east and drops precipitously on its south side for over 200 feet to the surface of Lake Champlain in Big Snake Bay. The steep cliffs that form the south edge of this bay are known as the Champlain Palisades. In the winter look toward 175° to see the village of ice fishing shanties that springs up annually on the Vermont side. There is no limit to the number of smelt that can be taken with hook and line on the Vermont side of Lake Champlain and this sport is very popular during the short season when shanties are safe on the lake. In the distance beyond the shanty village lies Snake Mountain.

Big Snake Bay takes its name from the timber rattlesnakes that inhabit the ledges north of the Palisades. Morris F. Glenn's *The Story of Three Towns* describes some of the local folklore associated with these snakes. Quarrymen in the nearby "granite" mine frequently encountered specimens four feet in length. While DEC biologist Walter Buckley has only seen two rattlesnakes in twelve years of field work and indicates that they were little or no problem, stories of them are enough to make you nervous if you try to scramble down the loose ledges to Big Snake Bay. And if the snakes are not a problem, the loose rocks are; this adventure is not recommended. And, because of the snakes, *camping or bringing dogs or children here is not advisable.*

From this point retrace your steps, and twenty minutes of uphill skiing on the tote road will bring you back to the intersection where you turn south toward Barn Rock Bay, 1.5 miles of moderate skiing away. At first the route heads south and then contours to the east, high above the drainage into Big Snake Bay. The road turns south again and after a steep section it crosses a height-of-land. Hemlock Mountain is on your right, west, and some bedrock is visible through the forest to your left. The road now continues south, descending gently as you head directly for Barn Rock Bay. The road here travels a north-south-trending inlier of Grenville marble that is surrounded by coarsely crystalline anorthosite. The inlier is easily eroded, which is why this valley trends north to south while most other

Barn Rock on Lake Champlain

valleys trend at right angles to the northeast-southwest trend of the Split Rock Mountain Range.

The gentle descent becomes moderately steep once you leave the inlier and reach an intersection. The road right is easily identified because it immediately crosses a small but very substantial stone bridge that was obviously built to carry heavy loads. This will be your way southwest after you visit Barn Rock Bay.

Stay left at the intersection; the roadway beyond is level but less distinct, and it crosses to the right bank of the drainage in a balsam forest. Some through-the-trees views of Lake Champlain appear. When the ground is not covered by snow, the remains of a small man-made channel and a very small stone bridge can be seen. From here the road becomes quite steep and skiers may wish to turn back. As the road descends you pass an elaborate section of dry wall on the right side of the road while the land drops off steeply on your left.

Soon you can see beautiful Barn Rock Bay on the left with Barn Rock forming its eastern edge. If you scramble to the west side entrance of the bay, the remains of an old stone wharf afford a place for a good view at lake level. The extreme north end of Barn Rock Bay is a sandy beach that is often favored by those who anchor large boats in the bay during the summer. From this beach a herd path leads south along the east shore of the bay. It follows the base of the steep cliffs at first, then gradually works its way up to the south to the top of Barn Rock. The views to the northeast, east, south, and southwest are completely unobstructed over a compass range of 180°. You see much of Lake Champlain and can distinguish many of the Green Mountains of Vermont. It is perhaps the most beautiful of all the wild near-shore views available to the public on the New York shore of this great lake.

The ledges of rock above Barn Rock were described as being the source of the "Barn Rock Harbor Monster" in the *Elizabethtown Post* in 1882. The petrified monster was reported to be six or seven feet long with pieces six to fifteen inches long that fit neatly together. The monster was found on a ledge of limestone above Barn Rock Bay. From its description, the monster sounds a lot like some straight nautiloid cephalopods commonly found as fossils in the Crown Point Limestone, a formation of the lower middle Ordovician age. These extinct animals are related to the modern chambered nautilus. Unfortunately, the monster disappeared after being on display for some years in Vergennes, Vermont. From a geological perspective, it seems possible that the Grenville marble described in the state bulletin might in fact be one of the much younger lower Paleozoic inliers. The rock outcrops are poor and badly weathered, so the distinction is not easy to make.

After exploring Barn Rock and its bay, retrace your route back up the steep road to the intersection by the stone bridge and head southwest and climb for 0.2 mile until you reach a prominent wall of stacked blocks of quarried rock on your right. This is the staging area that once was the top of a tramway to the head of Barn Rock Bay. The "granite" mine as it was called actually mined anorthosite beginning in 1880. The original company was the Champlain Granite Company, but the name changed several times in later years. The company erected the wharf in Barn Rock Bay and equipped it with a derrick to load quarry rock onto sailing canal boats. A boarding house, store, and cottages were built and blocks of stone were transported down the road you have just traveled over the stone bridge to the wharf. The company prospered and by 1887 had orders for $1 million worth of stone including an order for the then-new Philadelphia City Hall.

The short tramway was built in 1890 as a balanced, double-track affair that allowed a car on rails, loaded with eight tons of stone, to be lowered with the use of a steam-driven brake drum, while a second unloaded car was pulled to the top on the second track. On its very first trial on January 15, 1891, the brake drum failed due to icing and the empty car shot to the top of the tramway, smashing through the gate, killing four men. The Barn Rock Quarry shut down after this and never reopened. If you explore the woods east of the stacked blocks you will find some of the foundations and at least one of the "eye rings" of the loading area at the top of the tramway.

Just past the stacked blocks, an indistinct tote road on the right heads northeast to some of the foundations and a chimney base associated with the loading activities. A little farther along the main road to the south, another, better defined road comes in from the northwest. This is the route you take for 1.6 miles back to County Route 22J. The main road continues south to the end of state land and the posted land of the Rock Harbor Association of Westport.

Your route back to County Route 22J stays on state land, climbing to the northwest on a bearing of 355°. Shortly after you start you will notice an area of irregularly stacked blocks of rock to the left of the road. This was the location of the main mine for the quarrying operation, and if you explore here you will find much evidence of drilled and blasted blocks of quarry rock left as it was when the quarry was abandoned nearly a century ago.

Continue northwest on the road and follow it as it turns west and then enters a bog, after about twelve minutes of skiing from the last intersection. The road traverses the left, south, side of the bog to the middle and turns sharply right to follow the left, west, side of the bog to its north end. During the winter this is easy skiing. For hikers in dry years it is possible to pick your way along the road across the bog.

Once across the bog, the road continues uphill on a bearing of 330°. In five minutes you reach a more extensive marsh that forms a sort of horseshoe opening to the northeast. As you pick your way across with the aid of some well-placed beaver dams, you will cross the northeast-trending, sandy ridge of hemlock trees that forms the center of the horseshoe. The second limb of the horseshoe has some old pieces of iron culvert half buried among the beaver dams. It may take you twenty minutes to find your way across this marsh if it is not frozen.

Once you pick up the road again on the northwest side of the marsh, it will only take you another twenty minutes to follow the road northwest to County Route 22J. You pass through open gateposts and descend through a red pine and white pine forest to the ruins of a cabin at the head of a pasture. The pasture is not posted, but it is on private land. The owner will give you permission to cross the pasture if you ask in advance when you park your pickup vehicle. Alternatively, drop down to brook level, to the left, west, of the road, to the tributary of Beaver Brook whose left bank stays on state land all the way to County Route 22J and comes out across from the blue trailer.

This completes the 6.5-mile loop over Split Rock Mountain. If you have made the trip with one car, head northeast along the road back for the 0.9-mile trip back to the starting point. County Route 22J winds to the west around a promontory that causes the highway to swing out of line. The old road used to cut more directly over the promontory. It was in the woods, off this old section, where Henry Debosnys murdered his wife, the former Betsey Wells, in the summer of 1882. Mrs. Debosnys had been a well-to-do widow with four children when she married Mr. Debosnys. They were reported to have quarreled over the disposition of her farm property at Whallon's Bay. Mr. Debosnys was seen leaving the scene of the crime and his recently fired gun was found in his wagon. He was convicted of the crime and became the second and last person to be executed in Essex County when he was hanged in Elizabethtown in April 1883. By the time you have pondered these sad thoughts as you walk through the long shadows of late afternoon, you will have reached the starting point of this varied trip.

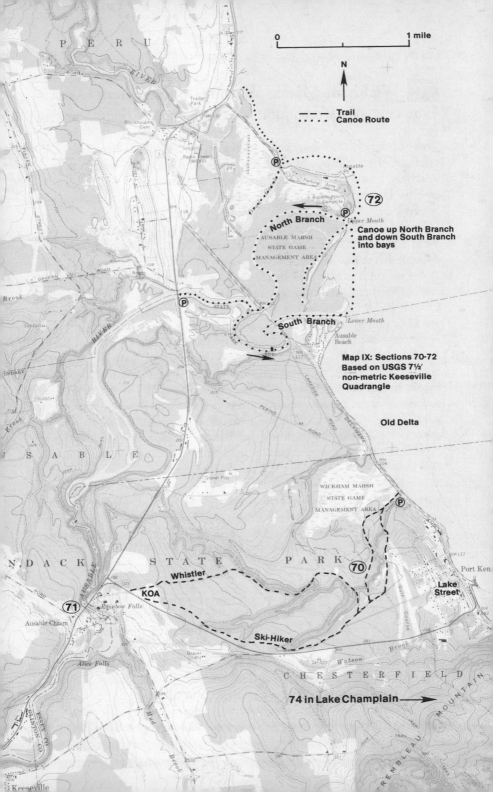

P E R U

RIVER

Trailer
Park

Blockhouse
Cem

BM 130

Ausable

Radio Towers
(WSAV)

BM 216

Trail .... --- ---

Canoe Route ....

N

1 mile

0

Parking
Area

Ausable Point
Campsite

72

North Branch

Upper Mouth

AUSABLE MARSH

STATE GAME

MANAGEMENT AREA

**Canoe up North Branch
and down South Branch
into bays**

DAVERN

ROAD

Brook

RIVER

STATE

BM

South Branch

Lower Mouth

Ausable
Beach

**Map IX: Sections 70-72
Based on USGS 7½'
non-metric Keeseville
Quadrangle**

BDY

BM
317

LAKESIDE

ROAD

DELAWARE

PLAINS

Old Delta

BM
186

BM
106

Gravel Pits

WICKHAM MARSH

STATE GAME

MANAGEMENT AREA

P

JEEP

BM 137

A D A C K   S T A T E   P A R K

70

Whistler

Lake
Street

KOA

Port Ken

71

Rainbow Falls

BM

Ski-Hiker

Watson
Brook

Ausable Chasm

Alice Falls

Gravel

C H E S T E R F I E L D

Mud

Brook

ESSEX CO
CLINTON CO

74 in Lake Champlain →

Keeseville

MOUNTAIN

70 Wickham Marsh Wildlife Management Area
Canoeing, picnicking, hunting, cross-country skiing, birding

This 862-acre wildlife management area on the shores of Lake Champlain offers an afternoon of canoeing and picnicking and is popular with bird watchers. In the fall, signs indicate that it is a designated public hunting ground. During the winter cross-country skiing is the main recreational activity.

To reach Wickham Marsh, head east from Northway Exit 35 on Bear Swamp Road. At 2.8 miles turn right, south, on NY 9. After crossing the Ausable River and climbing some former river deltas you reach NY 373 at 6.4 miles. Turn left and head east toward Port Kent. At 7 miles you reach a southern extension of state land which gives access to the Ausable Chasm, KOA Cross-Country Ski Area on the left. At 9.4 miles you see the D & H Railroad track ahead, and just before the tracks you turn left, north, on Lake Street. Continue north on Lake Street through Port Kent. At the north end of Port Kent the road drops down nearly to the level of Lake Champlain, and at 10.5 miles there is a sign and a road with a barrier indicating the Wildlife Management Area. This is the main foot access and there is room to park a few cars without blocking the access road. Those who wish to launch a canoe should continue north for another 0.3 mile and launch down the shallow bank on the left, west. Just beyond this point, the road climbs and bends to the left. At the intersection stay left and go another 0.2 mile. Here there is a short access trail to the north end of the marsh.

Skiers and hikers head southwest from the barrier, and at 0.2 mile a trail enters on the left. By following it as it climbs steeply to the south, you can reach the north end of the golf course on the south boundary of state land. Here you cross the distinctive old grade of the Keeseville, Ausable Chasm, and Champlain Railroad that connected with the D&H from 1890 to 1924.

You will enjoy skiing the steep run back. Incidentally, by skiing across the golf course to the southwest it is possible to connect with the Whistler and Ski-hiker trails of the KOA. Those planning to do this should register and pay the fee at KOA.

If you do not choose the side trail at 0.2 mile, you can continue southwest on the level to a log landing area, just beyond which there are some beaver dams. The trail continues past the beaver dams and begins to climb to the southern boundary of state land. It is again possible to connect with the KOA trails in this direction, but the route is not well marked.

Wickham Marsh

Wickham Marsh represents an earlier delta of the Ausable River that the river abandoned in favor of the present delta described in section 71. It extends for more than a mile out into Lake Champlain to the northeast. The steep sand banks that border the marsh to the north represent a still earlier delta at the 200- to 240-foot level that formed at the base of Ausable Chasm in glacial times, when Lake Champlain Valley was connected to the Atlantic Ocean as the Burlington Stage of the Champlain Sea. The banks that border the marsh to the south at the 250- to 300-foot level represent still earlier deltas of the Port Kent Stage of the Champlain Sea that formed before Ausable Chasm was eroded. Geologists have identified six separate stages for the Champlain Sea and two additional earlier lake stages from glacial Lake Vermont.

Wickham Marsh is in Essex County, while Ausable Marsh is in Clinton County. The county line that extends across the northern edge of Wickham Marsh was once the site of a major military encampment. On October 12, 1759, Major-General Jeffrey Amherst was moving his British forces north to meet the French when an autumn storm sank twelve of his boats. The remainder took shelter for six days on the west shore of Lake Champlain where an encampment was made. According to local tradition, Amherst's encampment was located on the county line in the pine woods just north of Wickham Marsh. It is said that he set up apparatus to manufacture pine tar to use in repairing his boats. This same location was also used for manufacture of pine tar by Commodore MacDonough's fleet in 1814.

71 Ausable Chasm
Scenic gorge, commercial site

Private facilities are not usually included in the *Discover* guides, but Ausable River Chasm is one of America's great scenic wonders and it should not be missed. You take a self-conducted 0.75 mile walking tour through the chasm and, if the river is not too high, a boat ride to complete the 1.5-mile trip.

You reach Ausable Chasm from Northway Exit 34 or 35. It is 1.5 miles north of Keeseville on NY 9 or 12 miles south of Plattsburgh. Ausable Chasm is open daily to visitors, mid-May to early October, for a reasonable admission fee.

An estimated 500 million years ago, the Potsdam Sea formed the northern and eastern boundaries of the Adirondack Mountains. On the floor of the sea, layer upon layer of sand, mud, and sediment formed Potsdam Sandstone, which was several hundred feet thick in some places. The Ausable River, plunging east from its headwaters near Mount Marcy, found a fault in the bedrock. This powerful river eroded the sandstone deeper and deeper until it created the high sandstone cliffs that make up the chasm. In some places the river is compressed to a width of less than fourteen feet; in spring flood waters in the river sometimes rise forty feet in these restricted places.

Your walk begins with steps down to Horseshoe Falls. Along the walkway you pass large stone formations sculptured by nature into shapes called Pulpit Rock, Elephant's Head, Jacob's Ladder, Cathedral, and Table Rock. It is damp and cool in the chasm, which creates a special climate for ferns and other nonflowering plants. Look for the small delicate fronds of maidenhair spleenwort, *Asplenium trichomanes*, in the crevices.

The walk ends at Table Rock where you can either climb steps to a bus back to the start or take a boat ride through the Grand Flume and Whirlpool Basin. Another bus returns you to the start. The complete trip can be made in an hour, or you can take as much time as you wish to study the formations and read the informative signs.

72 Ausable Point Campground and Ausable Marsh Wildlife Management Area
Camping, swimming, canoeing, windsurfing, birding

An attractive, well-planned campground and swimming beach is operated by DEC on a sandy point near the mouth of the Ausable River. There are facilities for day-use swimming and picnicking and for overnight camping. It is a safe place for children as the sandy beach drops off very gradually and lifeguards are on duty. Beyond the point on the east side of the campground, you can launch windsurfers, small sailboats, and canoes. As you paddle along the beach, you will understand why the French called the river *au sable*, meaning "to the sand."

If you wish to see marsh-dwelling wildlife, wildflowers, and ferns, then you will be rewarded by a quiet paddle in the nearby wetlands. The only drawback to these lakeshore public lands is the frequent flights of aircraft from the Plattsburgh Air Force Base; Ausable Point lies directly under takeoffs to the south, which causes considerable noise during the daytime—although it is somewhat less on weekends.

You reach Ausable Point Campground by driving east from Northway Exit 35 on Bear Swamp Road. In about 3 miles you reach NY 9; turn left, north, cross the Little Ausable River, and in less than 0.2 mile take a right, east, turn at the sign for the campground. It is 8 miles south of Plattsburgh on NY 9. There is a charge for day-use and overnight camping. Sites 10-38 overlook the lake, sites 39-47, 2E-13E, and 82-87 face the North Mouth of the river. The campground is open from Memorial Day through October 14, but since it is popular, it may be full on weekends.

One of the main attractions of this area is the marsh and wetlands of the Ausable River delta immediately to the south. If you are staying at the campground, you can put in your canoe (no motors are permitted) at two places between campsites along the river. Paddle upstream, west, on the wide shallow river. Very little current flows over the sandy clear bottom, so it is easy paddling. Soon you are away from the campground and the serenity and beauty of the wetland begins. In late July purple loosestrife, cattails, and square-stemmed monkey-flower grow profusely along the banks. On the high levee, luxurious green plumes of ostrich ferns dominate the rich plant life. Branches of silver maple overhang the water. Paddling beside this mass of foliage you have the feeling of the tropics. The ridged sands below your canoe are dark brown and coarse, ribbed with strips of black grains—pieces of Potsdam Sandstone eroded over time from the Ausable Chasm a few miles upstream.

As you paddle along, more wildflowers appear on the bank. Nightshade with its swept-back violet petals and protruding yellow beak is entwined among moist thickets; the yellow flowers of pale St. Johnswort stand tall; red petals of a cardinal flower glow brilliantly; and the two-lipped white turtle head nods underneath a mass of growth. You paddle slowly, from one side of the river to the other, flower book in hand to identify the seldom-seen species. Hidden birds sing melodious tones. After an hour you pass under a railroad bridge and the vegetation (and beauty) of the stream changes. The river forks; follow the right channel upstream, where, after twenty more minutes, you reach the NY 9 bridge. (You can also put in here on the south side below the bridge if the lake is rough; it is 1.5 miles south of the entrance to the campground on NY 9.) Willow and cottonwood trees are more common in this area. On the north bank of the river, below the bridge, stands a gigantic sycamore. It is unusual to see this species so far north, but the marsh contains several. There are small rapids upstream from the bridge so this is as far as you can paddle.

Paddling downstream, take the right fork just before the railroad bridge. This is the south branch of the river, and you are headed toward the lake. The stream meanders around, revealing delightful secluded sand beaches for sunning and picnicking. Turtles slide into the water from streamside logs. After passing under another railroad bridge, there are signs of habitation on the right bank, part of the summer colony called Ausable Beach. Sensitive ferns under a high canopy of trees line the public land along the north bank. Soon you paddle out onto the lake. Herring gulls and sandpipers rest and feed along the shallow sandy beach. There is usually a great blue heron standing motionless in the shallows. Paddle north and there is an isolated beach for swimming and sunning. Continue north and you come to the north branch of the river and the campground, completing the loop. It is a memorable two- to three-hour paddle.

If the campground is full, you can put a canoe in along the access road to the campground. There is a place to park at the water crossing just before reaching the entrance booth, or at several boat-launching openings along the north side of the road. Paddle east in front of the bathing beach and around a rock jetty and head south. (If there are waves and a wind off the water, it will be rough going past the jetty.) After you paddle past the campground on the right, you will see the north mouth of the river, which will take you on the loop described above. If you look left, before going up the river, you will see another water opening, which leads to a large wetlands complex. This area is more varied than the river, harboring a mixture of aquatic plants, wooded swamps, dead trees, and shoreline plants. Wood ducks, mergansers, and mallards hatch young here in spring; hawks perch on tall snags watching for frogs or snakes. Pickerel weed and bur reed grow in the rich mud. Along the banks there is royal fern. In the spring the wooded swamp attracts warblers, flycatchers and other insect eaters on their northern migration; Canada geese may rest here in the fall. Paddle this quiet area at dawn or dusk to appreciate fully the abundance and diversity found in this mixed habitat that harbors both upland and wetland wildlife.

If you still want to explore after you paddle back to your car, there is more. Paddle west along the reedy lake shoreline where fishermen cast for pike and pickerel, and you will reach the mouth of the Little Ausable River. You can paddle up it a little ways through a profusion of trees, shrubs, vines, and ferns. Or carry your canoe across the road from your parking spot onto Dead Creek, to enjoy another marshy pond. This diverse area of sand, water, marsh, river, and sky can be enjoyed in all four seasons and repeatedly produces new and memorable experiences.

73 Valcour Island
Hiking, camping, swimming, canoeing, sailing, cross-country skiing, snorkeling

Valcour Island, a 980-acre Primitive Area on Lake Champlain, is one of the most beautiful jewels of the Park—a green gem in an azure blue setting. Recreation on and around it takes many forms and covers all four seasons. It is a popular hiking and camping area in the summer and has many sheltered bays for sailboats. A 7.5-mile hiking trail circles and crosses the island, skirting cliffs with crashing waves, a heron rookery, and many scenic coves and secluded beaches. And when the 1-mile channel between the island and the shore is frozen, there is a delightful cross-country ski loop from the mainland. The trailhead for the ski trip and for launching canoes is the Peru State Boat Launch, 4 miles south of the Plattsburgh city limits on NY 9.

The island has a varied and interesting history. Its bedrock is mostly made up of the limestones in the Chazy Group, deposited in the middle Ordovician period about 450 million years ago. These have been modified by later faulting and uplift and most recently eroded by glacial advances over the last 100,000 years or so. The limey, shallow soils together with the harsh windy climate of Lake Champlain and the shallow soil produce a fascinating assortment of rare and fragile plants. White spruce dominates the southern half of the island and provides some protection from the wind and waves that hit the southern coast. Here, a threatened species of lady's-slipper and other special wildflowers can be found growing in the humus under these evergreens. White-tailed deer and small mammals inhabit or visit the island but the most notable wildlife is the great blue heron. These large, long-legged shore birds nest in colonies on the island. Arriving at the rookery in late March or April, they lay their eggs in wooden-twig nests forty to 100 feet above the swamp. They feed in the shallows of the island and the nearby mainland beaches, such as the sandy mouth of the Ausable River, and regurgitate fish, frogs, and snakes for their nesting fledglings. Black-crowned night heron also nest here; it is one of the major rookeries in New York State.

Off the southwest corner of the island, the fledgling American Navy fought the British in one of the decisive battles of the Revolutionary War. In October 1776, an American naval force under Benedict Arnold fought a large British fleet in the straits between the island and the New York shore. Arnold's flagship, the Royal Savage, was sunk and his navy destroyed;

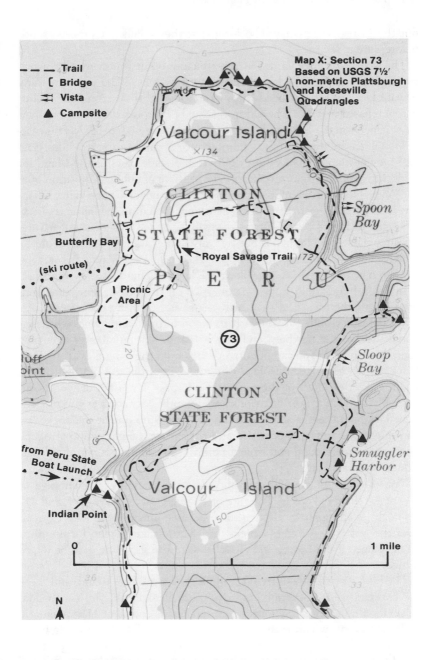

Trail
[Bridge
Vista
▲ Campsite

Valcour Island

×134

CLINTON

Spoon
Bay

STATE FOREST

Butterfly Bay

Royal Savage Trail /72

(ski route)

P E R U

Picnic
Area

(73)

Sloop
Bay

CLINTON

STATE FOREST

Smuggler
Harbor

from Peru State
Boat Launch

Valcour Island

Indian Point

0   1 mile

N

but the British were delayed so long that they could not proceed south before winter set in.

The island was once farmed as private land; but it is now wholly owned by the State of New York and is managed by DEC. The last remaining private land, which included the picturesque lighthouse on Bluff Point, was purchased in 1986. The Clinton County Historical Association owns an easement on the lighthouse, which was first manned in 1872. This easement will ensure the continued maintenance of this historic structure. Several previous landowners retain rights to use some parts of the island for a specific period of time. Credit for a large share of public acquisition goes to Wayne H. Byrne, past Chairman of the Adirondack Conservancy Chapter. In 1972, a 129-acre portion of the island, including the heron rookery, belonged to Henry Seton. Seton was willing to see this beautiful natural resource pass to public hands but he wanted a guarantee that it would be managed well and protected. He approached his friend Wayne Byrne, who worked out the details. A year later, the land was purchased by the state. The Seton home, built from rock quarried on the island, now stands unused among the trees near the southwest shore, awaiting plans for its use.

A permit is required if you wish to camp in one of the eighteen designated sites on the northern end of the island. The number of sites may soon be increased. You can obtain a permit from the caretaker at the Peru Dock, which is located on NY 9 directly across from the old lighthouse, about 2.8 miles south of the railroad underpass if you are driving down from Plattsburgh. Power boats or canoes can be launched at the modern new dock, and there is ample parking. If there is no one at the dock, you can select an empty camping site and the Forest Ranger, who patrols by boat, will come around and issue a permit. No camping is permitted outside a designated site.

One of the most popular uses of Valcour is for sailboat anchorage in one of the sheltered coves. They are often overcrowded, however, and toilet facilities and garbage disposal have become a major problem. Control over the waters is shared by several jurisdictions and a plan for use must be developed if the beauty and cleanliness of the shoreline is to be maintained.

The hiking or cross-country ski trail circles most of the island, and there are two east-west cross trails. Starting from Peru Dock, you can paddle or ski for 1 mile across the narrows on a compass course of 115° magnetic to Indian Point, which is the first point south of Bluff, identifiable by its lighthouse. There are picnic tables and a fireplace at Indian Point for day use. Go inland, east, for several hundred yards across the clearing and you will pick up the marked trail. Turn right, south, through conifers and then an open area where the path is mowed by DEC and then back into the woods. You will pass another picnic area and be close enough to the shoreline in places to watch the waves on the rocks. In about 0.5 mile you will come to the stone Seton House in the woods, boarded and unused.

From Seton House, the trail swings east and climbs to the southern end of the island, somewhat back from the high cliffs. Here is where the white spruce grow thick, sheltering the land from the wind, but an alpine or sub-alpine climate still exists. Search about for bearberry, pink and yellow lady's-slippers, and other rare plants. You can reach the cliffs by a short walk through the woods. After walking for 1 mile and entering a hardwood forest you come to an overlook to the south. The trail then goes north and passes a small cover, called Smuggler Harbor. In the summer many sailboats anchor in this idyllic spot. The 0.8-mile cross trail back to Indian Point, where you started, goes west just north of the harbor.

Continue north along the east side of the island and there are more bays to view and more places to swim. Sloop Bay is the large anchorage and side trips can be made off the trail to water level. As you hike the trail near the shaded limestone rocks, look for the bluish-green walking fern with its triangular fronds that sprout new plants from the tips.

You will come to the second cross-island trail, called the Royal Savage Trail, which goes west just north of Bluff Point. The circle trail north continues north and slightly right to an overlook, then down to lake level. After 3.5 miles on the trail, you are at the north end of the island and can see across the channel to mainland buildings. From here the trail goes along the north end of the island, passing the camping sites, to Butterfly Bay in the northwest. There is a day-use picnic area here.

If you are on skis, go south and just before you reach Bluff Point with the lighthouse, head across the ice to Peru Dock where you started, passing north of the lighthouse. If you wish to return to Indian Point, you continue south to the Royal Savage Trail, take it east across the island, then south to the other cross-island trail, and take that west to Indian Point. In this way you cover all the trails on the island with a total distance of about 7.5 miles, plus the 2-mile round trip across the channel if you are skiing.

Whether you ski or canoe, a word of caution about the weather is necessary. Pick a good day with light wind for the trip. The narrows can become very rough and windy and the crossing not only becomes difficult, it is dangerous.

74 Schuyler Island Primitive Area
Hiking, canoeing

Schuyler Island is a jewel of 123 acres in Lake Champlain just south of Port Kent and east of Trembleau Mountain. It is a relatively flat island of black, limey, and carbonaceous shales in the Stony Point Formation. They were deposited 435 million years ago in the Ordovician Period and are separated by a geological fault from the much older rocks of Trembleau Mountain to the east.

For many years the island was actively farmed and today foundations of the house and farm buildings can be seen. The island is now owned by New York State and consists of overgrown pastures, some wetland areas, and small stands of hardwoods and conifers. The latter provide shelter for a few resident deer.

There are no sheltered bays and no designated camping sites on the island and it is only occasionally visited. When wind conditions are right, it is possible to beach a boat or a canoe on one of the several rocky beaches. In some years, it is possible to ski across the ice from Port Kent to the island. Be very careful if you decide to ski because the deep water in the narrow channel between Schuyler Island and Trembleau Mountain frequently has thin ice, even in years when the rest of the main lake has a thick ice cover.

75 Bluff Point
Nature trails and cross-country skiing

The historic grounds and site of the former Hotel Champlain include about 2.5 miles of old carriage roads that make a lovely afternoon of strolling or cross-country skiing. Today the grounds are part of Clinton Community College and are open to the public for day use; motorized vehicles and overnight camping are not permitted.

To reach Clinton Community College drive south on NY 9 from the main gate of Plattsburgh Air Force Base at the corner of U S Avenue and New York Road in Plattsburgh. U S Avenue becomes NY 9 as you head south. The college entrance is 2.1 miles south of the intersection. Turn left and follow the long entrance road as it winds up to the parking area in front of the main college building. Parking is limited on weekdays when the college is in session and a guest parking permit is required. This is not needed at other times.

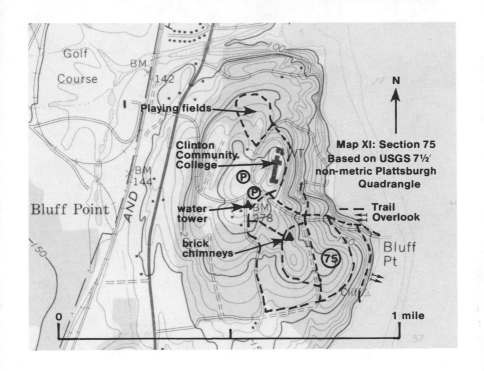

Map XI: Section 75
Based on USGS 7½'
non-metric Plattsburgh
Quadrangle

The main college building is an impressive reminder of more luxurious days now past. The first major building on the spectacular site was constructed by the Delaware and Hudson Railroad in 1890. The original hotel was constructed on a grand scale with three towers, the central one ten stories tall. The interior was elaborately decorated and the extensive grounds included riding stables and what is now the third oldest golf course in America. Many famous guests stayed at the hotel, including President McKinley. The original wood frame hotel burned in a spectacular fire in 1910 and the present, steel-frame structure was opened in 1911.

The present building is smaller than the original; it is built according to the plans of the former Fort William Henry Hotel of Lake George that burned in 1909. Despite its famous guests and all attempts to keep it open, its days as a hotel were numbered and it became first a Jesuit Seminary, then in 1969, the college.

Before you begin your hike you may wish to enter the main college building and go up to the second floor student lounge. From this vantage point you have a panoramic vista of Lake Champlain, with historic Crab Island and Cumberland Bay to the north and northwest. To the southeast lies the larger Valcour Island, section 73.

To reach the hiking and skiing trails, head south from the small parking

lot located at the south end of the main building. The routes are marked on the sketch map. The main downhill run heads southeast to the site of the old steamboat dock at Bluff Point, while side trails circle other points of interest. A turnout just before the dock leads through an old quarry to the overlook at the "Cliff" survey point.

Time and the elements have almost removed the old dock site. At one time the dock extended out far enough for steamships that cruised Lake Champlain. Just north of the dock was the hotel beach, known as the "Beach of the Singing Sands." Cliffs of Day Point Limestone of Ordovician age lie south of the dock. It was quarried at Bluff Point for the pinkish fossiferous zone that once sold commercially as "Lepanto Marble."

Return uphill and take the perimeter trail south and west. Land south of this trail is privately owned, but you can follow the perimeter trail to a restaurant, then north toward a water tower that is a short distance from the parking area where you started the trip.

76 Point au Roche State Park
Hiking, cross-country skiing, swimming

Point au Roche State Park, on the shore of Lake Champlain, is comprised of 840 acres of mostly undeveloped land that the state purchased in 1974 and opened as a park in 1986. It consists of former agricultural fields and forest on a series of peninsulas that jut out to the south into Lake Champlain, creating over 5.5 miles of shoreline. That makes it the longest section of public shoreline currently owned by the state on Lake Champlain. During the summer the park operates a bathing beach with bath house and playing fields. (There is an admission fee. In the future there will also be camping for a fee.) During the other three seasons, the interpretive center and trails are open free of charge.

To reach Point au Roche, leave the Northway at Exit 40, turn right and head east on County Route 456. At 0.6 mile you turn right, south, on NY 9. At 1 mile turn left heading east on Point au Roche Road. The main entrance at 2.7 miles is currently reserved for summer use, and those planning to use the beach must stop at the entrance building. When the park is completed this will be the entrance for all seasons.

At present, if you are visiting the nature center, hiking, or cross-country skiing, continue east past the main entrance and at 3.2 miles you will see

Conner Bay at Point au Roche State Park

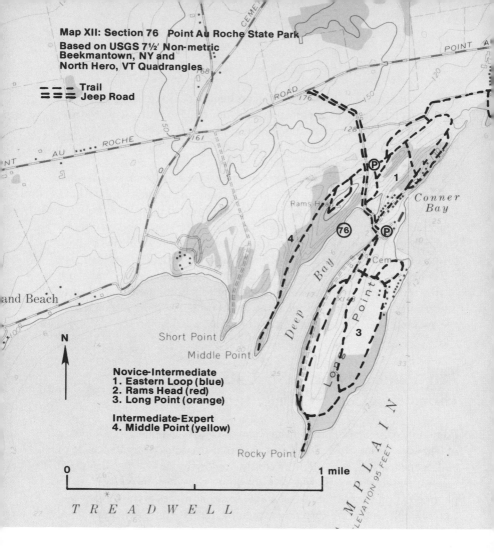

Map XII: Section 76   Point Au Roche State Park
Based on USGS 7½' Non-metric
Beekmantown, NY and
North Hero, VT Quadrangles

--- Trail
=== Jeep Road

N

Novice-Intermediate
1. Eastern Loop (blue)
2. Rams Head (red)
3. Long Point (orange)

Intermediate-Expert
4. Middle Point (yellow)

0   1 mile

a sign "Point au Roche Outdoor Interpretive Center—Trails." Turn right, south, to the center where you can register and pick up a copy of the free trail map or examine the map posted at the parking lot.

As you hike or ski the nature trails you pass through forest, brushland, wetland, and shoreline habitats. Each provides its own species of wildlife to the observer. Preliminary surveys have identified forty mammal species, twenty-three reptile and amphibian species, and 169 bird species. Through most of the park a calcium carbonate-rich shale of the middle Ordovician age, known as the Cumberland Head Argillite, lies just below the surface. The rock is well known as a headland former on Lake Champlain and is also responsible for the wetlands and two small ponds in the park. In

Point au Roche

addition to forming Cumberland Head itself, the rock produced the erosion pattern that makes Long, Middle, and Short Points. By walking along
the rocky shores of Deep Bay you can view the beautiful sailboats that
anchor there while you examine the shales for the Ordovician fossils that
are fairly common.

77 Cumberland Bay State Park
Plattsburgh City Beach
Swimming, cross-country skiing, canoeing, birding

A mile of beach on Lake Champlain awaits the visitor to the north end
of Cumberland Bay on Lake Champlain. It is located just a few minutes
from the Northway. Take Exit 39 and head east across NY 9 on County
Route 314. At 0.5 mile turn right on Beach Road. During the summer
season nonresidents of Plattsburgh must pay a fee to enter. Parking for
swimmers is carefully controlled and a bath house and concession stand
can be found on the beach. During the winter it is seldom crowded, and
you are free to explore the area on cross-country skis.

To the southwest of the Crete Memorial Civic Center you will find a
small, stone marker "In memory of 13 unknown soldiers who died of chol-
era in 1812 and were buried near this spot." Another marker recognizes
Honorable John Keady Collins, whose gifts helped to create this park. The
view from the beach is spectacular: you can see Cumberland Head and
the Green Mountains of Vermont, Providence Island, Valcour Island, Crab
Island, Pokamoonshine, Plattsburgh City, and Whiteface Mountain.

Another 0.5 miles east of Beach Road on County Route 314 brings you
to Cumberland Bay State Park. The developed portion of the park allows
tent and trailer camping, picnicking, and swimming for the standard New

York State fee during the summer. During the winter, the parkland, beach and unplowed parking area are available for cross-country skiing. North of County Route 314, 1.5 miles of undeveloped wetlands stretch to Woodruff Pond and over to Allens Bay on Lake Champlain. This remarkable wetland can be explored on cross-country skis and provides excellent birding for those who gain access from Allens Bay by canoe.

78 King Bay Wetlands Management Area
Birding, limited cross-country skiing, lake access

Approximately 380 acres of wetland on the shores of Lake Champlain are most attractive to the birder. The area is reached by leaving the Northway at Exit 41 and heading east on County Route 191. Turn left, north, at 0.9 mile at a T intersection with NY 9 in Chazy. At 3.5 miles turn right on NY 9B, following the signs for Rouses Point. At 6.5 miles you can see King Bay and Lake Champlain on your right. At 7.4 miles turn right on Point au Fer Road and follow it to the head of King Bay. The entrance

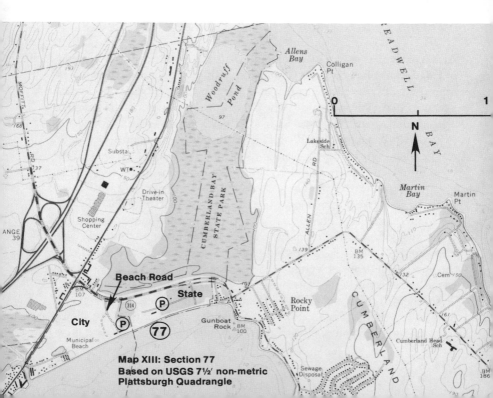

Map XIII: Section 77
Based on USGS 7½' non-metric
Plattsburgh Quadrangle

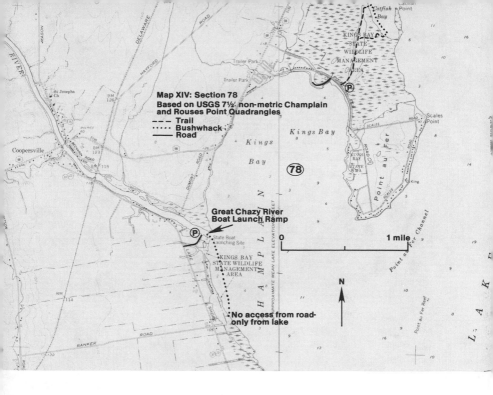

Map XIV: Section 78
Based on USGS 7½ non-metric Champlain
and Rouses Point Quadrangles
– – – Trail
• • • • Bushwhack
——— Road

to the Game Management Area is at 7.9 miles. Just before it there is a short access road that sportsmen use to reach King Bay.

If it is plowed you can turn left on the access road to a parking area. Barriers here limit trail use to snowmobiles and all-terrain vehicles. The red trail heads north along the ridge of an upland island in the midst of the extensive wetland. This ridge is underlaid by Stony Point Shale, a middle Ordovician resistant cliff–former, seen also at Stony Point to the north. At a junction at 0.4 mile, the red trail turns right and reaches Catfish Bay in another 0.2 mile. The route ahead is not open to vehicles but can be skied for another 0.2 mile before it peters out near the shore of Catfish Bay. By bushwhacking a short distance to Catfish Bay and skiing south you can make a small loop. Catfish Bay takes its name from the catfish that inhabit its reedy waters. It is a well-known ice fishing and bird hunting area.

A small, discontinuous piece of the Wildlife Management Area lies farther south on the west edge of King Bay. It is not accessible by road, but it can be reached from the Great Chazy River Boat Launch Ramp on Lake Shore Road, 1.3 miles southeast of NY 9B. King Bay is formed by Point au Fer which probably derives its name from the French for "point of signal fires."

Wayward Peaks

NUMEROUS SMALLER MOUNTAINS range north from the Jay Area. Parcels of state land cover the tops of a half dozen or so of these peaks, whose only common theme is the fact they are scattered among settlements and large tracts of private land—hence, their wayward nature.

79 Clements Mountain
Bushwhack

This 780-meter (2560-foot) mountain is west of and separated from the Jay Range. There are views to the northeast, north, and (to a limited extent) west from the multi-peaked summit. However, the summit is heavily wooded and the scenery is not as sweeping as from the peaks in the Jay Range. There is public access to the mountain from both the north and the southwest, each leading to short but challenging bushwhacks.

You reach state land on the north by going east out of Upper Jay off NY 9N on Trumbulls Corner Road. There is a Forest Preserve sign on the right, south, as you cross a brook at 1.8 miles. Drive on up the hill about 200 yards and you will see another Forest Preserve sign and then a stone wall, marking private land. This spot is 0.6 mile from the intersection with Glen Road, coming west. You are at 350 meters, 1150 feet, at the point where you begin the bushwhack.

Hike in along the stone wall, which runs about 200° magnetic. You reach the end of the wall after walking for less than five minutes, but you can follow a less obvious old wall for another five minutes. Then take a bearing south, uphill. In twenty minutes you cross an old logging road. Above it there is an interesting open forest of maple and hop hornbeam, remarkable in that a grove of the latter is an infrequent sight.

On this bearing you reach irregular ridges that you must detour around; on the rocky slopes you find several varieties of ferns. In circling around the slopes, you may cross a yellow-blazed Forest Preserve boundary line, which means you cut across the corner of private land. After climbing for twenty-five minutes, you will be at 1700 feet, still following roughly 180° to 200°. You climb over rocks covered with an especially beautiful moss whose branches resemble little Christmas trees.

Ice Wall on Pokamoonshine

After fifty minutes red spruce blowdowns make the going slow. Detours are necessary to get around them and steep rocky walls. Thirty minutes later you reach a striped maple and balsam thicket through which your progress will be slow at best. Occasionally, your way may be blocked by cliffs; in such places, generally work your way to the right, though keeping on the north face. The northern peak (there appear to be five equal knobs) is reached in an hour and fifty minutes.

There is a clear view up the valley of the Ausable River and toward the hamlet of Jay. To the northeast the ridge along Jay Mountain stands out; the slides and ski runs of Whiteface Mountain can be seen through the trees to the west. The summit is uneven and rough, but ten minutes more should provide a better view to the west. There does not appear to be a view to the east.

It is prudent to follow your path through the balsam thicket when you descend; it is easier and will avoid backtracking around steep drops. It will take an hour and fifteen minutes to return to your car, 1.2 miles from the summit.

There is state land along Glen Road, which is also called Styles Brook Road, southwest of the summit of Clements. It appears the mountain could be climbed from there by going north and then northeast to the ridge, and then up the ridge continuing in a northeast direction. This route involves a longer traverse to stay on state land, but would provide different views to the west and southwest.

80 Mt Fay
Bushwhack

Mt Fay is the high point of a particularly interesting group of mountains on a 700-acre parcel of Wild Forest Land that extends eastward from the extreme northeast corner of the Jay Wilderness Area. With the exception of the Seventy Road, which crosses the eastern portion of the parcel in a southeast-northwest direction, there are no trails in this mountain group. Mt Fay and the other mountains in the group are short bushwhacks that give exceptionally rewarding views. This guide describes the approach to Mt Fay by way of Little Fay Mountain and leaves to your imagination the routes to discover Blueberry and Carson mountains and Carson Ledges.

The introduction to the chapter on the Jay Mountain Wilderness Area tells you how to get on Wells Hill Road heading west from Lewis. You turn right, north, 1.6 miles from NY 9 on the unpaved Johnson Road.

At 2.1 miles you cross Derby Brook and continue straight past the "Seasonal Use—Limited Highway" sign. Park at 2.5 miles when you reach a large A-frame camp on the right, and begin the hike by following the extension of Johnson Road to the northwest. The first part of your hike is on unposted, private land and you will not be aware of the Forest Preserve boundary, which you cross on the lower slopes of Little Fay Mountain.

Johnson Road quickly becomes a woods road that climbs moderately through a white birch, striped maple, and balsam fir forest. At an intersection where there is an abandoned car, you continue northwest on the less-traveled road. Your road heads northwest 320° to reach another fork. Take the left, west, fork and your route will again bend to the northwest. You may hear the vehicles at the wollastonite mine about a half mile to the west. Johnson Road ends after 0.4 mile, a twenty-minute walk, at an elevation of 440 meters (1445 feet).

Take a bearing of 315° magnetic and begin your bushwhack uphill. At forty minutes, you reach the first ledges; work around them to the east and you will begin to get excellent views of Slip Mountain and the wollastonite mine to the west. After an hour and a quarter you reach the summit of Little Fay Mountain by circling the summit cliffs to the left. The summit, over 640 meters (2100) feet, has a remarkably lovely grove of red pine interspersed with striped maple. Mt Fay itself can be seen to the north beyond the col, and its steep cliffs look quite forbidding. To reach them, head off Little Fay's summit to the west, then by turning north, drop into the shallow col.

Once in the col, head east through the minor blowdown and make your way to the northeast edge of the col. The cliffs of Mt Fay can be avoided by circling to the east as you climb. It is still pretty steep, but there are good views to the east of Lake Champlain as you climb. In less than two hours total hiking time, you will emerge through the red pine to the bare, rounded summit of Mt Fay. Orange hawkweed grows in profusion on the summit. A small wood stake with the letters "AE" is guyed into a small crevice at the summit, whose elevation is 703 meters (2305 feet).

For a less than two-hour bushwhack of little more than a mile, you are treated to an exceptionally rewarding view that extends through 300° without obstructions, from Pokamoonshine at 15°, through north, west, and south to the Green Mountains of Vermont at 75°. In the foreground, you can see Carson Mountain at 65°, with the cliffs of Carson Ledges to the right and Little Fay at 150°. In the middle distance you can easily identify the major peaks of the Jay Wilderness, including Bluff at 305°, and moving to the left, Beech Ridge, Death, parts of US mountain, Jay, and Slip

at 240°. By walking over to the western edge of the summit you can look directly down on Fay Bog and further north to Hathaway Swamp. On a clear day this is truly a view to savor and share for several minutes.

To return simply retrace your route to Little Fay and after descending west around its summit ledges, you continue your route down the slope on a bearing of 155°. From the summit of Fay to Little Fay will take about a quarter hour, a little more than a half hour to the base of Little Fay and the woods road, hardly an hour to where you parked.

81 Daby and Jug Mountains
Paths, bushwhack, cross-country skiing, hiking

Logging operations have established an interesting network of roads in the triangle bounded on the east by the Trout Pond Road and on the south-west by Green Street. Although the road network is mostly on private land, very little is posted and it is well worth taking time to explore. Within the area, the state owns sections 29, 20, and 71 of Maule's Patent, totaling about 500 acres of Forest Preserve classified as Wild Forest. The state land includes the summits of Daby Mountain, about 620 meters (2034 feet), an unnamed summit of 864 meters (2178 feet), and Jug Mountain, 741 meters (2430 feet).

To reach these lands, begin at the T intersection of Trout Pond Road with Green Street as described in section 63, the Seventy Road. Head southwest on Green Street past Grove Road on the right at 2.9 miles to Black Mountain Road on the left at 4.3 miles. Turn left onto the unpaved Black Mountain Road and continue south. It is only plowed a short distance to the last house and you can park at the end of the plowed stretch. In summer you can drive 1.2 miles from Green Street, though the surface of the road is rough in places. Be sure to park off the traveled portion of Black Mountain Road since the road is used regularly for log hauling.

From your parking spot continue south along the dirt road. About 1.4 miles from Green Street, where the road is bending east, the road forks. The way left is a fairly recently built logging road that heads generally east along the south slopes of Ellis and Bald mountains north of the Gulf. At first the road climbs steeply; within 0.3 mile, as the road levels off, you will see a small knob on the right. It is open and has views along The Gulf and across to Daby and Black mountains. The road connects with others that can be explored all the way over to Trout Pond Road.

Cliffs on Mt Fay from Little Fay

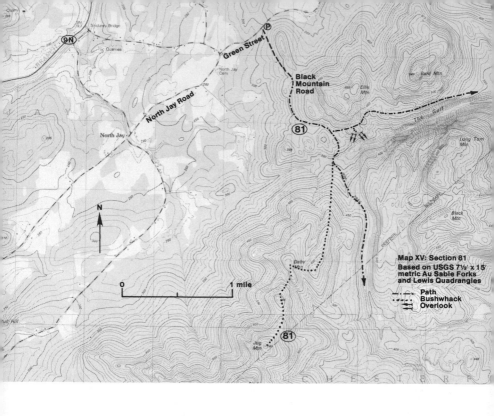

Map XV: Section 81
Based on USGS 7½' x 15'
metric Au Sable Forks
and Lewis Quadrangles
Path
Bushwhack
Overlook

If you go right at the fork, you continue downhill heading southwest. You descend about 50 meters (164 feet) to a drainage. To the left, the upper reaches of Durgan Brook enter the steep-sided chasm of The Gulf. On the right, the faint remains of a tote road head up the long nose of Daby Mountain, while the main road continues south through a narrow valley, finally reaching private lands. You can explore south for quite a distance before reaching posted, private lands that can be explored on cross-country skis.

If you take the faint tote road toward Daby, you find it climbs steeply following a generally southerly direction up the northeast ridge of Daby before it peters out. The eastern of the two wooded summits of Daby is reached after a bushwhack of a mile and a climb of 275 meters (900 feet) from the main road. The western summit can be reached by bushwhacking down 50 meters (164 feet) on a bearing of 300° magnetic. From this wooded summit follow the ridge south on a bearing of 180° until you can see the summit of the unnamed peak to the southwest. Head toward it on a bearing of 230°, dropping into the col and up to the summit. From the summit of the 664-meter peak head south at 185° magnetic along the ridge, climbing gradually at first and then more steeply as you gradually turn right to a bearing of 235° before you reach the summit of Jug Mountain. To the south lies Bitch Mountain at 801 meters and to the west of that lies Lincoln Mountain at 716 meters, both on private land. While neither Jug nor Daby have open summits, both have ledges and outcrops with views, especially when the leaves are off. However, there are usually a number of deer hunters in this area, so forgo a trip during hunting season.

The return to the jeep road from Jug Mountain is 2.1 miles over the unnamed peak and Daby. Round-trip time for the bushwhack from the jeep road is about four hours.

82 Pokamoonshine and Carl Mountains
Marked trail to Pokamoonshine, bushwhack to Carl
1 mile, 1 hour, 384 meters (1260 feet) to Pokamoonshine

The trail to the fire tower on Pokamoonshine Mountain is a somewhat steep but popular hike with commanding views of the Adirondacks and the Green Mountains in Vermont. The bushwhack to the higher and even steeper Carl Mountain to the west is more challenging but has exhilarating views of rocks cliffs and The Gulf. The towering, geologically interesting rock cliffs of Pokamoonshine command your attention as you drive along the Northway between Exits 32 and 33.

The origin of the unusual name is not certain but may be a combination of two Algonquin words, *Pohqui* and *Moosie*, which meant "broken" and "smooth." Those words certainly depict the breaks in the 1000-foot granite gneiss cliff on the eastern side of the mountain, which are intermingled with large, smooth rock areas. Rock climbers can often be seen on the cliffs in summer, and the ice falls just above the campground provide challenging technical ascents in winter.

The trailhead is 3 miles south of Northway Exit 33 on NY 9. From Exit 32, head west for 2 miles, then north on NY 9 for 9.3 miles. A sign at the south end of the campground indicates "Forest Fire Tower, Pokomoonshine Mountain, Elevation 2162 feet, 1.0 mile." (DEC spells the name of the mountain in a different way than the USGS, which is used in this book; the spelling for the campground is a third version.) There is adequate room to park cars along the shoulder of NY 9.

The trail up Pokamoonshine begins in a southwesterly direction up a rocky, worn trail. It is easy to follow in all seasons as there is a large number of red DEC trail disks. The trail zigzags up, going right toward a cliff where there is a view north when leaves are off the trees. You climb steeply under the cliffs and then level off somewhat in a wooded draw. After an-

Map XVI: Sections 82 and 83
Based on USGS 7½ x 15' metric
Au Sable Forks Quadrangle

Path
Trail
Bushwhack
Road
Overlook

other steep stretch, in less than half an hour, you reach a level cleared area and the standing chimney and foundation of the fire observer's cabin. About 200 yards away to the west is a lean-to, which at this writing has a large hole in the roof.

The route to the summit goes north from the old chimney. Water flows from a pipe in a spring beside the steep path, which goes sharply up a rock chimney to a level area, then winds east to the fire tower. Another route leads away from the clearing to the west and takes a gentler and longer circle around to the tower. On the top you have sweeping views from the open rock summit, with Lake Champlain and the Green Mountains to the east. Deerfield Mountain can be seen in the southwest and beyond it the open ridges of the Jay Range. Carl Mountain to the west is hidden by trees when you are at the base of the tower. In winter, rime ice forms a thick crust on the tower, trees, and shrubs and provides photogenic pictures well worth the short climb.

You can add a challenging bushwhack to this climb if you have compass, altimeter, and topo map. Return west on the official trail for about 300 yards until the trail bends south. Then take a bearing of 290° magnetic. The woods are too dense to see the summit of Carl, but keep on this heading for the gradual downhill. In about 0.5 mile, fifteen minutes, you will see openings to the south through the trees. When you explore them, you will find you are on the top of a cliff line with a sharp drop at 580 meters (1915 feet). Openings can be found in this area to view the top of Carl Mountain at 310° across the valley. Drop into the valley and look for the easiest way up the cliffs on Carl; there are at least two places to scramble up using rocks and trees without danger of falling. You will reach a wide area below the summit, and from it you can continue up a steep area from the east or contour around to the south for an easier climb to the 681-meter (2240-foot) summit.

The view is worth the hour hike from Pokamoonshine. The land falls away to the west into the valley of Trout Pond Brook and the beginnings of the North Branch of the Boquet. Across that valley is an extremely sharp defile, "The Gulf." You can appreciate this spectacular cleft only from this perspective. To the southwest the entire sweep of the Jay Range is visible, and beyond it Hurricane Mountain; Whiteface is to the right. The view exceeds that from Pokamoonshine and you no longer hear Northway traffic. A small rock cairn on the summit reminds you that you are not the first to stand here, but not too many people have made this climb.

The easiest way back is to retrace your steps to the east, keeping the cliffs on your right. Another way is to go west off the summit, then south, and then swing east just before you reach the draw between Carl and Deer-

field mountains. This route takes you under the cliffs, but you should stay high enough to avoid the swamp in the valley. Beyond the swamp you may come across stone walls and several dry wall cellar holes in a white pine forest, a very secluded area for a homestead many years ago. Continuing east over a ridge you will reach a jeep trail, the access road to the fire observer's cabin. You can follow this down to NY 9 at a point 1.1 miles south of the trailhead. The jeep road crosses posted, private land, however, before it reaches NY 9. If you go north on the jeep road you will reach the lean-to and can go back down the official trail. From the summit of Carl back to the car is an hour and a half to two hours, depending on the route.

The jeep trail has been described as an expert cross-country skiing route. This book does not recommend it because the bottom portion of the road is posted and gated. Furthermore, some sections are very steep and narrow. Other trails on public land are available and equally rewarding.

83 Rocky and Old Rang Mountains from Trout Pond
Roads, bushwhack, skiing, hiking

South of Clintonville and east of Trout Pond Road the state owns about 100 acres that includes the summit of Rocky Mountain. In addition, Old Rang Mountain lies on the north edge of the block of state land that includes Pokamoonshine Mountain. Both of these peaks have cliffs on their southeast sides that provide views, and both can be reached from Trout Pond Road.

From the T intersection of Trout Pond Road with Green Street as described in section 63, the Seventy Road, head south on Trout Pond Road for 2.6 miles to Trout Pond, which lies to the right, west. At the south end of Trout Pond, at 3.5 miles, a logging road enters from the left, east. You can park here along Trout Pond Road at an elevation of 271 meters (889 feet).

Head southeast along the logging road and across a brook flowing left to right. After 0.15 mile, turn left on another tote road and head steeply northeast up the left bank of the brook you just crossed. At 0.5 mile, the tote road crosses the brook and comes to a T with yet another tote road. Turn right, crossing the brook a few times as you continue northeast to a col at an elevation of 580 meters (1900 feet). From this col there are several options.

If you are interested in a bushwhack to the summit of Rocky Mountain, 660 meters (2165 feet), head northwest along the base of the cliffs of Rocky Mountain. By continuing northwest and climbing more to the right as opportunities present themselves, you can climb Rocky Mountain from the west. The flat, wooded summit must be crossed to the southeast to obtain the views from the anorthosite cliff on the southeast side. The total bushwhack is 0.5 mile and 80 meters (265 feet) vertical. Retrace your steps to return to the tote road.

Those interested in a bushwhack to the summit of Old Rang Mountain at 695 meters (2280 feet) should begin by heading 125° magnetic from the col at the top of the tote road south of Rocky Mountain. The bushwhack is fairly level for about half a mile and then climbs moderately to the flat, wooded summit of Old Rang. The anorthosite cliffs on the southeast side provide interesting views of Notch and Carl mountains to the south and Pokamoonshine with its fire tower to the southeast. Retrace your route to return to the tote road.

A third option is to continue beyond the col to the northeast to the Alec LaMountain Mountain Road. To do this, leave the tote road where it ends in the col and bushwhack down to the northeast. Note that this is a possible ski bushwhack—the woods are open—but the trip is strenuous. Stay to the left, northwest, of the boggy area south of Barber Mountain. Once past the boggy area, follow the right bank of the drainage from the bog to the point where you pick up the road. It is about 1.3 miles from the col to the road and an additional 1.5 miles down to the limit of passenger car travel on Alec LaMountain Mountain Road. The last option from the col requires having a pickup vehicle on that road, or else you must retrace your steps back to Trout Pond Road.

Clinton Parks and State Forest

NEW YORK STATE Forest in Clinton County comprises several parcels of state land, none of which are Forest Preserve. When the Blue Line of the Adirondack Park was extended in 1972, Terry Mountain fell within the Blue Line but was not designated Forest Preserve land. Other parts of Clinton State Forest are outside the Park, so logging can and frequently does occur on all of them, as well as on Terry Mountain. This means that the network of roads is constantly changing as different areas are logged. Only two parcels within the scope of this guide have recreational opportunities, Burnt Hill and Terry Mountain, although others appear in the Northern guide in this series. In earlier years, Clinton State Forest No. 1 (Macomb) on the east side of Burnt Hill was open to the public. However it is currently leased to the Turtle Island Trust for the exclusive use of a community of Mohawk Indians.

Several other parcels of state and private land with public trails, all of which are best suited for cross-country skiing, are found in Clinton County.

84 Terry Mountain
Road and bushwhack, hiking, views

Terry Mountain, at elevation 2067 feet, dominates the west end of Peru and is easily identified from the Northway between Keeseville and Peru as the ridge on the western horizon with the television broadcasting towers on top. Although a few acres of the summit and the access road are privately owned by WPTZ-TV of Plattsburgh, most of the mountain is part of the 4800-acre Terry Mountain Reforestation Area.

From Northway Exit 35, turn left, west, on Bear Swamp Road for 1.4 miles to a T intersection with NY 22 in Peru. Turn right, north, on NY 22 and cross the Little Ausable River. Just across the bridge at 1.6 miles turn left, west, on NY 22B. At 2.7 miles turn left, west, on Mannix Road to the intersection with Calkins Road or Peasleeville Road. Turn right on Calkins and continue to a T intersection at 5.6 miles, where Peasleeville Road continues left, west. Continue past the road on the right at 7.1 miles, which leads to Macomb State Park, section 88. Continue past Patent Road on the left at 8.4 miles. Peasleeville Road winds about, intersecting other

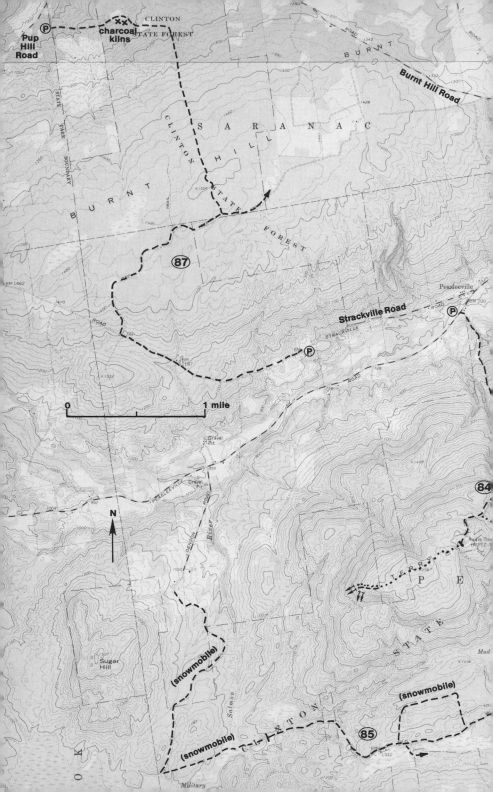

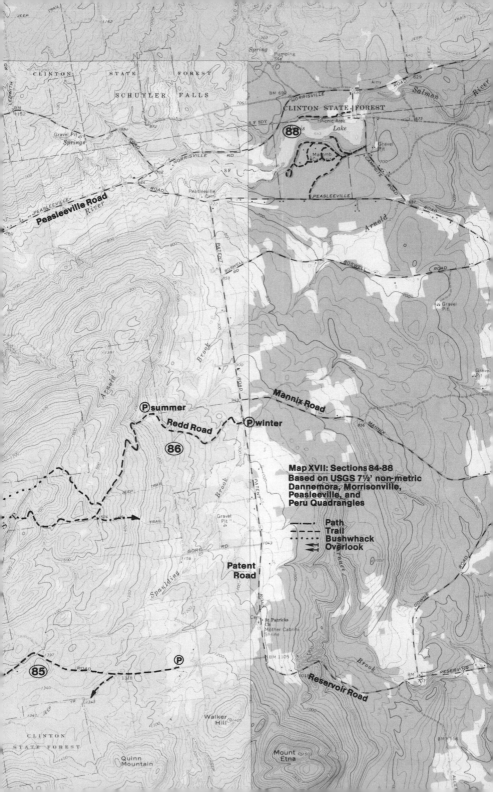

Map XVII: Sections 84-88
Based on USGS 7½' non-metric
Dannemora, Morrisonville,
Peasleeville, and
Peru Quadrangles

Path
Trail
Bushwhack
Overlook

roads. At 8.9 miles you are in the valley of the Salmon River between Burnt Hill to the right, north, and Terry Mountain to the left, with the tower plainly visible. Continue through Peasleeville, past the Zion United Methodist Church on the right at 10 miles, and take the left at the Y intersection with Strackville Road at 10.8 miles. At 11.1 miles there is a road left marked "Private Road Do Not Enter."

This is the access road to the tower and there is room to park, but be sure not to block the access road. The public may not drive on it, although hiking is permitted. It is too steep for skiing.

Starting at elevation 710 feet, walk south along the road and immediately an all-terrain vehicle track forks left leading to private land. The road twists and turns south through a white birch, poplar, and white pine forest, crossing several times under the power lines for the tower.

You will hear an unnamed tributary of the Salmon River off to the right, west. You cross a bridge with a cascading brook and just west of it reach a possible rest stop where two other brooks join in. Just beyond the bridge, the road turns sharply left, 1.1 miles and fifty minutes from the start, at an elevation of 1420 feet. After crossing the brook again, the road makes a sharp right turn, the first of a series of turns and zigzags that ends at the towers at 2 miles, an hour and a half from the start, and elevation 2000 feet.

This is not the true summit. To reach it, follow the guy wire that is stretched out toward 265° magnetic from the main tower, skirting right around a small spruce bog. From here a 0.2-mile gradual climb brings you to the summit, which is located in a red pine forest. It is marked with a copper bolt, which is in remarkably good condition with the inscription "Adirondack Survey—VC 30—1878," inserted in the mossy gneiss. Verplanck Colvin's description of his visit appears in his Seventh Annual Report of 1880. He seemed to prefer the name Norway Mountain for Terry, but both names are used. His surveys were done in November 1878 with snow on the ground, and it is interesting to note that his barometric surveys led him to report a summit elevation of 2666 feet, nearly 26 percent higher than current maps.

For the best views, follow the summit ridge for 0.3 mile to the cliffs on the west end of the ridge on a bearing of 260°. The tops of the cliffs make an excellent lunch spot. You can identify Jay Mountain in the distance at 185° with Whiteface to the right. Below at 255° you can see the Military Pond that marks the western edge of the Terry Mountain Reforestation Area.

To return, bushwhack easterly on a bearing of 80° magnetic toward the tower. This will take forty minutes, but the hike down the service road will only require fifty minutes.

85 Old Military Road
Cross-country skiing
8-mile loop, 4 hours, 250-foot elevation change

The Old Military Road is an enjoyable cross-country ski trip across the southern portion of the Mountain Reforestation Area.

Start from Northway Exit 35 as described in section 84 turning on NY 22B, but leaving it in front of the Peru Central School to go straight west on River Road. Just past Burrell's Apple Storage, turn right on Barney Downs Road. At 3.5 miles from the Northway, Barney Downs Road intersects Calkins Road and you turn left, south. At 4.4 miles turn right, west on Reservoir Road. You can catch a glimpse of Mount Etna on the left. A century ago blast furnaces in the Furnace Brook Valley gave Mount Etna the appearance of a volcano when seen from a distance. At 5.7 miles you enter the Park, and at 6.3 miles Barney Downs Road forks right. Immediately past the intersection, you pass a reservoir dam on Furnace Brook on the right. The Reservoir Road twists and turns as it climbs out of the steep valley of Furnace Brook and makes a right turn at the top of the hill. At 7.3 miles turn left on the Old Military Road as Reservoir Road turns right to become the Patent Road.

Drive west on Old Military Road, which is unpaved though open to vehicles. The road narrows and gradually gets rougher at the limit for winter plowing. Park here, leaving room for other vehicles to pass.

Mileages are given for the trip west along the Old Military Road west. After 0.6 miles of fairly level skiing, a road enters from the left. Although the road is posted, the state has right of access to a 240-acre parcel of land in the reforestation area that only connects with the main parcel at its northwest corner. A network of tote roads can be skied by turning left at this point.

Your route continues straight and after bending to the right at 1.1 miles, a road enters from the right, north. The northwest corner of this intersection is shown on the F.W. Beers county atlas of 1869 as the site of School No. 17. Bear left and continue to 1.7 miles, where a beaver pond outlet flows south from right to left.

Just beyond this drainage there is a well-defined tote road on the right. By following the tote road right for ten minutes toward the northwest you will come to the east end of Mud Pond. There is a campsite here that has been used by the U.S. Air Force base at Plattsburgh for survival training. Mud Pond is the headwater of the Salmon River at elevation 1528 feet and has some bullhead fishing.

Continue west on the Old Military Road, and at 1.9 miles you cross the outlet of Mud Pond as it flows south into a major wetland that stretches for 1.5 miles along this upper part of the Salmon River. You can identify Big Nineteen Mountain on the far side of this wetland. At 2.4 miles a snowmobile trail enters on the right. This trail climbs gently north for 0.3 mile before turning west for 0.4 mile and then back south for 0.3 mile to rejoin the Old Military Road at an unofficial sign calling it Mastic Road.

At a large borrow pit on the right, a road enters from the left at 2.9 miles. This road immediately crosses the Salmon River on a new log bridge and leads to logging operations south of the Salmon River wetland. Beyond the turnoff, the Mastic Road snowmobile trail completes its loop on the right.

Farther west there are three camps of a private inholding. At the west end of the wetland, the Old Military Road turns right, northwest, and at 3.2 miles begins to lose elevation. A logging road enters from the left just before a private camp on the left; beyond which the road narrows and drops, providing a downhill run for skiers. On the right to the north you can see the cliffs of the west end of Terry Mountain and the tower.

The Old Military Road bends left and continues downhill. A right turn-off leads to a camp. The Old Military Road begins to peter out in a boggy area where the J&J Rogers Company of Ausable Forks once had one of their charcoal-making operations. From here you can retrace your 3.9-mile route back to the trailhead.

86 Redd Road on Terry Mountain
Road, snowmobile and cross-country skiing

Redd Road provides access to the eastern slopes of Terry Mountain and makes an easy half-day cross-country ski exploration. To reach the road, start from the intersection of Patent Road and the Old Military Road described in section 85. From this intersection go north past Mother Cabrini Shrine at 0.3 mile to a fork at 1.7 miles where Redd Road forks left, west. For those traveling from the northeast, Redd Road is 0.1 mile south of the intersection of Patent Road and Mannix Road and 1.6 miles south of the intersection of Patent Road and Peasleeville Road, referred to in section 84. In heavy snow you will have to park on Patent Road at an elevation of 960 feet.

The ski trip on Redd Road heads west, climbing gently, and soon turns northwest and then makes a right-angle turn to the southwest. After 0.5 mile the road turns sharply right to the northwest again and continues bending, just a little, to the left. At 0.9 mile a logging road that is not on the topographic sheet comes in on the left, south, and Redd Road dips to cross a drainage. Beyond the drainage, the road bends right and then swings left to an old borrow pit on the right at elevation 1120 feet. This flat area is the limit for passenger cars in summer and a good place to park in dry weather.

On the left across from the borrow pit, yellow on red snowmobile signs mark Cross Road forking left, south, as well as Redd Road, which continues west, now climbing steeply and bending slowly to the right, north, to a sharp U-turn to the left. It continues south, turns sharply right, northwest, and climbs to a log landing where it turns sharply south. These switchbacks bring you to an elevation of 1340 feet.

Redd Road now levels off slightly and climbs gradually southwest. After 0.7 mile, a jeep road comes in on the left, east, and about 0.1 mile farther a tote road not indicated on the map comes in from the northwest at an elevation of 1500 feet. You have been skiing for thirty minutes to cover the 1.2 miles from the dry weather parking area.

You can take this tote road northwest as it climbs moderately to steeply past a culvert and crosses into state land. It ends at a log landing at an elevation of almost 1700 feet, just below the main northeast-southwest-trending ledges of the east side of Terry Mountain. A fifteen-minute scramble up the ledges is rewarded with a panoramic view over Plattsburgh Air Force Base to the Champlain Valley and the Green Mountains of Vermont. A bushwhack of 1.25 miles on a bearing of 265° through the open summit woods, skirting some boggy areas, will bring you to the tower described in section 84. For skiers, the return trip downhill makes this tote road a worthwhile side trip.

After returning to the intersection of the tote road and Redd Road, continue southwest on Redd Road. After a short distance you reach an intersection with a jeep road on the left at 1524 feet elevation. Although you can see a posted corner from there, the side road can be followed downhill to the east on state land for 0.75 mile.

Redd Road now turns due west and stays on state land with posted signs on the left, south. The forest is mixed deciduous with some spruce and white pine. You can see the television tower ahead to the west. If the snow is not too deep, you can see dark red sandstone rocks in the road bed. These are pieces of the basal part of the Potsdam Sandstone of late Cambrian age. The road passes through a gravel area that was once a borrow pit. It then narrows and turns right to the northwest, to climb gently up with a drainage on the left.

About an hour and 2 miles from the dry-weather parking site, Redd Road reaches the head of the drainage at an elevation of 1720 feet. In another five minutes it peters out. From here it is only a 1-mile bushwhack to the tower on a bearing of 275°. You might want to use this alternate approach to climb to the towers on Terry Mountain and go out on the road to a pickup car as for section 84.

To return to the start of this winter ski trip, be careful to watch for snowmobiles, especially in the area of the switchbacks.

87 Pup Hill, Burnt Hill
Old roads, snowmobiling and cross-country skiing

Pup Hill is the local name for Clinton State Forest No. 2 on the west side of Burnt Hill. Since the Macomb section of Burnt Hill was closed to the public, Pup Hill has become a popular cross-country ski and snowmobile area. Burnt Hill is the northeast-southwest-trending ridge of sandstone of the Potsdam Group of Upper Cambrian Age. It is visible southeast of the Saranac River and NY 3 between Cadyville and Redford and lies northwest of Peasleeville and Terry Mountain, separating the Saranac and Salmon River drainages.

This trip crosses Pup Hill from north to south and is described as a through trip with a two-car shuttle. To find the trip's southern end, start from the Peasleeville Zion Methodist Church, as in section 84, and head southwest on Peasleeville Road for 0.7 mile to Strackville Road which enters at a sharp angle on the right. Turn onto Strackville Road and follow it for 1.3 miles to the point it narrows; there is a road on the left and a driveway on the right. Leave your pickup vehicle here, return to the Methodist Church, and continue northeast on Peasleeville Road. At 1.1 miles from the church turn left on Norrisville Road; then at 1.3 miles turn left again on Burnt Hill Road, which climbs northwest, makes a dogleg to the left and right, and continues to climb. At 3.1 miles, at the crest of the hill where Downs Road comes in on the right, there is a lovely vista of Lyon Mountain across the Saranac River valley to the northwest. At 6.7 miles make a very sharp left turn onto Soper Road at the place where Hardscrabble Road also crosses.

If you are not doing the through trip, you would start at the north end. The easiest way to the northern trailhead starts from NY 3 at the Saranac Central School at Saranac (Picketts Corners), 18 miles west of Plattsburgh. Head southwest on NY 3 for 0.3 mile and turn left, south, on Bowen Road. After crossing the Saranac River and following its right bank, you reach a T intersection at 1.5 miles. Turn right to go west on Hardscrabble Road until you reach the intersection with Burnt Hill and Soper roads. Here, at 2.1 miles, turn left onto Soper Road.

As you continue southwest on Soper Road, you can see the surge tower of the penstock for High Falls Dam on the left. At 7.7 miles, make a sharp left turn at a borrow pit onto Pup Hill Road, which begins to climb steeply. You can see Russia Mountain, 1404 feet, on the right. At 8.6 miles Pup Hill Road turns sharply right and you leave it heading left, south, on an unnamed road, which drops sharply to cross a tributary of Ryans Brook. You reach a second unnamed road on the left at 8.8 miles and park here along the road.

You begin at an elevation of 950 feet by heading east on this second unnamed road. A sign indicates you are entering the 1574-acre Burnt Hill State Forest. Continue east and pass several side roads on both sides. The forest is mainly second-growth white birch, poplar, and small red pine. You cross two tributaries of Ryans Brook, and at 0.6 miles you pass an area on the right that had charcoal kilns according to F.W. Beers' 1869 *Atlas of Clinton County*. Evidence of these old kilns can still be found by scratching for charcoal.

You continue east on a section of road that has been constructed recently and does not appear on the USGS map. You cross another tributary of Ryans Brook on a small causeway before the road swings south at 1 mile. Your route now climbs moderately and you should turn about to enjoy the views of Lyon Mountain behind you to the northwest. After half an hour of climbing generally south, the road levels off at 2.2 miles from the start, and you are not far from the highest point of Burnt Hill at an elevation of 1506 feet.

A yellow and red sign marks the Eagle snowmobile trail, which forks right, west. A few minutes later, another sign marks the crossing of the Bluejay snowmobile route heading east and west. As you continue south you find the road zigzags several times, then climbs a low ridge and turns right to come to a T intersection at 2.7 miles, an hour and a half from the start. This jeep road is marked on the USGS map. It winds southwest to northeast to cross the State Forest. To the left it winds northeast fairly level to join horse trails on private land east of the State Forest.

Your route at the T leads right and you descend slightly. The road makes several gentle turns and reaches a Y intersection. The route right heads east and is the Grosbeak Snowmobile Trail. Your unmarked route goes left, west, making a sweeping turn as it descends to an intersection with the Deer Snowmobile Trail, which heads north, crossing just west of the highest part of Burnt Hill. You have come 3.5 miles and two hours from the start, depending on snow conditions.

Your route now turns left at the intersection and heads south then south-west as it descends gently and bends west. About twenty minutes from the Deer trail, turn left, south, past the remains of an old cabin on the right. At this point the route becomes narrower and begins to twist and turn as it descends steeply downhill to the south.

The steep downhill section ends at a T intersection with Strackville Road at elevation 1284 feet, 4.8 miles and three hours from the start. Turn left and head southeast on Strackville Road, which descends southeast and after 1 mile bends east, then north of east, descending more steeply. After crossing a brook flowing from left to right and a borrow pit on the left, the Strackville Road passes a pond. During the winter this last half mile on Strackville Road provides a lovely, wide, downhill cross-country ski run back to the pickup vehicle at elevation 913 feet, 5.3 miles from the start.

88 Macomb State Park
Camping, picnicking, swimming, cross-country skiing

A small dam on the Salmon River forms 68-acre Davis Lake. This small lake is the focal point of the 500-acre Macomb State Park. Fees are charged in summer, but in the winter the entire park is open to cross-country skiing.

To reach the park, turn right on Campsite Road from Peasleeville Road, 7.1 miles from Exit 35 on the Northway, section 84. The campground entrance is 0.6 mile from Peasleeville on the left, west. A short distance beyond the campground entrance, Campsite Road turns sharply left and crosses the Salmon River just above the Davis Lake Dam. After turning sharply right, you reach the separate entrance to the picnic area on the left. The campground and its swimming area occupy the south side of Davis Lake, while the picnic area and its swimming beach occupy the north side. Both areas make excellent, level cross-country ski opportunities. A network of old roads for skiing extends south to Peasleeville Road.

89 Rugar Woods
Walking, birding, cross-country skiing

Rugar Woods is a delightful natural area owned by the State University of New York's College at Plattsburgh on the north shore of the Saranac River. Camping and motorized vehicles are prohibited, but it is otherwise open to the public.

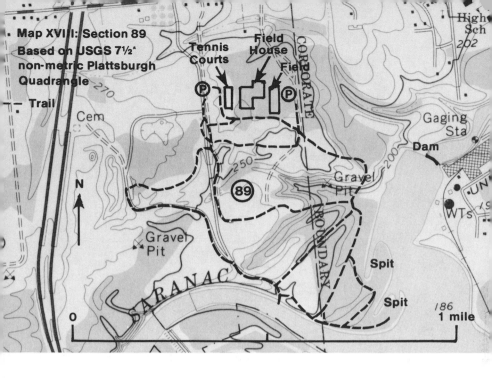

Take Northway Exit 37 to the NY 3 intersection. Turn left, west, on NY 3 and 0.2 mile from the intersection turn left, south, on Hammond Lane. At 0.8 mile turn left, east, on Ruger Street and continue across the bridge over the Northway. Turn right, south, at 1.8 miles at the western-most entrance to the SUNY Plattsburgh Field House. Just as the loop drive begins to bend left in front of the field house, you turn right to a parking area. Park here or, if it is full, in the lot to the east of the field house.

Rugar Woods has about 3.0 miles of trail in 120 acres of undeveloped land behind the field house. The clockwise loop begins at the southwest corner of the parking area. South of the baseball fields, you may find an old foundation. Some say it was a British fort in 1814, but it is probably younger and may be a farm building. Just beyond the foundation is the "buried treasure" apple tree.

By following the trails generally south you will reach the Saranac River. At this point the river is actually a pond created by a power dam. Sedimentation has formed a pair of spits that can be explored on skis.

As you ski upstream, you reach an old access road to the river. Up the road to the northwest you pass electronic landing instruments that guide aircraft to Plattsburgh Air Force Base. This can be a spectacular and noisy location—wake turbulence from the aircraft frequently creates small wind storms on the ground. Past here, at the westernmost point, the trail turns east to join the route back to the field house.

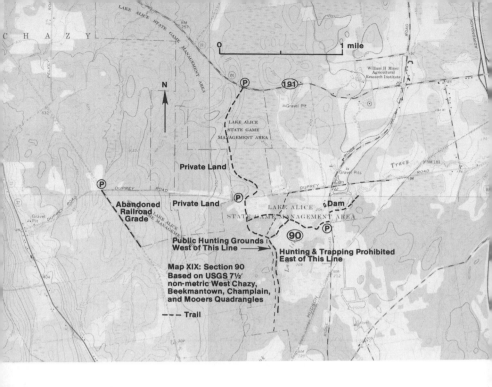

Much of Rugar Woods was once farmland with crops and orchards planted on the flat terrace. The main terrace is at an elevation of 240 to 300 feet and was formed in glacial times as part of the depositional delta of the ancient Saranac River during the Port Kent stage of the Champlain Sea. Today the area is gradually returning to a wild state. Off the trails you may see study plots set up by college faculty and students. Please do not disturb them.

90 Lake Alice Wildlife Management Area
Walking, birding, cross-country skiing

This Wildlife Management Area occupies 1468 mostly undeveloped wetland acres on the shore of Tracy Brook. The Lake Alice area, once part of William H. Miner's farm, was a gift to the state. Miner was a successful businessman who patented devices that cushioned the couplings of railway cars. These and other devices made him a wealthy man. He chose to return to the area where he was raised and developed Heart's Delight Farm to pursue his agricultural interests, which are still pursued at the William H. Miner Agricultural Research Center.

To reach the wildlife area, drive west on County Route 191 from Northway Exit 41. At 0.3 mile you reach Ridge Road with the Miner Center Campus of the Center on the north. Turn left and head south on Ridge Road. You cross Duprey Road and Tracy Brook, then at 1.7 miles there is a sign for the Lake Alice area and a small parking area. This is the main entrance, but other entrances are noted below. At the registration box you can pick up a checklist of plants for the area. A barrier limits motorized access to the road, which can be followed west to an intersection, then south, past a second intersection along the west shore of Lake Alice for 1.4 miles. This road is the boundary between the posted "No Hunting and Trapping" area around Lake Alice on the east and the larger public hunting ground on the west and north. Many wood duck boxes dot the marsh.

A small loop trail connects the two intersections at the northwest corner of the lake. From the northwest corner of that loop, a new trail continues north passing a series of beaver ponds. It leads to Duprey Road, intersecting it 0.8 mile west of Ridge Road. After crossing Duprey Road you can continue to County Route 191, 1.5 miles west of Ridge Road.

The western boundary of the area south of Duprey Road is an abandoned railroad grade that can be followed for 0.6 mile south from Duprey Road. The rail route was once the Plattsburgh and Montreal Railroad that connected Plattsburgh and Mooers Junction in 1852 and served as the main Delaware and Hudson line until it was bypassed by the more direct West Chazy-Rouses Point route in 1876.

A small dam creates 100-acre Lake Alice. It was one of a series of small dams in the complex hydraulic system whose turbines and generators supplied water and electric power to William H. Miner's Heart's Delight Farm and parts of Chazy.

There is a series of delightful birding ponds downstream from Lake Alice. They were also created by the dams in Miner's hydraulic system. To reach them, cross to the east side of Ridge Road and follow Tracy Brook down to the old powerhouse. The nearby tower was a surge tank to equalize pressure in the penstock.

Ridge Road follows the Ingraham Esker, a twenty-three-mile-long ridge that was formed by glacial sediments laid down by a river flowing in the ice during the time when the continental ice sheet was melting back.

References and Other Resources

References

Barnett, Lincoln. *The Ancient Adirondacks.* New York: Time-Life Books, 1974.

Brown, George Levi. *Pleasant Valley, A History of Elizabethtown in Essex County, N. Y.* Post and Gazette Print, 1905.

Carson, Russell M. L. *Peaks and People of the Adirondacks.* Glens Falls, NY: The Adirondack Mountain Club, 1973.

Essex County Historical Society. *The Reveille.* Vol. 5, No. 20, Elizabethtown, December 1960.

Everett, Allen S. *Briefly Told: Plattsburgh, New York, 1784–1984.* Clinton County Historical Association, Plattsburgh, NY, 1984.

Goodwin, Tony. *Northern Adirondak Ski Tours.* Glens Falls, New York, The Adirondack Mountain Club, 1973.

Glenn, Morris F. *The Story of Three Towns: Westport, Essex and Willsboro.* Privately printed, 1977.

Glenn, Morris F. *Coon Mountain, Westport, New York. Glenn's History of the Adirondacks.* Volume 3. Privately printed, 1986.

Hill, Ralph Nading. *Lake Champlain Key to Liberty.* The Countryman Press, Woodstock, VT, 1977. Paperback Edition 1987.

Hurd, Duane Jamilton. *History of Clinton and Franklin Counties, New York.* J. W. Lewis & Co. 1880. Reprinted 1978.

Jamieson, Paul F. *Adirondack Canoe Waters North Flow.* Glens Falls, New York, The Adirondack Mountain Club, Inc., 1975.

Kirschenbaum, Howard et al., Ed. *The Adirondack Guide.* Taquette Lake, New York, Sagamore Institute, 1983.

Kudish, Michael. *Where Did the Tracks Go: Following Railroad Grades in the Adirondacks.* Saranac Lake, New York, The Chauncey Press, 1985.

McKibben, Alan and Susan, Ed. *Cruising Guide to Lake Champlain.* Burlington, Vermont, Lake Champlain Publishing Co., 1986.

Palmer, Peter S. *History of Lake Champlain, 1609–1814.* Fourth Edition, 1886. Reprinted: Harrison, New York, Harbor Hill Books, 1983.

Royce, Caroline H. *Bessboro, A History of Westport.* Essex County, 1902.

Smith, H. P., Ed. *History of Essex County.* Syracuse, New York, D. Mason & Co., 1885.

Sullivan, Nell Jane Barnett and Martin, David Kendall. *A History of the Town of Chazy*. Clinton County, New York, 1979.

The Lake Champlain Committee Conservation Fund. *Exploring Lake Champlain and Its Highlands*. Burlington, Vermont, Land Press, 1981.

Warner, Charles B. and Hall, C. Eleanor. *History of Port Henry, New York*. Rutland, Vermont, The Tuttle Company, 1931.

Watson, Winslow C., "A General View and Agricultural Survey of the County of Essex." *Transactions of the New York State Agricultural Society, Volume XII*, pages 649–898, 1852.

Watson, Winslow C., "A supplement to the Report on the Survey of Essex County." *Transactions of the New York State Agricultural Society, Volume XIII*, pages 699–741, 1853.

Watson, W. C. *Pioneer History of the Champlain Valley*. Albany, New York, J. Munsell, 1863.

Weston, Harold. *Freedom in the Wilds, A Saga of the Adirondacks*. St. Huberts, New York, Adirondack Trail Improvement Society, 1971.

Other Resources

New York State Department of Environmental Conservation (DEC) 50 Wolf Road, Albany, NY 12233

For trails:
DEC Regional Office, Region 5 (includes Essex and Clinton counties), Ray Brook, NY 12977

For hiking groups:
Adirondack Mountain Club, 172 Ridge Street, Glens Falls, NY 12801

For other things to do in the Adirondacks:
New York State Department of Commerce, Albany, NY 12245 or 90 Main Street, Lake Placid, NY 12946, "I Love New York" series: Camping, Tourism Map, State Travel Guide.

For history:
Adirondack Center Museum, Elizabethtown, NY, 12932 Heritage Museum and Gallery, Montcalm St., Toconderoga, NY 12883 Clinton County Historical Museum, City Hall, Plattsburgh, NY 12901

Index

Guidebooks from Backcountry Publications

For information on other regions of the Adirondacks covered in the "Discover" series, please see the back cover.

Walks & Rambles Series
Walks & Rambles in Dutchess and Putnam Counties, by PeggyTurco $10.95
Walks & Rambles in Rhode Island, by Ken Weber, Second Edition $11.00
More Walks & Rambles in Rhode Island, by Ken Weber $9.95
Walks & Rambles in the Upper Connecticut River Valley, by Mary L. Kibling $10.00
Walks & Rambles in Westchester (NY) and Fairfield (CT) Counties,
　　by Katherine Anderson, revised by Peggy Turco, Second Edition $11.00
Walks &Rambles on Cape Cod and the Islands, by Ned Friary and Glenda Bendure
　　$10.95
Walks & Rambles on the Delmarva Peninsula, by Jay Abercrombie $10.95

Hiking Series
Fifty Hikes in the Adirondacks, by Barbara McMartin, Second Edition $12.95
Fifty Hikes in Central New York, by William Ehling, $11.95
Fifty Hikes in Central Pennsylvania, by Tom Thwaites, Second Edition $10.95
Fifty Hikes in Connecticut, by Gerry and Sue Hardy, Third Edition $11.95
Fifty Hikes in Eastern Pennsylvania, by Carolyn Hoffman, Second Edition $12.00
Fifty Hikes in the Hudson Valley, by Barbara McMartin and Peter Kick $12.95
Fifty Hikes in Lower Michigan, by Jim DuFresne $13.00
Fifty Hikes in Massachusetts, by John Brady and Brian White, Second Edition $13.00
Fifty Hikes in New Jersey, by Bruce Scofield, Stella Green, and H. Neil
　　Zimmerman $12.95
Fifty Hikes in Northern Maine, by Cloe Caputo $12.00
Fifty Hikes in Northern Virginia, by Leonard M. Adkins $12.00
Fifty Hikes in Ohio, by Ralph Ramey $12.95
Fifty Hikes in Southern Maine, by John Gibson $10.95
Fifty Hikes in Vermont, by the Green Mountain Club, Fourth Edition $11.95
Fifty Hikes in Western New York, by William Ehling $13.00
Fifty HIkes in Western Pennsylvania, by Tom Thwaites, Second Edition $11.95
Fifty Hikes in the White Mountains, by Daniel Doan, Fourth Edition $12.95
Fifty More Hikes in New Hampshire, by Daniel Doan, Third Edition $12.95

We offer many more books on hiking, walking, fishing, and canoeing in the Midwest, New England, New York state, and the Mid-Atlantic states—plus books on travel, nature, and many other subjects.

Our titles are available in bookshops and in many sporting goods stores, or they may be ordered directly from the publisher. Shipping and handling costs are $2.50 for 1-2 books, $3 for 3-6 books, and $3.50 for 7 or more books. To order, or for a complete catalog, please write to The Countryman Press, Inc., P.O. Box 175, Dept. APC, Woodstock, VT 05091, or call our toll-free number, (800) 245-4151.

Dennis Conroy is a writer and photographer who makes his home in North River, New York. He is an avid cross-country skier and white water canoeist, which, along with his fondness for hiking and camping, led him to settle in the Adirondacks a number of years ago.

Prior to this move, Dennis worked primarily on African economic development. He has lived in Iran, Ethiopia, Tanzania and Washington D.C., and has traveled extensively in the Middle East and Africa. He continues to do consulting work for the Agency for International Development.

Dennis has written widely on the Adirondacks for several periodicals on subjects ranging from Park Agency affairs to local crafts people.

Having contributed to three other guides in this Series, Dennis has provided much of the material for this volume, and is currently working with Barbara McMartin on a forthcoming "Discover" book.

in the Adirondacks, as well as sailing on Lake Champlain. He is a professor at the Center for Earth and Environmental Science, State University of New York at Plattsburgh, and his expertise as a geologist has enriched this series.

Jim is well known as an active conservationist, chairs the Adirondack Land Trust, and serves The Adirondack Council, Environmental Planning Lobby, Association for the Protection of the Adirondacks, the Lake Champlain Committee. He is a member of NYS-DEC's Forest Preserve Advisory Committee, and a past president of the Adirondack Mountain Club. Jim's strong interests in the history of the region are reflected in his service as Chair of the Adirondack Research Center of the Schenectady Museum, and President of the Clinton County Historical Association.

Jim has contributed to several volumes of the Discover Series, and in this guide has prepared the material on areas surrounding his Peru home. He has also shared his extensive knowledge of Lake Champlain.

James C. Dawson and his wife Caroline are outdoor enthusiasts who enjoy hiking, canoeing, cross-country skiing and fishing